THE POLICE ESTABLISHMENT

WILLIAM W. TURNER

THE POLICE
ESTABLISHMENT

G. P. Putnam's Sons

New York

To Mark Peter and his new era

Contents

THE POLICE ESTABLISHMENT

1

The Police Crisis

That American law enforcement is in crisis is one of the most obvious and distressing facts of this nation's contemporary life. The crime rate is accelerating—at a pace, the FBI reports, five times faster than the population growth—while the rate of crime solution by the police remains fairly static, portending the opening of a "crime gap." Reacting to the role of scapegoat, the police have set up a chorus of protest over court decisions they feel handcuff them and coddle the criminal. Public apathy, ridicule and at times outright hostility, the police contend, have hampered them in their thankless task.

The never-smooth relations between the police and minority groups have been inflamed by recurrent charges of police brutality and unwarranted incursions on civil liberties. While both sides bristle with resentment, demagogic politicians raise the specters of "violence in the streets" and "crime waves" and propose saturating the cities with police, a nostrum that would create a virtual garrison state. Understandably, the police look upon themselves as an embattled group and realize now more than ever the relevancy of the old adage: policing a dictatorship is easy, policing a democracy is hard.

And it grows harder as our society becomes more complex. No longer is the police function merely to patrol a beat and investigate crimes. "Crime in the streets," cautioned the President's Commission on Law Enforcement and the Administration of Justice in its 1967 report, "is an inaccurate label for the bulk of serious crimes in this country, most of which are committed inside buildings and often in places where the police have no right to go until after a crime is committed there." The police themselves concede that anywhere from 50 to 90 percent of modern police work is of a noncriminal nature.

Yet most police stubbornly cling to the old concepts of their role. They disclaim any sociological role on the grounds that their mission is solely to enforce existing laws, overlooking the fact that they are de facto sociologists. They are baffled and frustrated by the curbs imposed on their powers by a society they are sworn to serve and protect. To much of the police community, the recent Supreme Court ruling that narrowed police latitude in questioning suspects was the last straw. "I guess now we'll have to supply all squad cars with attorneys," complained Quinn Tamm, executive director of the International Association of Chiefs of Police. In Oakland, California, police responding to a shooting call carried the ruling to its *reductio ad absurdum* by stiffly advising the dying victim, a housewife, of her rights before asking who shot her. "My husband," she gasped just before she died.

The poverty of these attitudes has been recognized by the more visionary elements of the police establishment, including Don L. Kooken, a former captain of the Indiana state police who is now a professor of police administration at Indiana University. In *Ethics in Police Service* he admonishes:

> The public in the past have naïvely avoided consideration of the fact that the principal difference between a democracy and a totalitarian form of government is not so much in the laws under which they operate as it is in the manner by which the laws are applied. The public is slowly awakening from its passivity toward the principles of personal liberty. Illegal invasions of the sanctity of private homes, unreasonable deten-

tion of persons suspected of crime, and withholding from the innocent and guilty alike the right of due process of law, are bringing increased criticisms of enforcement officers both from the public and the courts.

Thus, by failing to measure up to the emergent standards of conduct, thinking and procedure expected of them, the police are simmering in a cauldron of their own making. It is fatuous for the police to grouse, as many do, that society has lost its respect for law and order. What has happened is that society is reasserting its respect for the law in its most viable and equitable form and is aggressively seeking a police system that will respond to its standards.

The reluctance of the police to adapt to new conditions is all the more critical because of the indispensability of their role in society. Even the most vociferous critics of the present system would hardly advocate its abolition (although ultraconservative newspaper publisher R. C. Hoiles of Santa Ana, California, contends that the police should be privately organized). A story told by former San Francisco Mayor George Christopher illustrates the citizens' love-hate syndrome with regard to the police. "At a '49er football game a drunk ran out on the field and interfered with play," he recounted. "A policeman chased him, to a lusty chorus of boos from the crowd. I had an announcement made that the game would be held up until the man left of his own accord. The booing stopped, and the policeman escorted the man from the field, to the accompaniment of loud cheers."

To acquire the broad base of public understanding that is necessary for effective police work, the police image will have to be drastically upgraded from that of the bumbling, graft-prone "flatfoot" to one of a civil servant of professional competency and integrity. "As long as the average citizen enters a police station with a defensive chip on his shoulder, a feeling of hostility unlike the sensation with which he would enter some other welfare agency," wrote the late Harry Söderman, a detective of international repute, in *Policeman's Lot,* "there is certainly something wrong. A policeman does not enjoy the sensation of being looked upon as the enemy of the very people who hire him to protect them."

The mutual suspicion with which the police and the populace regard each other has its origins on both sides. There are pathological cop-haters; there are those who resent authority in any form; and there are many well-meaning persons who have lived in less democratic nations and retain an innate fear of police. But it is equally true that the police have not always conducted themselves in a manner calculated to earn respect. The President's Commission found that "a significant number of officers engage in varying forms of criminal and unethical conduct" and that incidents of rudeness and physical and verbal abuse are widespread. Moreover, even the more scrupulous police have a tendency to apply dual standards to "average" citizens and to nonconformists, members of minority groups and persons of unorthodox political and religious beliefs. "In police circles, conformity to the group opinion is often considered to be the equivalent of national patriotism," chides one police textbook, *Professional Police-Human Relations Training.*

The lack of popular support for the police can be put in even broader terms. Since its inception, the police establishment has conducted itself more as the agent of the power structure than the servant of a pluralistic society. Philadelphia unionists have not forgotten how effectively the police mounted patrol was used as a strikebreaking force—until workers got the idea of tossing ball bearings under the horses' hooves. The motto of the Chicago department is "We Serve and Protect," yet Negro victims of crime in the ghetto are resigned to the fact that the motto does not equally apply to them. Although the police did not create hard-core poverty, they physically contain it, the poor are prone to believe, with exaggerated zeal. The police enforce a white middle-class morality that is alien to broad segments of our population.

Thus the police have abdicated their duty to bring protection under the law equally to all. They remain badly out of step with mid-twentieth-century America, marching to a cadence set in a long-past era. "No single task is more urgent," affirmed the President's Commission, "than breaking down the wall of isolation that surrounds the police."

For the better part of a career I was behind that wall. On the morning of February 5, 1951, at FBI headquarters in Washington, I proudly raised my right hand and repeated the oath of the special agent to uphold the Constitution and investigate matters in which "the United States is or may be a party at interest." At twenty-three, I became a member in good standing of the law-enforcement club.

That membership was retained over the next ten and one-half years. As an FBI agent investigating for the most part criminal-type cases, I came in contact with a host of other federal agents and state and local officers from St. Louis to San Francisco, from the Northwest to the South. I worked with them, shared risks with them, exchanged shop talk with them and socialized with them. I was privy to their hopes and aspirations, their gripes and glories, their prides and prejudices— and I learned something about the intricate mechanism that makes the police personality tick.

The initiate to the fraternity is soon impressed with the strong bond of camaraderie and stick-togetherness that accounts for the solid front presented to the outside. Officers at all levels of law enforcement are bonded by a mutual empathy —and the mystique of the badge and the gun. Their job is a special one; their problems are unique; and the pride in cracking a tough case is universally shared. Understandably, the police are skeptical of the motives of "outsiders," who they feel cannot possibly fathom the nature of the police job. Crime is horrible and sordid; the plight of the victim is to be considered; crime solution cannot always be accomplished under Marquess of Queensberry rules; and one mistake can mean a life. The vocation is one that deals constantly with trouble, and in that sense it is unique.

Not the least factor behind police clanishness is the physical danger lurking behind every trouble call, every arrest. I can recall my own baptism of fire on a balmy spring morning in Seattle on March 12, 1954. Three gunmen wearing false noses and spectacle frames held up the Greenwood branch of the Seattle-First National Bank. They methodically emptied the cash drawers and forced a bank official to open the vault. They were about to escape with $90,000 when the first policeman, summoned by a silent alarm, arrived. As he came in the front door, shotgun in hand, Sgt. Howard Slessman was stopped by a .45-caliber slug smashing into his neck. The gunmen raced for a rear exit, where they encountered two more officers, Frank Hardy and Vernon Chase. Hardy and Chase were also gunned down.

I was the first FBI man to arrive on the scene. Shots reverberated somewhere. Someone pointed to a broken window— one of the gunmen had dived through it. I gave chase, but the last of the retreating gunmen was just scrambling into the getaway car as it accelerated out of the parking lot. The getaway was clean. Hardy was dead and Slessman and Chase greviously wounded. The gunmen dropped $80,000 in their frantic escape.

There is an unwritten code among police officers that cop-killers must be caught at any cost, and we investigated that case relentlessly. It was not until nine years later, after I had left the FBI, that the first arrest was made. But the code had been lived up to, as it usually is in the more than forty police murders each year.

In this sense, police clanishness may have some justification, but the net result is that the police have turned inward and become in effect a closed society. That society is jealous of its prerogatives, resentful of criticism and "outside meddling," and anchored to tradition. In many ways it has scarcely changed from the day in 1844 when the nation's first regular urban force, the New York City department, ignited its gas-lamp POLICE globe.

In police quarters, technological progress is often equated with adjustment to current times. It is only a partial adjustment; the attitudes which dominate law enforcement remain largely anachronisic. Take, for example, Thomas J. Cahill, the capable Irishman who is chief of the San Francisco department. Cahill is a totally clean cop; the word "graft" arouses him to rage. But he has carried on an unremitting crusade against establishments in his convention city that feature "topless" entertainment, despite court decisions informing him, in effect, that he is not to consider himself arbiter of the community morals. And take Sgt. Fred Cobb of the Nashville, Tennessee, department, who in July 1966 indignantly left a showing of *Who's Afraid of Virginia Woolf?*, the Academy Award-winning motion picture, and returned with a warrant charging the theater manager with showing "an indecent film. . . . I represent the thinking of the good people of this town," declared the sanctimonious sergeant, "and I just don't feel like they would approve of this type of film for the young people to see." Cahill and Cobb are not anomalies in their profession: the police community tends toward Victorianism in this permissive age.

This turn-back-the-clock ideology accounts in large measure for the punative frame of mind that dominates the police community. When the issue of abolition of capital punishment is raised, it is the police who argue the loudest for retention, even though their own statistics demonstrate that capital punishment is no deterrent to crime. Nor is police zeal ever more evident than in the pursuit of perpetrators of "crimes without victims"—drug addicts, alcoholic derelicts, prostitutes and other deviates from society's norms who harm only themselves. Excessive liberalism in the parole system is a common complaint of police executives, despite the fact that the rehabilitation phase is outside their province. When J. Edgar Hoover rails in florid rhetoric against the "hoity-toity professors" and "mollycoddling sob sisters," he is articulating the sentiments of the entire police establishment.

Recently, police attitudes have been brought most sharply into focus by the civil rights and Vietnam war protest movements. During my career in law enforcement I found that there exists a broad band of animosity toward political and racial minorities. In the FBI, for example, agents often referred to an automobile occupied by Negroes as "a load of coal," and scurrilous remarks of this nature are common in private talk among officers. In Los Angeles a motorcycle officer stopped a white doctor whose car displayed a sign in favor of an open-housing measure. "I thought only niggers had those signs," the officer sneered.

As the various movements have gained momentum, police prejudices have become sharpened and manifest themselves in dual standards of enforcement. The inebriated convention-goer is quietly driven back to his hotel in a police car, for example, while "peaceniks" and racial-equality demonstrators are herded into Black Marias on technical charges such as "disturbing the peace" and "failure to disperse."

Granted that many allegations of police brutality are over-blown, physical duress, while not as prevalant as two or three decades ago, is far from extinct. A San Francisco public official whose father was a policeman reveals that in his handball sessions with police officers there is constant boasting, as if it were a mark of honor, of beating administered to recalcitrant suspects; this in a city whose chief has categorically denied the existence of brutality on his force and who became incensed when various groups pushed for a civilian review board. In an article entitled "The Case for the Cop" in *Harper's* magazine (April 1964), former Deputy Commissioner Richard Dougherty of New York asserts: "It is hardly news that suspects of serious crimes often get 'worked over' in the back rooms of station houses." Nor are petty offenders whom the police particularly dislike immune from such treatment.

In the final analysis, the crudely manifested prejudices of the line officer are not substantially different from the more subtle biases of the men at the top. Even J. Edgar Hoover, reputedly a model of impartiality, angrily labeled Dr. Martin Luther King "the most notorious liar in the country" when the Nobel Peace Prize-winner questioned the *élan* of FBI agents in investigating civil-rights violations in the South.

The most sickening photograph I have ever seen, other than that from a war, was taken by a *Life* lensman during the Newark riots in the summer of 1967 and published in color in the issue of July 29. It shows a Newark policeman leveling his shotgun at the fleeing figure of a young unarmed Negro. A *Life* reporter teamed with the photographer is cringing on the sidewalk, below the gun's muzzle. An older Negro stepping out of a tenement is recoiling as he almost enters the line of fire. At some thirty paces, the policeman fired into the youth's back, mortally wounding him. A twelve-year-old boy bystander farther down the line of fire was struck with pellets and seriously injured. The dead youth was William Furr, Jr. His crime: He had grabbed a six-pack of beer from a looted liquor store.

As mercenaries of the commercial establishment, the police tend to place property rights over human rights. In some jurisdictions elite "jack-in-the-box" squads lie in wait in warehouses and stores with shotguns, ready to blast to death would-be burglars. When a veteran San Francisco officer was suspended in

September 1966 pending an inquest into the fatal shooting of a juvenile fleeing from a stolen car—an incident that touched off rioting in a Negro district—1,000 of his fellow officers came to his support with a petition protesting the suspension and a demonstration on the steps of City Hall. Unnecessary shootings have been so frequent in New York City that the department has found it advisable to suspend automatically any officer who fires at a person without the element of self-defense being present.

The hypocritical rationale which employs the sanctity of law and order as a franchise for breaking the law has been an additional source of disrespect for law enforcement. FBI Director Hoover, for one, has repeatedly proclaimed the majesty of the law and deplored civil disobedience; yet he had no compunctions about ordering his agents to install electronic listening devices in Las Vegas casinos in wanton violation of Nevada law. A number of times during my own career I was dispatched to break and enter a premise, in direct violation of state criminal statutes, in order to install electronic "bugs." Yet the FBI cannot be singled out for special censure — the use of lawlessness to uphold the law is widespread.

In a sense, the resort to illegal methods by the police is symptomatic of their increasing perplexity over how to cope with today's crime. The Dillinger-like desperadoes in the thirties were clear-cut adversaries who could be disposed of with the burst of a machine gun or the snap of the handcuffs. Now the organized-crime labyrinth and the slick professional criminal pose an infinitely more complex challenge.

Concomitantly, as the complexity of our urban society increases, the black and white absolutes in which the police have traditionally dealt are becoming totally inadequate. Because the greatest part of police work is now concerned with noncriminal matters, the police are confronted with a bewildering array of new problems for which their stereotyped views are hardly a match. Thus ill equipped to solve problems, the police have developed a vindictiveness toward those elements of society they feel are responsible for their plight. Not long ago two Long Beach, California, officers arrested a college art professor as he was sipping a beer in a tavern and worked him over on a slow ride to headquarters. The only "crime" ever adduced was that he was wearing a beard—in the policeman's book a grating symbol of nonconformity.

Rather than putting themselves through the wringer of self-criticism and reappraising the assumptions upon which they operate, most police have shifted the blame for their predicament to outside influences. Overlooking the fact that adverse court decisions originate with police abuse, they complain of being hamstrung by courts packed with ivory-tower or "pinko" judges. When a palpably guilty defendant is acquitted, they decry "technicalities in the law" and allude to "smart liberal lawyers" who have exploited the technicalities. The authoritative police text, *Introduction to Law Enforcement*, whose authors, Dr. A. C. Germann, Robert R. J. Gallati and Frank D. Day, have been policemen themselves, chides police spokesmen who vocally denounce the police review-board concept as "a scheme from the Communist handbook" or "the work of Communist-led or -inspired groups." Such statements, the authors reprove, are "*at best,* pusillanimous nonsense, *at worst,* malicious subterfuge, and *never* serve the best interests of law enforcement." Yet police declamation against the concept remains general and high-pitched.

A disturbingly large number of police officers have found identification with chauvinistic organizations that pander to their gripes. John Rousselot, former public relations director of the John Birch Society, made the claim in 1965 that 2,000 law-enforcement officers in Los Angeles County alone were members of the society, which may be a slight hyberbole. But the society unquestionably holds an attraction for many a hard-pressed policeman by virtue of its sympathetic propaganda. For example, a Birch Society mailer disseminated in North Hollywood in 1965 declaimed: "Demands for police review boards, false allegations of police brutality, rash Supreme Court decisions, demands for recall of police administrators, and numerous other acts of harassment have made the police officers' job tremendously more difficult in these times of lawlessness in the streets." The irresistibility of this kind of appeal has been manifested in Bircher-disrupted departments from Philadelphia to Santa Ana, California.

One of the most critical problems facing the police system is a dearth of qualified applicants. Most departments are operating below authorized strength, and some have been virtually crippled. The President's Commission estimates that 50,000 police jobs are going begging throughout the country. Police executives attribute much of the shortage to a waning respect for law and order coupled with an increasing reluctance on the part of young men to accept the rigors and hazards of police work.

Such simplistic explanations fail to consider that respect must be earned and do a disservice to a generation that has distinguished itself in other rugged types of endeavor. Normally a career combining vital public service, an interesting and unusual challenge, and a dash of adventure would be a highly sought prize, especially since police salaries have been brought more closely in line with private enterprise (the largest cities, where the manpower shortage is most severe, pay approximately $7,000 per year to start).

One obstacle is the stigma that still clings to the police image. In large measure, it stems from the betrayal of the public trust by the few. Chicago and Denver, for instance, are still trying to rid themselves of the scourge of 1960, when police burglary rings were exposed in both cities. Criminality and venality are not limited to the ranks. "Most police officials are honest," the President's Commission concluded, but it added that "a significant number" are not.

Yet the main impediment to recruitment remains the system itself. Most departments advertise perquisites such as "security" and "fringe benefits" to lure applicants. To an ambitious young man seeking a rewarding vocation, these terms are synonymous with a straitjacket. They mean being locked into an archaic civil-service system whose shibboleth is seniority. To all but the cloddish, the light at the end of the tunnel seems dim and distant.

The experience of a bright young man of my acquaintance shows how disillusionment eventually besets those who enter law enforcement hoping for personal achievement and public service. Having obtained a degree in law enforcement from Indiana University, he joined the Oakland Police Department and at the same time attended the graduate school of criminology at the University of California. The Oakland department is typical of the police paradox; housed in a gleaming new edifice and outfitted with the most advanced equipment, it is run in hidebound style by ultraconservative administrators. Assigned to the Planning and Research Bureau, the young man found himself pressed into service with helmet and nightstick as part of the famous "Berlin Wall" erected by the Oakland police to bar Vietnam protest marchers from the territory of Oakland. Not long afterward, sorry but wiser, he took a position in the security department of an aerospace firm. And the police service lost a highly qualified, promising officer.

My own disenchantment was similar. I had originally intended to join the New York state police, but when the FBI opportunity came along I took it. I never did lose my enthusiasm for the work, but in time I became sorely disappointed with the system itself. The accent was on looking good in public rather than on objective enforcement. Once, for example, the local office insisted I defer seven arrests so that the offenders, all misdemeanants whose whereabouts were known, could be officially declared federal fugitives and apprehended as "fleeing criminals." The system seemed to run on pettifoggery administered by priggish bureaucrats. Promotion as often went to the sycophantic as to the able, and the airless environment bred a cult of the personality. It was a climate of moral absolutism carried to the point of being a religion in itself. It was not the place for an aspiring secularist.

This lack of a stimulating atmosphere in which to work was deplored by the President's Commission in these words: "At the present time, personnel is closely regimented in most departments and initiative is not encouraged. For example, there is far more emphasis on making arrests and following orders than on questioning traditional procedures or solving community problems. This is not an appealing environment for a person of professional stature."

Of late a number of police executives have awakened to the desirability of seeking out and keeping higher-caliber personnel rather than trying to keep abreast of mere manpower quotas. As in other fields, automation is tending to stretch the police day so that an officer can accomplish more during his shift. With the crime problem growing more intricate, the need is for a thoroughly professional force rather than one rated on size alone. Society insists upon high standards for its schoolteachers, medical personnel and other specialists; it should expect as much from the specialists to whom it entrusts the task of keeping law and order and the public safety.

It is the individual officer, alone on the street, who must make decisions involving human life and liberty by himself and without time for deliberation. Although he belongs to a quasi-military structure, the policeman cannot be an automaton responding only to commands. He must perform instinctively on his own initiative and make on-the-spot judgments. To shoot or hold fire; to arrest or desist; to use force or persuasion; to act or not to act. These are a few of the incessant questions to which he must instantly react. The officer needed today must not only be mentally and physically superior, he must possess the breadth of vision and social consciousness that will enable him to deal fairly and humanely with the disparate individuals he encounters. In other words, he must be as quick on the draw with reason as with a gun.

These are stringent requirements, and we are going to have to pay to get men who meet them. Federal Judge George C. Edwards, former Detroit police commissioner, told a law-enforcement gathering on October 1, 1966: "I look forward to the time, probably not too distant in history, when police induction requirements will include two years of college and when the fully trained and qualified police officer will command a salary of $10,000."

Upgrading the police profession necessarily means the weeding out of the indolent, lackluster types who drift from job to job before taking root in the security of the police system. It means the phasing out of the "gung-ho" bully to whom the authority of a badge and gun is a license to intimidate. And it means the termination of the sadists and psychopaths whose present numbers have provoked calls for psychiatric screening of all applicants.

Significant changes in the police system are inchoate, but there is a stirring. In 1953, some 10 percent of the nation's police had from one to four years of college training, an appallingly low ratio that is slowly edging upward. A few departments have insisted upon some exposure to the college classroom, and most are willing to arrange duty schedules to accommodate class schedules. Formal education is by no means a panacea, but studies indicate that the more education an officer acquires the less authoritarian he tends to be.

As educated, more tolerant officers rise through the ranks to administrative positions, the ancient attitudes that have so long dominated will yield and gradually be supplanted. This trend is well under way and, one hopes, is irreversible. There is still a long way to go, but the quality of policemen is perceptibly improving.

Indeed, the quality of our police system must be made to match the quality of our society, of which it is an integral part. This will require a complete restructuring of the police system and an entirely fresh police philosophy. It will also require an open mind on the part of society. "Police have been denounced as relentless manhunters, as oppressors of the weak and the helpless, and as the tools of sinister influences and interests," wrote the late Bruce Smith, a well-known police consultant, in his *Police Systems in the United States*. "They have also been described as largely ineffective agencies which fail to realize their objectives and in any case cost too much."

This public-eye view of the police has had all too substantial basis in fact. But the public must be prepared to meet the police halfway as reforms are realized. And the public must be prepared to pay out of pocket for those reforms, as freely as it has for fine libraries, cultural centers, medical facilities, school systems, freeways, rapid transit and the other components of modern urban life.

For the matter of attitudes is a two-edged sword. Recently in a San Francisco suburb a well-dressed man driving an expensive late-model car with a bumper sticker proclaiming "Support Your Local Police" was halted for a traffic violation. He became incensed that *he* should be cited and in a fit of anger tore up the citation, much to the chagrin of *his* young local policeman.

Thus far I have tried to sketch roughly the shape and dimension of the police crisis in the United States. It is not the crisis as described by the police establishment, which visualizes one created largely by external forces. Nor is it the precise crisis imagined by the bulk of society, which has virtually abandoned hope that police reform and an end to "crime waves" are simultaneously obtainable goals.

But through the muddle of arguments pro and con, one imperative is clear: it is the police who must get in step with society, not vice versa. This they have not shown a disposition to do; the potent police lobby continues to pressure for greater police power within the present system, a rather frightening prospect.

So it is the masters of the police—the citizens—who must force the issue and bring about change by sheer weight of public opinion. In this book I hope to explore the police system, its character and its personalities, in sufficient depth to illuminate the problems that confront us. And I hope to offer meaningful answers and alternatives.

In the first part of the book I examine a number of the major police departments across the nation, describing briefly their history, their operations, their philosophy and attitudes, their strong points and weak ones. In the second part I attempt to come to grips with the salient issues affecting the police, most prominently the impact of court decisions, brutality and review boards, political extremism in the ranks, relations with the community, and the police lobby. The story is told in largely anecdotal fashion, so that the reader can make his own interpretations. While I have necessarily concentrated on a limited group of departments, the police establishment is strikingly homogeneous and what is true of one department is generally true of most.

2

New York: The Finest?

At 240 Centre Street in lower Manhattan, surrounded by a
drab cluster of buildings housing machinery dealers and hard-
ware wholesalers, stands the headquarters of the New York
City Police Department, by far the largest in the nation. The
forbidding, turn-of-the-century structure is the command center for some 27,500 sworn officers and 3,500 civilian personnel
responsible for bringing law and order to a metropolis of more
than 7,000,000 inhabitants.

In New York, as in most great cities, the police department
has expanded rapidly in the past decade, accelerated by the
pervasive fear of "crime waves." In 1954, when Mayor Robert
Wagner first sensed the growing apprehension of the public
and commenced his "war against crime," the Thin Blue Line
numbered 19,000. Now the line is a hefty one: there is one
policeman for about every 300 citizens. Because New York's
Finest have multiplied considerably in the years since I left the
FBI, I visited 240 Centre Street to obtain the latest statistical
profile. A visit is an experience in itself. Through the tread-
worn entranceway, one enters abruptly into the insular world
of the police. At the center of the gloomy marble foyer is a
desk with a sign challenging: "All Visitors Stop and State Business." Manning the desk that day was an older uniformed policeman probably superannuated from street duty. His voice

sounded bored as he directed: "The public information office is up the stairs and to the right." On the wall above the bifurcating marble stairway with its ornate balustrade is mounted a large bronze plaque with World War I doughboys in bas-relief and an honor roll of New York police officers killed in that long-ago conflict.

In the public information bureau I was eyed appraisingly, a strange face among the regular reporters on the police beat. "What kind of information?" the unsmiling man at the front desk wanted to know. He rang an extension number, and soon I was in the office of a ranking police official. A tall, sandy-haired man with penetrating gray eyes and the cop's quizzical stare, the official briskly asked for my identification. Lacking working press credentials, I produced a copy of a police-science text I had written. As a former FBI agent, I remarked, I had often worked with former New York City detectives who had joined the bureau; in St. Louis, I recalled, we had tracked down a fugitive wanted in New York as a "cat burglar." The official's suspicion melted. I was one of the fraternity.

The mention of "civilian review board" to a policeman is like waving a red flag in front of a bull, and I casually inquired how the men felt about the defeat of the New York civilian review board (it had been trounced in the general election of November 8, 1966). "They were pleased," he said, smiling. Then his face hardened. "I think it's illegal. The cop [New York police call themselves cops] has to testify, and they could use it against him later in court." The official was repeating a common police argument, but it fails to make the distinction between administrative discipline decided by either police officials or civilians, and criminal prosecution.

"How is Operation Friend going?" I asked. The pioneer community relations program was started in 1963 in Spanish Harlem to ease tensions created by the shooting of two Puerto Ricans by a policeman. "Fine," he replied. "We hope it will

lower antagonisms so we can make arrests without a mob collecting." This kind of cynicism is so deeply ingrained in most
police officers that it has become subliminal. The police are
consummate pragmatists who, as one New York bluecoat put
it, "live on the short run and don't see the big scene."

During my discussion with the official I was somewhat startled to notice a baited mousetrap in a corner of the room, but
in a way this almost obsolescent contraption was symbolic. New
York's is the nation's oldest police force, and it has not intrin-
sically changed from the day in 1845 when the Star Police first
pinned on their eight-pointed copper badges. The first destination of many of the waves of sturdy young men from Cork, Gal-
way and Killarney was 240 Centre Street, where the legend of
the plodding Irish cop was born. The Irish Catholic tradition
has always dominated The Finest, despite the numerical parity
the Italian-Americans have achieved in recent years. The force
is still known as "The Irish Mafia" or "Spellman's Army"; the
notion that it is virtually a Catholic club persists to the degree
that some Negro policemen become converts to Catholicism on
the theory that it will enhance their chances of promotion.

Not unexpectedly, the Irish have maintained a stranglehold
over the years on the ranking positions within the department,
and it would be as unthinkable to have a non-Irishman as commissioner as it would be to have an Englishman as pope. But
of late it has become increasingly apparent that this virtual
nepotism, with its built-in inertia, has prevented the force from
responding to the needs of a modern cosmopolitan city. The
police brass, competent enough in the fundamentals of their
profession, have simply failed to display the vision and imagination required to cope with the manifold problems of contemporary police work.

This deficiency was recently enunciated by the Mayor's Law
Enforcement Task Force, a blue-ribbon panel appointed by

Mayor John V. Lindsay and chaired by retired federal Judge
Lawrence E. Walsh. "There is public apprehension with respect to personal safety and the safety of property," its report
declared. "There is social tension, and this tension in part centers upon community relations with the police. There is, if not
apathy, at least a lack of strong public support for the police
in the performance of their duties." The Task Force study
found that "so many practices and procedures are either out-
moded, inefficient, or undesirable that we have no reservations
as to the need for a thoroughgoing reevaluation of the department's operations." New York's Finest, the report stated with
finality, "must be subjected to an unrestricted and unstinting
review of long-standing traditions, attitudes and practices."

The essential anachronism of the department was well
known to Lindsay when he took office. He had in fact made a
campaign promise that he would create a civilian review board
to handle complaints of police malpractice, an unmistakable
sign that the days of the old guard were numbered. Although
Lindsay's opponents claimed that his review-board stand was
a political move aimed at the minority vote, the later defeat of
the board by referendum showed that the issue stood to lose
him more votes than it gained. The principle of civilian review of alleged police misconduct is perhaps the single most
controversial issue in the tug of war between preservers of the
police status quo and would-be reformers; the police themselves are unanimously and unalterably opposed to what they
view as civilian "meddling" in police affairs.

While the subject of civilian review will be discussed in a
later chapter, it should be mentioned here that it is broader in
scope than considerations of conduct—it involves the question
of civilian ascendency over the police. And it was civilian
ascendency that Lindsay was determined to assert. He was well
aware of the traditional police argument that the department

must function autonomously, unencumbered by City Hall interference. But he was also aware of the dangers inherent in giving the police free rein.

Inaugurated in January 1966, the progressive Lindsay clashed almost immediately with the philosophy of the "Headquarters Irish Mafia," as the department's command level was called. The incumbent commissioner, Vincent L. Broderick, had replaced the familiar, personable Michael J. Murphy, a practitioner of the old school, a year earlier. Murphy, more noted for speech-making than innovation, had become disillusioned with the lack of popular support for the police position in the civil rights strife. "The police officer, too, belongs to a minority group—a highly visible minority group," he complained to the New York chapter of the American Jewish Committee at a luncheon shortly before he retired, "and is also subject to stereotyping and mass attack. Yet he, like every member of every minority, is entitled to be judged as an individual and on the basis of his individual acts, not as a group. . . . We as police object to being second-class citizens."

Broderick, a blunt, articulate man who had served as the department's chief legal officer, could see the force for its faults. On July 2, 1965, he took the occasion of a promotion ceremony for forty-seven police officials to deliver a stinging rebuke against bigotry within the ranks. Certain passages in his speech are the kind of talk rarely addressed by one police official to another:

> If you believe that a police officer is somehow superior to a citizen because the citizen is a Negro, or speaks Spanish—get out right now. You don't belong in a command position and you don't belong in the police department.
>
> If you will tolerate in your men one attitude toward a white citizen who speaks English, and a different attitude toward another citizen who is a Negro or who speaks Spanish—get out right now. . . .

If you will tolerate physical abuse by your men of any citizen —get out right now. . . .

If you do not realize the incendiary potential in the racial slur, if you will tolerate from your men the racial slur—get out right now. . . .

I have since received reports that some members of this department, at City Hall last Tuesday, made disparaging remarks —racial slurs—concerning proponents of civilian review.

Let me make this very clear. We live in the year 1965. For too many years the Negro members of our society have been deprived of their rightful place. For too many years they have been denied the respect which is due them as fellow citizens, as individuals, and as creatures, like us, of God. . . .

I will not tolerate, and I charge you at your peril not to tolerate, verbal brutality by any police officer against any citizen. . . .

The unthinking tongue, in 1965, can be the worst enemy which this department has—it can undo so much we do that is constructive. . . .

Undoubtedly Broderick would have wished that his straight-from-the-shoulder edict could have been enforced. But in a large department police officials have little practical control over their men. At the precinct level the amorphous blue masses deport themselves according to their own codes rather than the department's. The vast gulf between the commissioner's office and the precincts was suggested in parting salutes to the retiring Broderick published in the police magazine, *Spring 3100* (named after the first telephone number assigned to the department) in April 1966. The correspondent from the 60th Precinct in Brooklyn extended best wishes even though "on a precinct level we have virtually no personal contact with the P.C.," and the 105th's commented, "I know of no member of our command who ever spoke to our former P.C. Vincent Broderick in person."

The confrontation between Lindsay and Broderick revolved about the issue of civilian review. Broderick argued that while he could accommodate himself to the civilian review board as such, it represented an encroachment by City Hall on the internal affairs of the department and thus constituted "political meddling in police affairs." In a biting seven-page letter to the mayor, Broderick stated: "An outside civilian complaint review board has become a rallying cry, Mr. Mayor, with some deceptive political appeal. But it is, I repeat, a cruel hoax. . . . Is it not time, Mr. Mayor, for you to say that you renounce political expediency; that you realize that the principal effect of an independent civilian review board will be to depress the morale of your police department and hence impair its capacity to prevent crime?"

The doctrine of separation of police and politics in New York dates to more than half a century ago, when a major police scandal rocked the city and led to the election of a reform mayor and a Republican governor. It was laid down by the Tammany Hall leader, Charles Francis Murphy and has been religiously adhered to ever since. Ironically, it was brought about not because City Hall taint had rubbed off on the police department, but the other way around.

While the doctrine may have been desirable in the days of machine politics, it is largely irrelevant in terms of the present. For one thing, it is founded on two false assumptions: that the police can ever be totally divorced from politics, and that they can police themselves according to a civilian set of values. The exclusion of the police from civilian scrutiny, be it by City Hall or by a review board, perpetuates a system that is apt to assign a higher priority to preserving *esprit de corps* than eliminating malpractice. As Albert Deutsch pointed out in *The Trouble with Cops*, "A perverse sense of loyalty tends to brand as a traitor to his group any police officer who publicly exposes dishonest colleagues. To an amazing degree, crimes that would send an ordinary citizen to prison are punished by mild reprimands, transfers, light suspensions without pay or requests for resignations. Dismissals are rare, and criminal prosecution even rarer."

Although Broderick expressed a desire to stay on as commissioner, his contract, which expired February 21, 1966, was not renewed by Lindsay. As he departed to join the famed Louis Nizer law firm, Broderick asked tauntingly, "Who is to run the police department?" His answer came in a ringing reassertion of civilian control, made by Lindsay in appointing a new commissioner: "These desperate voices which have spoken in the past few weeks about the relationship between the police department and the mayor have come perilously close to missing the basic principles of a democratically elected government. They have suggested—no, they have stated—that the police department is a law unto itself. They have stated that the duly elected civilian government of New York is not responsible for the police department as it is for the other departments in the city. The ultimate responsibility lies with the mayor, and I intend to exercise that responsibility."

Lindsay's choice as his new commissioner was Howard R. Leary, whose twenty-six-year span of police service had been capped by his appointment as Philadelphia's commissioner in 1963. During his three-year tenure as head of that 7,000-man department, Leary had shown an aptitude for adopting modern technology to police work and applying fresh approaches to nagging problems. But it was clearly his willingness to coexist with civilian review that caught the mayor's eye. The stumpy, quick-tongued Irishman was admittedly not comfortable with the Police Advisory Board that had been in existence in Philadelphia since 1958, but, he said, he had "learned to live with it."

As an outsider and a Lindsay appointee, Leary was not exactly welcomed by the old guard. His choice of a chief inspector, the key line officer who runs the department on a day-to-day basis, only widened the breach. It was Sanford D. Garelik, a Jew who had been inspector in charge of the Detective Division's special squads and who was leapfrogged over a number of more senior brass. Doubly rankling was the promotion of Deputy Inspector Lloyd G. Sealy, a Negro, to assistant chief inspector to serve as "an advisor on race relations to the commissioner."

Coupled with an internal restructuring that, in Leary's words, "will be more sensitive to community needs and more responsive to specific crime situations," the naming of Garelik and Sealy consolidated the new commissioner's grip on the department and broke up the Headquarters Irish Mafia. Charging that the appointments were "not routine" and resulted from "City Hall interference," several of the department's top officials promptly retired, as did a few lesser links in the chain of command. Although Leary later elevated three popular old-line officers to key positions, resentment over the Garelik and Sealy promotions still lingers.

Yet, below the ripples on the surface, the almost unfathomable mass of the department hardly undulates. With some 31,000 employees, it ranks behind only the Board of Education and the Department of Hospitals in size. The Patrol Division, by far the largest segment, consists of close to 19,000 patrolmen working out of eighty precincts in the five boroughs. Headquarters is honeycombed with specialized units ranging from the Narcotics Bureau, Safe, Loft and Truck Squad and Bomb Squad, which are part of the Detective Division, to the Emergency Service Division of rescue specialists, the Youth Division, and the Hack Drivers Bureau, which processes cab-driver applications.

In short, the New York force is a sprawling bureaucratic complex of almost unmanageable proportions. While the commissioner sets policy and reassures the public, while the Bureau of Public Information hands out press releases and guides visitors through headquarters, and the police band and marching units put the department's best foot forward, it is the faceless cadres in the precincts who stamp the force with its character.

Ethnically, the rank and file are not numerically representative of New York's melting-pot image. Men of Irish and Italian heritage are in the vast majority. Jews account for 6 to 7 percent, Negroes for 5 to 6 percent, and Latins about 3 percent. While minorities have never sought the police career in large numbers, the ratio of Negroes on the force seems disproportionately low. New York City has a Negro population of 1,257,500, or 15.8 percent. By comparison, the Philadelphia and Chicago departments are about 20 percent Negro, a figure which corresponds roughly to the population ratio.

The promotional record of Negroes is likewise suspect. There are but 8 Negro detectives out of 283, 45 sergeants out of about 1,700, 20 lieutenants out of 1,000, and 1 captain out of 278. The mercurial rise of two Negroes, however, has distracted from the overall picture. Following the 1964 Harlem riots, Commissioner Murphy appointed law-educated Lloyd Sealy captain in charge of Harlem's 26th Precinct, and a year later Broderick promoted him to deputy inspector in command of patrol forces in Brooklyn North, which covers the touchy Bedford-Stuyvesant slums. In designating Sealy an assistant chief inspector, Leary actually created a position. Eldridge Waith has moved up fast to the command of the Sixth Division, which embraces three Harlem precincts.

The tendency of policemen to stick together can be seen in the various ethnic, religious, fraternal and patriotic clubs under the department aegis. There are no fewer than thirty-one, and their memberships are practically a demographic chart of the department. The largest is the Holy Name Society, with 17,000 members, a testimonial to the pervasive Catholic influence on the force. Of the religious clubs, the next largest is the Protestant St. George Society, with 4,500 members, followed by the Jewish Shomrin Society with 2,270. Proudly bringing up the rear is the 450-man St. Paul Society of Eastern Orthodox communicants.

The plurality of the Irish over the Italians is suggested by the Emerald Society's 8,500 members to the Columbia Association's 5,000. Next in line are the German Steuben Association with 1,600, the Negro Guardians Association with 1,600, and the Slavic Pulaski Association with 1,250. The Spanish Hispanic Society claims only 350 members, inordinately small in view of the large Puerto Rican population in the city. There is no organization representing the smattering of Orientals on the force.

There are also police chapters of national organizations. The Anchor Club is composed of 1,124 members of the Knights of Columbus, and the Square Club of 1,000 Masons. Five military veterans' posts boast a membership of 4,500. Within this social and fraternal milieu, the police are inveterate joiners; most belong to two or more organizations.

Like those of police in other cities, the socioeconomic backgrounds of The Finest are confined to a fairly narrow spectrum. Most policemen are products of a lower-middle-class environment that stresses such virtues as frugality, cleanliness, punctuality and conformity, insists on participation, if only token, in organized religion, and seeks status and security. Many are first- or second-generation Americans, raised in households where foreign tongues are spoken, old-country traditions and family ties are strong, and the usual suspicion of other nationalities and cultures prevails. Thus the policeman tends to be politically conservative and socially conventional, a striver whose most conspicuous trait is his lack of conspicuousness.

From this reservoir, a variety of personality types enter police service. Some are quick-witted and intelligent; others are not. Some are brave, even reckless; others are not. Some are industrious and conscientious; others are lazy. Some are ambitious; others prefer to languish in the ranks. Some are of sound moral principles; others are not. Some are swaggerers; others wear authority with grace.

There is also a multiplicity of motives for joining the force. In New York particularly, many follow a family tradition of police service, although the day that the badge brought automatic status in the neighborhood disappeared with the new affluency of the blue-collar worker. The romantic aura of adventure and sleuthing draws many, especially military veterans who find the transition from olive drab to blue hardly perceptible (after World War II, discharged veterans flocked to the department in such numbers that they comprised 78 percent of the uniformed patrol). A number of veterans have had experience in the military police or military investigative and intelligence branches, which gives them an edge in gaining the coveted detective's rating.

The police service also attracts its share of plodding, pedestrian types who shun more individually demanding jobs for the anonymity of the blue ranks. Since most applicants are young (New York's age limitation is twenty-one to twenty-nine) and not highly educated (only a high-school education or its equivalent is required), the badge often means an appreciable increase in earnings. Although figures for New York are not available, a 1966 survey of the Washington, D.C., metropolitan police revealed that 96.4 percent of the applicants were then earning less than the starting police salary, indicating that police wages are not the pittance they once were. Probably the largest single group attracted to police work is men with a mild inclination for the nature of the job coupled with a strong desire for civil-service security. "Most cops are personally insecure," asserts Donel E. J. MacNamara, a former government investigator and now a New York police consultant. "The service gives them security."

The badge and the authority it represents have inevitably been a magnet for gun-happy swaggerers, pathological bullies, sadists and others with severe personality defects. Although no comprehensive study of the problem has been completed, a Los Angeles survey some years ago hints at its scope. During the period 1953-1957, 760 applicants were given psychiatric tests. A startling 11.3 percent were rejected as not meeting acceptable psychiatric standards; more than half the rejectees were diagnosed as latent or borderline psychotics and almost one quarter as schizoid personalities.

Paradoxically, it is the civil-service system that has prevented effective screening of potential troublemakers. In many jurisdictions, preinduction psychiatric testing is proscripted by civil-service regulations; a 1961 survey by the International Association of Chiefs of Police determined that only 50 of 300 departments queried conducted the tests, and presumably in some cases the lack of testing was involuntary. Once inducted and safely past a probationary term that usually does not exceed one year, the misfit is sheltered by civil-service tenure that precludes his removal for all but the most flagrant and provable offenses. Some departments, Boston's for one, partially circumvent the civil-service restrictions by having a psychiatrist present at physical examinations in the hope of detecting the more obvious deviants and rejecting them on one excuse or another. But such ploys are no more than a stopgap measure, and the essential problem continues to plague American law enforcement.

Whatever his background and origins, the New York recruit is molded into the image and likeness of The Finest by subtle processes of the society into which he has entered. The phenomenon was observed by former deputy commissioner Richard Dougherty in his novel *The Commissioner*. By the end of his indoctrination, Dougherty wrote, the recruit had become, no matter what his origins, thoroughly Irish in character. "His

point of view, his way of seeing and judging the world, became
a cop's point of view and that was a darkly Celtic thing—suspicious, untrusting, and fearful." That fear, said Dougherty,
was chiefly of "civilians"—the millions of New Yorkers who
were not members of the department.

The introverting process begins with training. The Police
Academy, formerly housed in a musty converted school building at 7 Hubert Street, now occupies a new $8,000,000, eight-
story complex on East 20th Street. It also has as tenants a combined 13th-15th Precinct station house, the nation's first and
possibly still the best police crime laboratory, the Medical
Bureau, and the College of Police Science of the City University of New York. Though the program of instruction reflects
modern advances, the philosophy remains the essential product
of an earlier day.

The philosophy stresses physical prowess and militarylike
regimentation. A departmental booklet describing the Police
Academy informs: "During the Draft Riots of 1863, the training of policemen paid off. Disciplined, well-drilled cops took
rapid-fire military orders—'By the right flank, company front,
double quick, charge!' A training lesson learned in these riots
was that in close contact with a mob no weapon was as effective
as the club. Inspector Carpenter's famous formula was: 'Strike
quick and strike hard.' Training with a nightstick has been
standard practice ever since."

The supremacy of physical force is a theme that dominates
the rookie's four months at the Academy. It is drummed into
him that, by virtue of his selection and training, he is superior
man to man to a possible foe and must always take the initiative and "command the situation." He is afforded intensive
training in firearms at the academy's indoor range and on an
outdoor range at Rodman's Neck in the Bronx. Accent on the
physical is constant. "Physical training at the academy is geared
to develop an above-average degree of strength, endurance,

agility, coordination, and skill," the department's *Self Portrait* declares, "in preparing the new patrolman for the rigors of a job that at times taxes his physical being to the utmost."

Modern police work also taxes the intellect to the utmost, yet there does not seem to be a comparable emphasis on this faculty. For example, the police have been delegated many discretionary powers, including the use of deadly force. The number of homicides by police, some of which have sparked racial disturbances, is a matter of more than passing concern. Until recently, New York State law, which conforms basically with that of other states, permitted a policeman to shoot to kill "if he reasonably believed that the person at whom he shot was committing a felony or escaping from a felony."

The law was ambiguous and loose and necessarily avoided the profound moral considerations involved in taking a life. A juvenile who steals a car for a brief joyride is a felon and could be legally shot in the back while fleeing from it. The possession of marijuana is a felony punishable by up to three years in prison in many jurisdictions, and a suspect running away with a single reefer in his pocket could be stopped by bullets. The only reasonable and moral criterion should be whether the suspect clearly is a threat to the physical being of the officer or other persons.

Effective September 1, 1967, New York State tightened restrictions on the use of deadly force. Commissioner Leary revised his department's regulations in accordance with the law; deadly force, he explained, could be used "only in situations where the person against whom it is used has himself escalated matters by using or threatening deadly or other serious force." Among the potential situations, he elaborated, is a suspect trying to escape by using a deadly weapon or otherwise indicating that unless apprehended immediately he is likely to endanger human life or inflict serious physical injury.

Laudable as they are, such guidelines cannot possibly solve

the calculus of on-the-spot decision-making. Many a menacing bulge in a dead suspect's pocket has turned out to be an innocent object, and many a dead suspect has been not guilty of the crime. A fatal shooting in Oakland, California, illustrates how different the apparent can be from reality. A man ran from a tavern pursued by the barkeep shouting, "Stop! Robber!" A policeman took up the chase and, when the suspect failed to respond to his command to halt, shot him fatally in the head. It had not been an armed robbery after all: the man had merely not paid for a drink. To cover for the mistake, the dead man was accused of "defrauding an innkeeper," a felony no matter what the monetary loss. There was no public uproar because, as the policeman commented, the man had a long record and "nobody cares when you kill a rotten egg."

The New York Police Academy includes in its firearms training an electronic course which duplicates the kind of situation that occurred in Oakland. The rookie is confronted with fifty simulated situations flashed on a movie screen and is required to make an instant decision whether to shoot or hold fire. In one, he may be lulled into thinking he has the drop on a bandit when a confederate suddenly materializes from behind a door with gun blazing. In another, he may be ready to fire on a fugitive when children appear in the background.

I asked John T. Downer, the inspector in charge of the academy, whether rookies who showed a tendency to be trigger-happy were taken aside for special counseling. "There is no rule to that effect," he said. "The instructors may do it on their own, but we don't have much time to spend on each man because we handle some 12,000 a year." The rookie going onto the street from this police factory has received only a smattering of specific advice. "We tell them not to shoot unless absolutely necessary," Downer stated, "and the old hands in the precincts give them the same advice." Although New York police are permitted to shoot to disable (in the FBI we were not supposed to unholster unless we intended to shoot to kill), the point is largely academic under actual conditions. "There aren't many crack shots who can assure the difference," the inspector conceded.

The "instant judgments" police are called upon to make are basically reflexive actions conditioned by training and environment. The training instills aggressiveness in a policeman until it is second nature to him, and the semimilitary environment, with its regimentation and automatic response in place of individuality ("the department's manual on rules and procedures," declares the *Self Portrait* booklet, "becomes the learning policeman's Bible"), hardly sharpens the reasoning power. The combination often results in precipitous violence. A New York policeman described trapping a knife-wielding youth in a blind alley. "My first instinct was to shoot him," he said, "and if I had been fatigued or in a bad mood I'm sure I would have—it's that fine a decision. But I held off a second, and he didn't come after me. I told him to drop the knife. He did, and I effected the arrest."

With the College of Police Science now located within the confines of the Police Academy, the inquisitive air of the campus may prove a stimulant to more enlightened thinking. More and more policemen are now being exposed to the broadening effect of higher education, and changes, durable if not dramatic, are bound to come in time. Professor Alexander Smith has conducted studies which reveal that "college-oriented police are not, as a group, as authoritarian as others." But Donel Mac-Namara, the consultant who also teaches at the college, doubts that education can work miracles. "See those two detectives?" he asked, pointing to a pair of neat, sharp-looking men. "They have master's degrees. They're smart, personable and articulate. But their thinking is turn-of-the-century. The police as a group simply resist change."

In part, the inertia is attributable to the nature of the police bureaucracy. Its officials are men who have climbed step by step up the civil-service ladder; they inherently resist radical departure from the status quo. Like most bureaucracies, the police system is regulated by a surfeit of rules and a welter of red tape—the Mayor's Task Force found the department bogged down in a morass of 500 official and 2,000 unofficial forms, and commented wryly, "The proliferation of paper threatens police efficiency." To the chair-bound bureaucrat, however, forms are a kind of psychological warfare that intimidate policemen into "going by the book" and help to "fix responsibility" when an embarrassing incident occurs.

The bureaucracy is anchored to past traditions and empirical truths and suspicious of bold, imaginative thinking. Conformity is its most cherished virtue, for in conformity the image can be perpetuated. Not long ago, a New York patrolman was fired because his wife won an annulment on the grounds that he refused to have sexual relations with her, and a bachelor officer was given the gate for having sexual relations with a single girl—conduct, the department declared, its collective finger fairly quivering, that "tended to cause criticism detrimental to the department."

The nature of the police task encourages a kind of cynicism that hardly breeds visionaries. The policeman is a leading expert on grubby reality—the sordid, the squalid, the worst twists of human nature. He feels that in this *demimonde*, platitudes are dispensable. While there is a certain fundamental logic to this philosophy, it is vastly oversimplified. The world cannot be divided into "good guys" and "bad guys" with no shades of difference in between. In a time when control of wanton criminality constitutes only a fraction of the police function and the enforcement of sumptuary laws is a major part, it is an obsolete philosophy.

As soon as he "hits the bricks" in his assigned precinct, the rookie is shorn of his illusions. "Forget what they told you at the academy," is the standard advice of the veterans. "Here're a couple of tips. . . ." The tips may range from how to blackmail a whore to the tricks of hoodwinking headquarters and the advisability of carrying a hidden "toss-away" knife or gun that can be planted on a suspect to corroborate an excuse of self-defense. As he struggles to apply academy theory to the reality of the street, the rookie is frustrated even more. He has been taught that his job calls for the utmost discretion, and he is baffled by the seemingly limitless restrictions a democratic society imposes on his exercise of power. And when he does finally "bust" a criminal and the criminal soon returns to the streets, he is bewildered and angry over what he considers "turnstile justice."

Perplexed and disillusioned, all but the most resilient retreat to the security of the womb—the police society that the late Chief William H. Parker of Los Angeles termed the "shell of minorityism." To the general community it is an "out" society—as out, ironically, as youth gangs and hippies. The policeman's odd hours, the secretive nature of his work, and the social stigma that attaches to being a cop (even police executives are not as acceptable in men's clubs as their military counterparts) combine to encapsulate him. Among his own he can share the mystique and camaraderie that go with being a policeman.

Inside this society, the policeman becomes integrated into the fraternal whirl. Should he be, say, a detective, a Catholic, of Italian extraction and a military veteran, he likely will belong to the Detective's Endowment Association, the Holy Name Society, the Columbia Association and American Legion Post #1059, thus enhancing his internal standing and prestige. But even in this subculture, the lines of discrimination are often drawn, perhaps more clearly outside of New York, as in the case of an Oakland police fraternal organization that denies membership to Negro officers.

Nestled in the security of their own society, the police bravely confront their enemies on the outside. A measure of their solidarity can be gained from the reaction of two gatherings of The Finest to words they longed to hear. When the superarticulate William F. Buckley, the Conservative party's candidate for mayor in 1966, defended the tactics of the Selma, Alabama, police before a communion breakfast of the Holy Name Society, he received a lusty ovation. When the curmudgeonish Robert Moses, the former Parks Commissioner and World's Fair chief executive, told a communion breakfast of the St. George Society that criticism of the police was Communist-inspired, he was roundly applauded.

3

New York:
Behind the Image

The day is past when police departments are content to sit back and answer press inquiries and scramble to cover up or minimize a bad blunder or nasty scandal. Perhaps inspired by the tremendous success of the FBI in applying Madison Avenue techniques to the creation of an image, they have taken the offensive with aggressive publicity campaigns. New York is no exception. It has hired Sylvan Fox, a former newspaperman with the defunct *World-Telegram and Sun*, as deputy commissioner in charge of press relations.* In this civilian post, he directs the Bureau of Public Information in programs designed to depict The Finest in the best possible light.

The BPI escorts visitors on tours showing off headquarters operations, the laboratory, a new police museum, and the Image-Maker, a optical device that can "sketch" a subject in minutes as opposed to the hours it once took a police artist. It produces publications such as *Self Portrait*, which acquaints the public with the many functions of the department, and prepares feature stories for media presentation. Under a Know Your Police Department program, police officers make appear-

---

* In 1967 Fox resigned and became a reporter on the New York *Times*. He was succeeded by Jacques Nevard.

ances at schools and invite classes to visit station houses. A children's coloring book, "What Does a Policeman Do?" and a comic book, "Your Friend, the Policeman," are widely distributed in the schools. In the final panel of the comic book, a teenager who has been on a tour of police facilities shakes hands with a bluecoat and comments, "A New York policeman risks his life a dozen times a day, and he does it for us! He's the enemy of the lawless, but to me and the millions like me . . . he's our friend and protector!"

To adult New Yorkers familiar with the history of the force, this kind of idealization strikes a slightly discordant note. At one time in the city it was virtually impossible to distinguish between the law enforcers and the lawless, a state of affairs uncapped by the celebrated Becker-Rosenthal case of 1912. Lt. Charles Becker and his band of police cohorts, operating with the subvert benediction of Tammany Hall, boldly maintained a stranglehold on the city's criminal rackets through intimidation, terror and, when necessary, murder. A crusading district attorney finally blew the whistle on the free-wheeling lieutenant after the murder of Joseph Rosenthal, a racketeer who refused to pay off. Following a sensational trial, Becker was convicted and went to the electric chair at Sing Sing prison.

The scandal did not curtail police-racketeers liaisons, it merely drove them underground. The racketeers operated under a sort of delimitations agreement, carving up the rackets territory along precinct lines, which prevented internecine warfare. Thus many an ambitious officer aspired to the rank of precinct captain, not for the prestige and slightly higher salary, but because it was to the captain that the "bagman" ordinarily delivered the police cut, and it was he who skimmed off the largest percentage.

While the day of extensive and organized police corruption is gone—most high police executives neither condone nor tolerate it—the tradition is far from extinct. In 1951 the biggest police-gambler alliance of modern times broke into the open when federal authorities arrested bookmaker Harry Gross, one of whose specialties was fixing college basketball point spreads. Gross' ring, it was revealed, had been paying the staggering sum of $1,000,000 a year to the police for protection, and more than 100 of The Finest, implicated in the payoffs, were dismissed or retired.

In 1960, the same year the citizens of Denver and Chicago were shocked to learn of police burglarly rings in their towns, Ted Poston and a team of New York *Post* reporters dug into The Pad, described by Poston as "the police-approved list of spots or locations where 'official protection' is guaranteed in the six-day-a-week operation of the numbers racket. . . . [Each] spot must be approved by the police for The Pad. And each spot on The Pad must be paid for in cash." According to Poston, the usual sum for the patrolman on the beat was $2 a day, with larger monthly sums being funneled into the hands of a bagman for distribution to precinct, division and headquarters brass in on the take. A police official is quoted as saying: "If you knew the actual amount of money involved, you wouldn't believe it."

Such was the greed of the police involved, the *Post* series contended, that small numbers operators were forced out of business, leaving a vacuum filled by the national crime syndicate, which was well able to afford the bite. For almost four years, the district attorney's office and the Confidential Investigating Unit, a crack unit reporting directly to the commissioner, carried on a silent probe into the payoff labyrinth. On June 25, 1964, ten policemen who refused to sign waivers of immunity and testify before a grand jury were dismissed. The development prompted the chief inspector, whose investigating unit was responsible for enforcement of the antigambling laws, to transfer his entire complement of forty-eight men; the unit had, he said with typical police understatement, "lost its effectiveness."

Eventually fourteen policemen were found guilty of perjury, and a veteran captain was suspended for "consorting with known gamblers." Yet the hard lessons seemingly have not reformed incorrigible "bad cops." The commissioner's elite unit still turns up incidents of payoff, shakedown, extortion and bribery. A streetwide observer can still watch policy-slip bankers, bar owners with after-hours action, and others on the fringe or wrong side of the law sidle up to patrol cars and drop packages inside during a brief exchange of banter. "New York cops are democratic," quipped one New Yorker; "they'll take ten dollars from anyone." A highly placed union official told me about a game played for higher stakes. "Whenever we schedule a picket line," he said, "we grease the precinct captain, and the police don't molest us. But one time a rival union paid off more, and damned if the police didn't rough up our pickets anyhow."

Widespread police venality, or at least citizen belief that widespread venality exists, has so corroded respect for the police that most citizens find it difficult to feel empathy with a "friend and protector" they fear may be on the take. The nature of the job is such that the police are constantly exposed to temptation. The policeman on the beat can elect to enforce ordinances or overlook them, and the vice-squad detective can omit a place from a raid list. These are only two examples of the discretionary powers the police can pin with a price tag.

Few policemen join the force with the express intent of using the badge for profit, but the manifold pressures to which the police are subjected can weaken all but the most resolute. Although departmental rules forbid the acceptance of gratuities, the taking of a bottle of liquor from a grateful storekeeper or, in the case of a detective, a television set in return for cracking a warehouse burglary is commonplace. From this relatively innocent beginning a process of rationalization is liable to set in. New York pays starting patrolmen $6,355 per annum, with a maximum of $7,806 after three years' service. In a locale with a high cost of living like New York, this amounts to a bare subsistence wage, especially so for a man with four or five children. Consequently a few dollars here, an item of merchandise there is viewed more as a rightful perquisite of an ill-paying job than an evil that in the end can be a consummate one.

Most police make a distinction between gambling and what they consider serious vices such as prostitution and narcotics peddling. Gambling, they reason, may be illegal but it is not immoral per se, and their cut therefore is "clean money" as opposed to the "dirty money" connected with prostitution and narcotics.

Once the policeman has taken a bribe or payoff, however, he is hooked just as surely as the narcotics addict. He gets in deeper and deeper, to the point where he cannot possibly extricate himself. Ted Poston of the *Post* reported that police officials told him some policemen had accumulated so much money from The Pad they did not know how to spend it without getting in trouble.

Abuse of authority is not limited to looking the other way. On February 18, 1966, two detectives burst into an East Side apartment without a search warrant to seize, they said, a quantity of marijuana in possession of the occupants. A private detective accompanied them, and it was subsequently alleged that the raid was no more than a pretext to allow the detective to take a photograph for a divorce suit. The apartment occupants were cleared of charges of marijuana possession, and, as of this writing, departmental charges against the officers remain pending.

The presence of uniformed officers about a business premises has an understandably deterrent effect on patronage, a fact the New York department has employed to drive out of business dance halls, hamburger joints, coin-machine emporiums and other enterprises catering to what it considers "undesirable elements." The same technique has been used by police on the take to persuade balky businessmen to "contribute." An episode in Harlem that dangerously increased police-community antagonisms apparently was an attempt to extort money.

A version of the episode was given in a press statement by Donald Smith, director of public relations for the Congress of Racial Equality, on February 28, 1966: "On the evening of February 20th, Mrs. ——* and a female companion were seated in a booth at Joe's Place, 449 West 125th Street, when four police officers entered—a captain, a sergeant and two patrolmen. Mrs. —— and witnesses report that one of the patrolmen walked to the table at which Mrs. —— and one of her friends were seated, grabbed her by the hand, dragged her into the kitchen of the bar and demanded that she 'identify herself as a woman.' Mrs. —— remonstrated with the officer, declaring that she was married, a housewife and mother of two children. Thereupon, according to Mrs. —— and one of her friends who stood nearby, the officer ordered Mrs. —— to lift her dress and exhibit incontrovertible evidence of her femininity. Embarrassed, frightened, and almost hysterical, Mrs. —— complied."

An affidavit filed by the victim agrees with this version. "I told [the officer] that I was a married woman with two children and that I was not a faggot," she swore on February 26, 1966. "He ordered me to lift my dress up and pull my panties down. He then looked at my exposed private parts, smiled, and left the kitchen. . . ."

* I have deleted the name of the victim, a Harlem housewife, from the account as it is not material.

The police contended they were concerned about homosexuals in the area, which, if true, hardly explains their unconscionable travesty of legitimate methods of investigation. But according to the bar owner, two police officers had been in the day before on a shakedown mission. He said he gave them $15, and was jestingly told to consider it "a contribution to the Police Athletic League." The next day they were back looking for another "contribution," and he refused. It was that night that the incident took place.

CORE did not allow the affair to drop, as the police would undoubtedly have preferred. It scheduled a revolving picket line on February 28, 1966, at the three precinct stations of the Sixth Division, the jurisdiction in which the incident had taken place. A division inspector, CORE later claimed, agreed to orderly picketing of the length of the precinct station houses. Nothing untoward happened at the first two stations, but at the third the pickets were blocked from assuming their picketing posts by a wall of blue uniforms. When CORE leaders led the pickets around the police line to take up positions as originally agreed, they were arrested and charged with "disorderly conduct." The police had reneged, they charged, in an effort to discredit the protest.

The handling of the affair by departmental brass gave little assurance that they were interested in anything except letting the storm blow over. CORE had made the reasonable demand that "this entire group of officers be removed from Harlem, that suspensions be applied and that charges be brought against the patrolman who is alleged to have done the cruel act. His removal from the force and strong guarantees that the department will not tolerate this kind of misconduct in the future are needed to allay the anger of this aroused community."

No apologies or guarantees were forthcoming from the department. Chief Inspector Sanford Garelik did transfer three of the accused officers, including the captain, who is still a supervisor of patrol in another district. But the transfers did nothing to resolve the question of the officers' conduct (although the victim has filed a civil suit seeking $300,000 damages for "extreme humiliation"). It has long been a source of irritation in Harlem that the department habitually consigns its least desirable officers there, and this case provoked William H. Booth, chairman of the City Commission on Human Rights, to deplore police "dumping" of problem officers in Negro neighborhoods. "What we don't want in Harlem," he said, "we certainly don't want somewhere else."

Internal discipline in the New York department seems to display the same dichotomy as that of other departments across the nation. Alleged malfeasance involving graft, bribery or complicity in criminal acts is vigorously but quietly investigated, although cooperation from the suspect officer's comrades usually is not forthcoming because of the peculiar code of silence, not unlike the Mafia's *ommerta*, that deems an informer a traitor to his class. Should the charges be substantiated, and if the case has not been exposed in the newspapers, the bad apple is removed from the barrel by means of the "negotiated resignation" in which he is handed his pretyped resignation and signs it—or else. No one on the outside is the wiser, but the offender escapes criminal prosecution and is free to move on to another department.

However, should the charges involve brutality or excessive force, the investigation ordinarily takes an entirely different tack. Such charges are viewed not only as a challenge to police prerogatives, but as an opportunity for minority groups, civil libertarians and assorted leftists to attack the police establishment itself. The department closes ranks behind the officer, and the inquiry is aimed not at incriminating the guilty but at deprecating his accuser, undermining the accuser's position, and gathering evidence to bring charges against him.

Aside from deflecting justice, this policy can produce tragic consequences, as the Harlem riots of 1964 seem to prove. Harlem had long seethed under what it felt was continuous and unwarranted police oppression. On April 17, 1964, there was a seemingly innocuous incident on Lenox Avenue in the heart of Harlem. Some children running down the street toppled a fruit stand; several began to pick up the fruit and replace it, while several others began tossing it playfully around. The police were called, and, had the children been white, they would probably have escaped with a stern lecture. But they were Negro, and the long hot summer that culminated in the July rioting was about to get under way.

Truman Nelson, who did exhaustive tape interviews with the children involved and their mothers, recounts in a book entitled *Torture of Mothers** what happened:

> The owner of the stand called the police. They came in force and fell on the children with drawn guns and flailing clubs, in an attack so fearful and merciless that the people came swarming out of their tenements in horror and shock.
>
> Some young Negroes, teenagers, felt compelled to come between the attackers and their defenseless victims, and became, in turn, the victims. These boys were handcuffed and beaten in the street and then taken to the precinct house, where, handcuffed, they were beaten again, mercilessly and incessantly by cops who exchanged uniform coats for sweatshirts so as to carry on with more comfort and efficiency. The boys were beaten steadily from four in the afternoon until around midnight, taken to the Harlem Hospital to be patched up, taken back and beaten again (handcuffed as usual), with the sweatshirted police working in shifts.

Frank Stafford, a thirty-one-year-old Negro salesman, and Fecundo Acion, a forty-seven-year-old Puerto Rican seaman, also had the temerity to intercede on the children's behalf. They too were manhandled and hauled off to the precinct station, where they were shoved into the detectives' office up-

* Newburyport, Massachusetts, Garrison Press.

stairs with the others. All were handcuffed behind their backs. "They came in with oranges and started smashing them in people's faces," said Stafford, "saying . . . you like fruit, you like oranges, well try these. . . . It went on for a while. About thirty-five I'd say came into the room and started beating, punching us in the jaw, in the stomach, in the chest, beating us with a padded club [blunt instruments are favored in police "interrogations" because they do not draw blood and injuries can be attributed to falls]. . . . They just beat us across the back, pulled us on the floor, spat on us, called us niggers, dogs, animals. 'You got what you deserve,' these are the things that they said to us."

Nineteen hours after the orgy of beatings started, Stafford was taken to the hospital, where for close to a month doctors struggled to save an eye. But he had been too badly beaten in that eye, and it finally had to be removed. He is now on the street again selling, with a patch over his eye, and he claims the police have pegged him a "cop hater" and stare menacingly at him. His lawyer has advised him to have a companion with him " 'cause the police may try to mess with me again." As a pretext to protect themselves against unlawful arrest charges, the police lodged three criminal charges against Stafford, including the incredible charge of assaulting the police.

For the three teenagers who intervened in the assault on the children the nightmare was not over. On April 29, the police came to their homes and dragged them off again. The mother of Danny Hamm relates that when the detectives came and her son readily acknowledged his identity, "right away—gun right to the head and slapping him up, one gun here and one here—just all the way down the hall—beating him and knocking him around with the gun to his head." Also arrested were three friends of the trio who were partners in a pigeon coop kept on a tenement roof. Even before the fruit-stand incident, the six had been shaken down by the police on the

roof; in Harlem the police are chary of rooftops, seeing them
as potential sniper's nests. After an all-night vigil at the precinct station, the mothers learned in the morning that the boys
were being charged with first-degree murder in the death of
Mrs. Margit Sugar, a Harlem used-clothing-store owner.

The police case rested largely on the "confessions" of the
boys, and it is not too difficult to imagine how they were obtained. The mood of the trial was set by the daily press, which
kept up a drumfire of innuendo depicting the boys as black
nationalists and racists, the *Times* going so far as to "identify"
them as members of a killer gang called the Blood Brothers,
the existence of which has never been documented. The trial
took place in March 1965. The prosecution approached first
the mothers, then the boys, offering to reduce charges in return
for guilty pleas, a sure sign of a flimsy police case.

The boys stuck to their pleas of not guilty, recanting the
"confessions." Nevertheless, they were convicted and sentenced to life imprisonment, and as this is written, appeals are
still pending. The case of the Harlem Six has become a *cause
célèbre* and a symbol of police persecution to the black community of New York.

Regardless of the guilt or innocence of the Harlem Six, the
issue of police conduct still remains unresolved. If the version
told by the victims and eyewitnesses is substantially accurate,
there is displayed here an arrogance and cruelty reminiscent
of the Gestapo. It is scarcely to the department's credit that it
refused to "dignify the charges" with a public explanation.
Nor is the department's credibility enhanced by the reply it
furnished, apparently at the instance of Mayor Lindsay, to the
inquiry of Don R. Baumgart of Seattle, Washington. Profoundly disturbed by *Torture of Mothers*, Baumgart wrote the
mayor asking if the incidents described were true, and, if so,
what action was being taken. Three months later he received a
reply from Michael J. Lonergan, an inspector in the office of

the chief of staff. The matter had been "duly investigated," said Lonergan, "and no evidence existed that the persons mentioned in the article written by Mr. Nelson were the subjects of the actions described in the articles." And, solemnly declared the police spokesman in what reads like gallows humor, "No complaints were made by any of the individuals described in the articles nor any members of their families alleging police brutality of any kind."

The fruit-stand incident raised Harlem temperatures to the flashpoint, and the fatal shooting of a fifteen-year-old Negro schoolboy on July 16 by an off-duty police lieutenant was the incendiary spark. The officer, Thomas R. Gilligan, claimed that James Powell had attacked him with a knife without provocation, and a grand jury accepted his story that he had acted in self-defense. The grand jury transcript shows that a knife was found in a nearby gutter, although no witnesses placed it in the boy's hand and accounts of the incident were conflicting.

The grand jury's exoneration of Gilligan was a foregone conclusion in Harlem, since it is axiomatic that police officers who plead self-defense are *never* indicted. Posters bearing Gilligan's photograph and the heading "Wanted for Murder" blossomed throughout black Harlem. On the night of July 18 there was a protest demonstration and a mob, spurred by heated oratory, rampaged through central Harlem attacking whites, pulling fire alarms, looting stores and generally venting its rage. For three nights violence reigned. On the third night it spread to the slums of Brooklyn's Bedford-Stuyvesant district.

The police responded to the rioting with a firm, disciplined hand, and incidents of police overzealousness were relatively few. One stratagem they used was to transport those arrested into other precincts for booking, on the theory this would eliminate milling hostile throngs around the station houses. When the riot toll was counted, many whites heaved a sigh of relief and were thankful to the police for forcefully containing the violence. But hardly anyone pressed for an inquest to consider police responsibility in causing the riots in the first place.

The grievances of tenement and slum dwellers against the police go far beyond physical maltreatment; they embrace all the slurs, indignities, degradations and double standards men with badges can impose on minority peoples. "For many years," asserted a CORE statement, "CORE has pointed out that New York City has two kinds of law enforcement—one for the respectable white majority, another for Negroes, Puerto Ricans and people that might be called nonconformist or bohemian."

The dual standards are evident even in such a simple area as traffic-law enforcement. The neatly dressed white offender is ordinarily treated, provided he does not become obstreperous, with crisp courtesy by The Finest and goes his way with a summons or warning. But take the case of a man we shall call James Parson, who happens to be Negro and who happened to display a CORE sticker on his automobile. Not long ago James Parson was halted in Harlem for running a stop sign. Although he produced a valid driver's license, the officer ordered him from the car, frisked him, and searched the car, probably on a fishing expedition for narcotics. Then the officer marched him *at gunpoint* to the precinct station because, the officer claimed, Parson did not have sufficient identification. He was held for close to two hours without any charges being made. "Must have been every cop in the place came by and called me a nigger motherfucker and stuff like that," recalled Parson. "There were times when I didn't think I was going to get out of there alive." Finally he was taken upstairs to a captain, who decided his identification was in order. He left without a bruise to manifest his ordeal.

Repeated incidents of this kind have left the white policeman in Harlem stereotyped as a swaggering, arbitrary bully. A 1964 publication entitled *Youth in the Ghetto*, produced by

Harlem Youth Opportunity Unlimited, Inc., aired viewpoints representative of this consensus. A man of thirty-three complained:

> The white cops, they have a damn sadistic nature. . . . We don't need them! They don't do the neighborhood any good. . . . They start more violence than any other people start. A bunch of us could be playing some music, or dancing, which we have as an outlet for ourselves. We can't dance in the house, we don't have clubs or things like that. So we're out on the sidewalk. . . . Right away here comes a cop! "You're disturbing the peace!" No one has said anything; you understand; no one has made a complaint. Everyone is enjoying themselves. But here comes one cop, and he'll want to chase everyone. And gets mad. I mean he gets mad! We aren't mad. He comes into the neighborhood, aggravated and mad.

A man of thirty-five recapitulated:

> Last night, for instance, the officer stopped some fellows on 125th Street, Car No. ———, that was the number of the car, and because this fellow spoke so nicely for his protection and his rights, the officer said, "All right, everybody get off the street or inside!" Now, it's very hot. We don't have air-conditioned apartments. . . . We can't go back in the house because we almost suffocate. Now where are we going? But he came out with his nightstick and wants to beat people on the head and wanted to—he arrested one fellow. The other fellow said, "Well, I'll move, but you don't have to talk to me like a dog." I think we should all get together—everybody—all get together and every time one draws back his stick to do something to us, or hits one of us on the head, take the stick and hit *him* on *his* head, so he'll know how it feels. . . .

One of the most redundant complaints is that Harlem has become a catch-basin for police who have gotten into trouble elsewhere or fail to meet customary standards. "Downtown the cops are sharp-looking and wear white gloves," griped one Harlem resident. "We get the sloppy, seedy ones here." Jus-

tifiably, Harlem residents feel they are entitled to police service of an order equal to other sections of the city. Most Negro
crime is directed against other Negroes, yet many Harlem
businessmen and citizens allege that police protection is virtually nonexistent. Through either indifference or incompe-
tence, the "wall-to-wall cops," as one detractor has put it, have
failed to contain the lawless elements in Harlem while har-
assing its law-abiding citizens.

One of the more mortifying harassment techniques is the
street stop, which several years ago was cloaked in legality by
the passage of the "stop-and-frisk" law in New York. Advocated by the police and lobbied into being by an association of
district attorneys, the law avowedly is a crime-prevention
weapon and a means for the police to discover concealed weapons that might be used against them. It authorizes a police
officer to search the person of anyone he has "reasonable suspicion" to believe has committed a crime or is about to commit
a crime.

In practice, "reasonable suspicion" is the kind of abstract
term that opens the door wide to abuse. The policeman can
shake down a citizen on no more than a visceral feeling that
something is amiss or even with malicious intent, yet have little
difficulty in "justifying" the action by placing a suspicious con-
notation on the circumstances of the moment. John Pember-
ton, Jr., national executive director of the American Civil Liberties Union, takes a dim view of giving police the right to
force people to explain their presence on his beat. "How can
you have probable cause to believe a person guilty of a crime
that hasn't been committed yet?" he asked on the *Playboy* panel
discussion, "Crisis in Law Enforcement." *

* The validity of the stop-and-frisk statute was upheld by the New York Court
of Appeals in 1965 in the case of *People vs. Rivera*, a decision the U.S. Supreme
Court refused to review. As a result, a number of states have or are in the
process of adopting similar laws. However, further testing of the constitutionality
of such laws is in the offing.

It is impossible to convince the Negro and Puerto Rican communities that the stop-and-frisk law was not aimed solely at them. Terming the law "a nefarious example of class legislation," civil rights leader Bayard Rustin on the *Playboy* panel argued that "that kind of brusque police action is reserved for the poor and minorities like Negroes and Puerto Ricans." The police do not ordinarily frisk well-dressed businessmen on Wall Street, he said, but they do frequently frisk their well-dressed Negro counterparts in Harlem.

New York's police and prosecutors have promoted another piece of dubious legislation, the so-called no-knock-and-enter law. It empowers police to burst into and search a suspect's home or business premises without either knocking or announcing themselves as police officers. The law was designed primarily to enable police to preserve the evidence in narcotics cases; frequently the suspect would flush the narcotics down the toilet while police were announcing themselves outside. Defenders of the law point out that the police can act only on reasonable cause and must first secure a search warrant through normal procedures. Theoretically, an officer wanting a warrant must convince a judge that he has reasonable cause, but quite often in practice the warrants have already been signed and need only be filled in by the police or prosecutor. Of overriding consideration in laws of this nature is that they give police powers which chip away at the spirit and intent of the Constitution—powers which the police have yet to demonstrate they can apply with judicious concern for the rights of a free people.

Another grating symbol of police power in the ghettos is the Tactical Patrol Force, an elite squad which has its counterpart in other major departments in the country. The TPF was established in 1949 "to supplement the regularly assigned foot patrol personnel in any given area during periods when unusual crime conditions require reinforced manpower." It is a volunteer group of some 300 men, all unmarried six-footers trained in judo and imbued with a "gung-ho" spirit reminiscent of the Army's Green Berets. The TPF is the department's trouble-shooting corps. In one highly publicized special assignment, TPF members dressed as women acted as decoys to lure sex molesters and purse-snatchers in Central Park into the arms of police.

The TPF also has been thrown into the breach to quell insurrections in the ghetto, and the brusque, head-cracking tactics of its members have been a source of surly resentment. During the 1964 disturbances, for example, a pair of TPF men smashed their pistols through the window of Harlem CORE headquarters and ordered the occupants, who tried to explain they were giving first aid, to "get upstairs or we'll blow your brains out."

The bullying approach was decried by former Commissioner Vincent Broderick. "There are some who believe that a rough manner is a sign of strength which brings swift obedience," he once admonished his men. "They are wrong. . . . There is no need for such behavior by any policeman. . . . Those who have this incorrect attitude must change it and change it now." Broderick's words, however, seem to have fallen on deaf ears.

More typical of police thinking is the self-righteous indignation of Broderick's predecessor, Michael Murphy, over lack of public support for the police institution. "Why," implored Murphy just before he retired, "are the police regarded in some quarters as enemies and aggressors rather than friends and protectors? . . . Why, for example, in a demonstration aimed at protesting slum conditions, does the attack suddenly switch from the slumlord to the policeman? . . . Why are we equated with some other police forces in the civil-rights struggle [an apparent reference to Deep South police forces], when our methods and successful handling of such problems have been in such healthy contrast?"

Murphy's bewilderment betrays an ignorance of the rudiments of minority hostility. In the eye of the slum dweller, the New York police are not fundamentally more civilized than the police of Selma and Birmingham; they are merely more subtle in their methods and pretentious in their claims of being friends and protectors. Racial and ethnic prejudices abound on the New York force, as they do in practically every other police force in the nation. These prejudices manifest themselves daily in hundreds of incidents of rudeness, indifference, deprecation and dual standards of enforcement.

Moreover, the police have made it plain that their allegiance lies with the power structure, not the people. In an article called "A Report from Occupied Territory" in *The Nation* (July 11, 1966), Negro author James Baldwin eloquently expresses the ghetto's view of the police. In every Northern urban center, he writes, "the police are simply the hired enemies of the population. They are present to keep the Negro in his place and to protect white business interests, and they have no other function. They are, moreover—even in a country which makes the very grave error of equating ignorance with simplicity—quite stunningly ignorant, and, since they know that they are hated, they are always afraid. One cannot possibly arrive at a more surefire formula for cruelty."

Harsh as Baldwin's indictment may seem, it is essentially accurate, and so long as the police envision their role as that of mercenaries of the power structure, the root problem will remain. "This is why those pious calls to 'respect the law,' " explains Baldwin, "always to be heard from prominent citizens each time the ghetto explodes, are so obscene. The law is meant to be my servant and not my master, still less my torturer and my murderer. To respect the law, in the context in which the American Negro finds himself, is simply to surrender his self-respect."

Attempts by the department to establish equitable relations

with the minority groups have been so superficial or misdirected as to be meaningless. Although "human relations" training appears on the Police Academy agenda, no one, least of all the police, pretends that it is any more than a cursory stab at a prodigious problem. The community-relations programs in operation dwell largely on how the citizen can prevent his car from being stolen or avoid burglaries, an academic subject to those who own neither car nor property. In March 1966 the department began a pilot program in conjunction with the National Conference of Christians and Jews, but the program is still in the seminar stage and concentrates on three precincts which are not in the sorely troubled areas.

Operation Friend, started in 1963 to ameliorate bitterness over the shooting of two Puerto Ricans by a policeman, has shown some promise. Significantly, the program was initiated not by headquarters, but by Capt. Stephan J. Valle, then commander of the predominantly Spanish-speaking 24th Precinct (Valle has since been promoted to deputy inspector of community relations). Himself of Spanish derivation, Valle undertook, with the cooperation of the Board of Education and the Community Center, to establish a police-to-people program that would break down the barriers to communication. Some 250 officers in the precinct took off-duty lessons in Spanish language and culture. An exchange program sent police to Puerto Rico and brought children from there to live for two weeks with police families.

When a visiting police chief from the Dominican Republic told of the critical need for used clothing there, the station house was used as a collection depot and more than a ton of clothing was shipped. To build rapport with neighborhood children, the police escort busloads of youngsters on tours of the United Nations and other excursions. A lively interest in the program is maintained by a monthly Operation Friend award given by radio station WBNX.

But thus far the scope of Operation Friend has been limited to 1 precinct out of the 114, and its principle has not been extended to the black community. Moreover, the remark of Captain Glaser that "we hope it will lower antagonisms so we can make more arrests without a mob collecting" suggests an ulterior motive that is subversive to the spirit of the program.

Attempts to accommodate the New York police to their role in a pluralistic society have been, like attempts in most major cities, nothing more than temporizations. For example, there have been urgings that the department step up its recruitment among minority groups, and the department has responded by lowering height minimums to make more Puerto Ricans eligible and doing some proselytizing in the Negro community.

But these and similar measures are only tangential to the central problem. The Negro policeman, for instance, functions from within a police structure that is essentially archaic, and by reason of being both a Negro and a policeman he tends to deal more arbitrarily and brutally with his people than do white officers—this is his only way to acceptance within the police society. "If the Negro cop works in Harlem," elaborates Norman Frank, public relations counsel to the Patrolmen's Benevolent Association, "he is an Uncle Tom. If he works elsewhere, he is a freak."

What is needed is a thorough rejuvenation of the system, a prerequisite of which is vastly improved recruiting standards. As it is, police recruitment is primarily a quantitative process, designed to meet authorized strengths calculated on a "desirable" police-to-citizens ratio. Under this criterion, the department has experienced a chronic manpower shortage, and it is ironic that at a time when the President's Commission is counseling departments to set their sights on a college degree for every member, New York has resorted to a program in which high-school dropouts are accepted as police cadets, prepared for high-school equivalency tests, and then absorbed into the ranks.

Rather than ever-spiraling authorized strengths, the emphasis should be switched to obtaining the quality of man the city really needs to enforce its laws. More often than not the most brutal, bigoted and arrogant officers are the same ones who are on the take and involved in the protection rackets, and the fact that most victims of police malpractice realize this fills their bitter cup to overflowing.

Moreover, the investigative prowess of The Finest could stand upgrading, as the rash of miscarriages in 1964 demonstrates. In that year a Spanish Harlem housewife was wrongfully arrested for possession of narcotics and spent twenty days in the House of Detention for Women; George Whitmore, Jr., was coerced into signing a bogus confession to the double murder of Janice Wylie and Emily Hoffert; Detective John C. Devlin, seeking a murder suspect, shot the wrong man three times; and an innocent man was charged with a murder later found to have been committed by the knife-slayer of Kitty Genovese, who was killed before the eyes of thirty-eight unheeding apartment dwellers in Kew Gardens, Queens. "We definitely need a better grade of police officer," affirms the PBA's Norman Frank, "but men who have the education and qualifications are not interested."

That highly qualified men reject the police career reflects more on a department that is physically and mentally musty than on the job itself. Mayor Lindsay's Task Force has arrived at the inevitable conclusion that New York badly needs imaginative and courageous policemen who will apply the law equally and merit the respect of all citizens, but that it will not get them unless the city is willing to break with tradition and face up to the controversy that will ensue. High on the priority list of recommended changes, in addition to the elimination of red tape and modernization of methods and facilities, are a civilian-dominated review board and an end to the "nepotism" that governs promotions. Until radical reforms are realized, the character of the department will continue to straggle almost out of sight behind its image as The Finest.

4

William H. Parker: Los Angeles' Controversial Cop

The recent history of the Los Angeles Police Department centers about the forceful, dynamic personality of its late chief, William H. Parker, who, outside of J. Edgar Hoover, was perhaps the nation's best-known law-enforcement officer. Parker, who ran the Lost Angeles force from 1950 to his death in 1966, was a straight-from-the-shoulder spokesman of a fraternity that tends to be tight-lipped. A lawman's lawman, he transformed a mediocre force into one of the nation's most efficient crime-fighting machines. But it was not much more than a machine, for the inflexible chief was an utter failure at human relations. It was this failure that prevented Parker, a man rich in talent, from achieving the total professionalism he preached for so many years.

Parker epitomized the police establishment as vividly as any one man could. A Victorian in a permissive age, he was confounded by the manners and mores of mid-twentieth-century America. A perfectionist in the mechanics of his trade, he failed to comprehended the swirling tides of change and became hostile to them. An authoritarian who worshipped the letter of the law, he was an uncompromising antagonist of those who invoked its spirit. Incorruptible, an unflagging taskmaster who literally worked himself to death, he was perplexed by public indifference to the police and acutely sensitive to criticism of his department.

It was Parker who coined the phrase "The Thin Blue Line," and it was he who promulgated most effectively the exaggerated notion that the police are the last bulwark of freedom and civil order in the United States. "If law enforcement fails in this democratic republic," he once warned in his Spenglerian rhetoric, "anarchy will sweep the land and the fires of freedom will be extinguished, and slavery will again become the lot of all mankind."

In personality, Parker was as bleak and forbidding as the Black Hills of South Dakota from which he came. His manner was brusque, businesslike, and rarely lightened with humor. In private moments, it is said, he could be engaging, almost charming. But private moments were few; he was totally wedded to his job. When he became indignant, which was often, his voice would rise and his words would become barbed. His wrath, once aroused, was monumental. In a 1962 meeting with the police commission and Negro leaders to explore ways of lessening friction between the police and the Negro community, Parker exploded: "I didn't come here to be lectured to. I'm going." He returned shortly thereafter, mollified but hardly conciliatory.

Despite his propensity for public outbursts, Parker did not crave the spotlight for personal publicity. "Sometimes I just want to hide," he once told his administrative aide, Lt. Vernon Hoy. But Parker was a man with a mission, and any challenge to the discretion of William H. Parker, or to that of the Los Angeles Police Department, was a clarion call to battle which he stood ever ready to answer.

Responsible for millions of dollars in public funds, Parker

was personally austere. He lived with his wife (they had no children) in a modest home in the Silver Lake district of Los Angeles. He did not drink or smoke. His office in the pretentious, glass-paneled police headquarters was plain to the point of obsession. His walnut desk, of 1930 vintage, looked oddly out of place, and he protested, "I don't want a new one," when informed a new budget had allowed for one. He permitted himself an assortment of memorabilia: a Boy Scout paperweight (he was president of the Los Angeles council); a sword bestowed on him by the Republic of Korea (in 1953 he was made honorary chief of the Korean National Police); a walnut cabinet crammed with plaques and awards; and several photographs taken with visiting dignitaries (he was proudest of that with General Douglas MacArthur). An American flag and the California Bear flag flanked his desk.

Parker was born in Lead, South Dakota, on June 21, 1902, and left his native state after graduating from high school. He had a thin, somewhat esthetic face, with a paradoxical set to the jaw that in later years gave him the appearance of a stern headmaster of a boys' school. He was in fact an intellectual among his breed, articulate and versed in the lessons of history. He went to law school at night while pounding a beat in the daytime and obtained a law degree from the Los Angeles College of Law in 1930. Admitted to the California bar, he seemingly had ideas of practicing law instead of continuing with the department. "At that time, as I seem to dimly recall," he told the Legal Secretaries Association in an address at Glendale in January 1951, "there was a depression and thus fate decided that I should remain with the police department."

From the moment he joined the department on August 8, 1927, Parker was pegged as a tough, no-nonsense cop. He refused to bend with the expediency of the time. In the forties, many Los Angeles policemen, including some ranking officers, were carrying on illicit deals with local rackets characters. The top brass had a lucrative pact with Brenda Allen, the well-known madam, that left her free to run her posh operation and left them with a large supplemental income. In addition, the department's Gangster Squad members were openly consorting with their supposed targets such as mobster Mickey Cohen. Parker would have none of it. In defiance of his bosses, he picked off the streets pimps, prostitutes and hoodlums with reckless disregard for his own longevity.

But in 1949 the situation erupted into scandal, and a leathery retired Marine Corps general, William A. Worton, was co-opted as interim chief to bring about reforms. Worton did, but was prevented by civil-service law from serving more than one year.* In searching for a successor, Worton focused his attention on the unrelenting, scrupulously honest Parker. By this time, Parker had climbed steadily up the civil-service ladder. During World War II he had been tapped by General Dwight D. Eisenhower to formulate police and prison plans for the invasion of the Continent, and after the war was assigned to set up democratic police systems in the German cities of Munich and Frankfurt. He was precisely the type of candidate who would appeal to a former Marine officer.

Jumping him over several higher-ranking aspirants, Worton appointed Parker as deputy chief, from which position he acceded to the top spot when Worton stepped down. One of the new chief's first moves was to come to grips with the intricate menace of organized crime, a task many of his colleagues in other cities had shied away from because of the numerous tie-ins between the syndicates and political bosses. In part, Parker was aided by the lack of a political machine, in the

---

* To honor the custom of promotion through the ranks, most police civil-service systems bar what is called "lateral promotion," i.e., the permanent appointment of outsiders to administrative posts. Most, however, make exception for high posts such as chief. The Los Angeles system is particularly protective—not only must a permanent chief be appointed by the police commission from inside the ranks, but a permanent chief can be removed only for reasons of gross malfeasance or criminal conduct.

Eastern sense, in Los Angeles, but it was his evangelical fervor and personal courage that made the difference in the end. He rejuvenated the old Gangster Squad, manning it with his brightest young detectives and renaming it the Intelligence Division. The key to coping with organized crime, Parker knew, was a painstaking, systematic program of intelligence gathering.

In November 1959 I caught a glimpse of the Intelligence Division's operations while in Los Angeles as a member of an FBI inspection team checking on the local bureau office. My principal assignment was to do a critical analysis of the office's organized-crime program, part of a nationwide program hurriedly installed after the humiliation of 1957, when syndicate czars from all over the country held a conclave in Apalachin, New York, without the FBI's knowledge. I found, admittedly to my surprise, that practically all the intelligence of value in the FBI files had been beggared from the files of the police Intelligence Division. Spurred by the Kefauver hearings of 1950, the division had been patiently collecting information for nine years; its head, the late Capt. James Hamilton, had conceived and founded the Law Enforcement Intelligence Union, a working agreement with police in other cities by which national crime figures were kept under close scrutiny. The division's "open warfare" policy had driven the syndicates underground, where they functioned on a vastly reduced scale.

In his missionary zeal, however, Parker was able to justify about any means to crush "the lawless criminal army warring against society itself." When the Intelligence Division was unable to find concrete and legal evidence of a crime on the part of a suspect, it would substitute a campaign of harassment. Despite state law forbidding wiretapping, the Los Angeles department had a reputation in police circles for being one of the most prolific users of technical eavesdropping equipment. As a dodge, the department often contracted "jobs" to private detectives.

Parker was playing with fire, and in 1955 he got burned. He personally authorized the placing of electronic bugs inside premises used by suspected bookmaker Charles Cahan, necessitating illegal breaking and entering on the part of the police officers who installed the bugs. Cahan was convicted but on appeal was freed by the California Supreme Court, which laid down the law to Parker and his men in no uncertain terms:

> Without fear of punishment or other discipline, law enforcement officers, sworn to support the constitution of the United States and the constitution of California, frankly admit their deliberate, flagrant acts in violation of both constitutions and the laws enacted thereunder. It is clearly apparent that they casually regard such acts as nothing more than the performance of their ordinary duties for which this city employs and pays them.

The decision was doubly damaging to the reckless enforcers of the law, for it brought to California the long-delayed doctrine, called the exclusionary rule, which made inadmissible any evidence illegally obtained.

Ironically, Parker had argued the case for wiretapping and bugging a year before when he testified before the Appropriations Committee of the House of Representatives in February 1954. Conceding that a "fight fire with fire" philosophy could eventually ignite the Bill of Rights, he dauntlessly proceeded to advocate such a philosophy through the rationale of "the principle of ethics entitled 'the law of double effect.'" The principle posited, he said, "that when an action produces two effects, one good, one bad, as long as the good effect is intended, and as long as the means are either morally good or morally neutral, the act may be morally justified.

"Thus, when this nation was faced with the ethics of warfare in the use of the atom bomb, it was obviously morally justified. . . . In the case of the wiretap or dictograph [electronic eavesdropping] the identical rationale may be applicable." For a moral absolutist who preached strict observance of the rule of law and who could see absolutely no merit in civil disobedience for morally justifiable ends, it was strange logic. Even after the court decision on the Cahan case was delivered, he stuck to his guns of expediency. "The rule is extremely harmful to the law-abiding segment of society," he complained before the 36th Annual Conference of the Peace Officers' Association of California in San Diego on May 23, 1956. "The only one who really benefits is the criminal. . . . The criminal will continue to benefit and the law-abiding public will continue to pay the bill."

Parker's professional ability as an administrator and police-science practitioner was widely recognized, and he was summoned with almost monotonous regularity before Senate and House committees investigating various aspects of police work. As a law-enforcement spokesman, he frequently propounded his views at university seminars and conferences. In 1962, he was invited to participate in the President's White House Conference on Narcotics and Drug Abuse. His reputation transcended national boundaries, and in 1960 he was the only representative of local law enforcement in the United States to attend the 29th General Assembly of the International Criminal Police Organization, better known as Interpol. In 1964, under State Department auspices, he traveled to India to help redesign that country's police administration procedures. He is best remembered for his widely publicized veto of the plans of now-deposed Soviet Premier Nikita Khrushchev to visit Disneyland during his 1960 tour of the United States; the reason given was "security," and Khrushchev sent him a "no hard feelings" gift.

By 1964, when J. Edgar Hoover turned seventy and presumably would be retired, Parker's preeminence in the law-enforcement establishment was so firmly established that he was prominently mentioned to succeed the durable FBI chief. In personality and outlook he closely paralleled Hoover: dour, unrelenting, incorruptible, something of a martinet, prudish, archreactionary, an acerbic critic of the Supreme Court and other police bugbears, and an angry denouncer of his own critics. Perhaps inevitably, the monumental egos of Parker and Hoover clashed, and for years they carried on a running feud.* On Parker's part, standing up to the FBI director was a singular act of courage, for practically all his colleagues, whatever their private opinions, considered it foolhardy to incur the wrath of a man of Hoover's power and influence whose agency controlled the central fingerprint file and other vital police "services." Indeed, Parker paid the price: Los Angeles officers were not accepted at the prestigious FBI National Academy, on the excuse that quotas were full, although neighboring departments had no trouble getting men accepted.

While Parker was uniformly respected in police circles, he was not uniformly admired. Some executives found him supercilious, others thought his abrasive remarks ill-becoming to a public official. Significantly, two of his goals, becoming president of the International Association of Chiefs of Police and state commander of the California American Legion, in the end eluded him. Though police as a whole tend toward the conservative, many thought Parker had gone off the deep end.

---

* The origins of the feud are obscure, although one Los Angeles investigative source claims it started when Hoover, who vacations in the southern California area each summer, took offense at being shadowed by Parker's Intelligence Division. In December 1963, at the height of the Frank Sinatra, Jr., kidnapping investigation, the feud broke into the open. Parker, incensed at FBI secrecy, complained: "This is the first time that we were faced with a problem where there was criminal activity in the City of Los Angeles that was known to a law enforcement agency where we were not permitted to participate."

"He fell for the Birchers' 'Support Your Local Police' slogan," commented one chief, a top officer in his own right. "But then, he was hung up on patriotism."

As Parker saw it, patriotism was the last defense in America against the apocalyptic forces of our times. In 1962 he told Donald McDonald of Marquette University, who was conducting a study of the American character for the Center for the Study of Democratic Institutions, that he found it hard to believe "our society can continue to violate all the fundamental rules of human conduct and expect to survive. I think I have to conclude that this civilization will destroy itself, as others have before it. That leaves, then, only one question—when?"

This morose strain permeated Parker's philosophy. On the right-wing *Manion Forum* broadcast of May 30, 1965, he declared: "I subscribe to the theological premise that man is inherently corrupt; that his impulses along criminal lines must constantly be repressed." When the holocaust in Watts was at its height, he asserted, "If you just want to believe that the human being will respond to kindness with kindness, that he's not an evil thing, you are just living in a fool's paradise. And now reality asserts itself, and we're aghast."

To the boy from the Black Hills who had seen first-hand the seamiest and most sordid aspects of big-city life, society stood at the brink of a moral abyss. The permissiveness of modern society—"this hedonistic philosophy, this libertine existence" —appalled him, and he spoke vaguely of an overriding "natural law." He felt the simple values of a less complex age were disappearing and with them the rugged individualism of "free enterprise." The rise in crime, he told a meeting of the Texas Municipal Police Association in Dallas on August 21, 1964, was due to "the nation turning away from Victorian morality and culture in a transition from capitalism to socialism."

To Parker, the correlation between decaying moral standards and political liberalism was crystal clear. It was a meas-

ure of the man, therefore, that he should indulge in partisanship of the political right. It was also a glaring inconsistency
in his professed principles. Although he bemoaned what he
called the "lack of discipline" in the American character, he
was unable to discipline himself by subordinating his deep-
grained prejudices to his role as chief of police. In 1960 he displayed the acute bad taste of mounting a Project Alert platform during an anti-Communism rally a few minutes after retired Marine Colonel Mitchell Paige had called for the hanging of Chief Justice Earl Warren. In conduct that could be
construed as unbecoming an officer of the law, he participated
in the strident right-wing programs of Dr. Fred Schwarz's
Christian Anti-Communism Crusade and encouraged Los
Angeles officers to attend the Crusade "schools" at special police tuition fees. The right wing reciprocated with lavish pane-
gyrics. The Freedom Club of Los Angeles, for example, raved
that he had made an outstanding contribution to constitutional
government "that man might live free as a child of God, not
bound as a slave of the state."

Parker's overriding failure was his inability to solve the
human equation. He was by no means a pathological racist,
nor did his problem lie with interpersonal relationships. He
maintained equanimous relations with the two Negro members of his police commission (although Los Angeles Negroes
regarded the commissioners as Uncle Toms), and promising
Negro policemen found the door to promotion wide open.

But it was to minorities *en bloc* that Parker instinctively
reacted, for it was as a group that they posed a threat to his
ordered world of the rule of law, of authoritarianism and discipline, of the status quo. Parker viewed himself as a representative of the establishment and assumed the grandiose stance
that an attack on him was an attack on the establishment. And
he was hypersensitive to criticism of himself or his department,
refusing to consider its merits. "Criticism of the Los Angeles

Police Department is politically motivated," he categorically stated to the California Advisory Committee of the U.S. Civil Rights Commission on September 13, 1962.

One of his severest critics was the Los Angeles chapter of the American Civil Liberties Union, which he considered in the nature of a Communist front and with which he refused to have anything to do. When the ACLU set up four stations in the city to receive complaints of police malpractice—there is no civilian review board in Los Angeles—the chief smoldered in self-righteous silence and sent for the personal dossiers of ACLU functionaries, laboriously and somberly poring over them. When he could not duck emissaries from Negro or other minority groups, he met them with cold and curt suspicion and responded indignantly and categorically to their complaints. "There is no police brutality," he once stated in annoyance, despite a welter of evidence to the contrary. Allegations of brutality, he said on another occasion, were "deliberately manufactured" by the Negroes' "so-called leaders." It was all a device, he insisted, "part of their stock in trade of what I call the modern Pied Pipers of Hamelin."

Parker envisioned himself as white Los Angeles' defender against the black tide he predicted would soon engulf it in crime. "It's estimated that by 1970, 45 percent of the metropolitan area of Los Angeles will be Negro," he warned on a local television program on August 14, 1965. "If you want any protection for your home and family . . . you're going to have to get in and support a strong police department. If you don't do that, come 1970 God help you!"

Parker based his claim of an inordinately high crime rate among Negroes on his department's statistics, but bare statistics fail to show the contributing factors. For one thing, the Los Angeles department has a proclivity for arresting Negroes where in identical situations it would not arrest whites. Moreover, the department under Parker abdicated its responsibility

for crime prevention at the grass roots. "Law enforcement officers are neither equipped nor authorized to deal with broad
social problems," the chief is quoted in *Parker on Police*, an
anthology of his speeches and writings. "Our job is to apply
emergency treatment to society's surface wounds. We deal with
effects, not causes." To the end, he was hostile to the civil
rights movement and indigenous groups outside the official
structure which attempted to solve the problems. "Hell, the
police department isn't here to revitalize society," he told a
reporter shortly before his death, "and I'm critical of this
whole social revolution. It has created a cleavage between the
races."

It was his tactless remarks, often uttered at delicate times,
that made Parker a storm center of controversy. On January
26, 1960, he provoked a furor when, in the course of testifying
before the Federal Civil Rights Commission, he opined that
some minorities were "not far removed from the wild tribes
of Mexico" and "you cannot ignore the genes in the behavior
pattern of people." It sounded disturbingly like a superrace
theory.

When the Watts rioting began, Parker flatly refused to nego-
tiate with Negro leaders, even though it was immediately evident that much of the antagonism was directed toward the
police. "I am not going to sit down in any kind of mediation
and meet with any leaders," he announced. On television, he
used typically heedless similes in giving his version of how the
disturbances started: "One person threw a rock and then, like
monkeys in a zoo, others started throwing rocks." And when
the rioting temporarily subsided, before flaring into its final
and most savage stage, he goaded, "We are on top and they
are on the bottom."

Most neutral observers conceded that Parker's tactless and
unconciliatory remarks during the riots had an inflammatory
effect that contributed to their horrifying dimension. Governor

Edmund G. Brown commented that Parker was a "sincere man" but was "not without blame" for the riots. "I do think that his statements have been very unfortunate," Brown said. "I think they have hurt the whole cause of race relations in Los Angeles."

Ironically, the mayor at the time Parker was appointed chief, Fletcher Bowron, was not particularly sold on him, and Sam Yorty, in his first campaign for mayor in 1961, promised that, if elected, his first order of business would be to dump the controversial chief. Yorty's principal campaign issue was that Parker and the department had done a "very poor job of public relations" in the Negro community. An underdog against the moderate, colorless Republican incumbent, Norris Poulsen, Yorty eked out a victory on a wave of Watts votes. But instead of sacking Parker, the new mayor strengthened his hand.

The duplicity infuriated the Negro community, whose votes Yorty had wooed and won. Unperturbed, the resourceful Yorty, a leftist who had veered sharply to the right, pulled a flag from his sleeve: Any attack on the police, he cautioned, was part of the Communist "Big Lie" technique and an "attack on our American system." It was the kind of statement that was Parker's stock in trade, and the two became inseparable political allies. It is safe to say that their tandem power polarized the city into white and black camps—and pointed Los Angeles down the path to Watts.

After Watts, the pair remained intransigent. Rather than weighing the charge of Negro leader Rev. H. Hartford Brookins that the intensity and duration of the rioting was due as much to "unleashed police aggression" as it was to the Negroes' pent-up frustrations, they pressured for a dangerous piece of legislation giving the police virtual martial-law powers without a state of emergency. Testifying on behalf of the bill, called the Yorty Anti-Riot Bill, Parker said: "The police must have authority to put down riots before they occur by arresting those who would disturb the peace." To the people of Watts, the bill was nothing more than a bald attempt to cloak police harassment in legality.

When William H. Parker died suddenly on July 17, 1966, he became a martyr to those who supported the white status quo. "He is the white community's savior, their symbol of security," Otis Chandler, publisher of the Los Angeles *Times*, had observed not long before. Parker had been to the Mayo Clinic earlier in the year for treatment of a heart condition, but he would not curtail his arduous schedule. "I go home at seven," Lieutenant Hoy, his aide told me shortly after the chief returned from the clinic, "and he is still going—off to speak at a banquet or something."

It was at a banquet for the Second Marine Division that Parker suffered his fatal heart seizure. "I've become the symbol of the attack against the establishment," he had told his fellow veterans. "I'm not a brutal person, but remember the attack against the police has been used since time immemorial to attack the establishment." He had received a standing ovation, then succumbed.

At the funeral, presided over by Parker's prelate, James Francis Cardinal McIntyre of Los Angeles, Msgr. Patrick Roche eulogized: "Of such steel was he forged that its mettle could tolerate no compromise with principle, no traffic with expediency, no corrosion of authority." It was an apt description of a crusader who had waged a holy war against the infidels he saw in society.

But Parker was a crusader born far too late. His stewardship as a police chief in modern America is best appraised by two other eulogies:

> His death will be a loss in the sense he put together a strong, disciplined force. But I think his death will be a relief to the

minority community, who believe he woefully misunderstood
the social revolution taking place.

> —Thomas Kilgore, Western representa-
> tive for Dr. Martin Luther King's
> Southern Christian Leadership Con-
> ference.

His policemen have won a reputation for efficiency, but also
for implacable enmity toward the lower strata of society, the
poor, the ignorant, the unemployed.

> —Howard K. Smith, moderator, "Issues
> and Answers," ABC-TV, August 23,
> 1965.

5

Los Angeles: Parker's Legacy

The legacy of William H. Parker is the Los Angeles Police Department, a crack unit of 5,161 sworn personnel (according to the most recent available figures) with a nationwide reputation for efficient law enforcement. Its pay scale is one of the highest in the country, and in physical appearance it is one of the most impressive. Many members of the force are recruited from distant sections of the country by teams of traveling recruiters and newspaper ads extolling the balmy California climate. Others are recruited from universities offering law-enforcement courses; and military police posts are prime targets of the department's inducements.

In demographic character, however, the department does not correspond even roughly to the lines of the city it represents. It is only 4 percent Negro (Chicago's, for example, is 16 percent), compared with a Negro population of 13.5 percent; there is only a scattering of Mexican-Americans, although they comprise 24 percent of the city's population. The largest segment of the force is made up of men a generation or less removed from Oklahoma, Texas, Arkansas and the Deep South, and their attitudes retain many of the features of those sections of the nation.

The crime-busting proficiency of the department has been portrayed dramatically in the *Dragnet* television series. Its reputation for effective sleuthing is earned, as the department's high rate of cases "cleared by arrest" demonstrates. In the field of scientific techniques, the department ranks with the best. Under the recently retired criminalist Raymond Pinker, the crime laboratory achieved wide renown and pioneered in applying the relatively new analytical tool, nuclear activation analysis, to forensic problems.

The department functions with the smooth efficiency of a well-oiled machine, but it is not much more than just that—an impersonal machine. The department patrols its sprawling bailiwick almost entirely with cars, so that the police officer is a badge number, not a person, to the populace. A large portion of the men who man the cars are those who have failed to earn promotion or who have been demoted, a fact which does nothing to improve the relationship between police and public. The young patrolman quickly learns that the way out of the car is to write as many traffic citations as possible and to exceed an informal quota of "field interrogations" and misdemeanor arrests which is based on computer-derived crime projections.

This arrest consciousness and the premium placed by policemen on the "big pinch" have badly warped traditional concepts of equal and fair justice. The issuing of traffic tickets for marginal offenses is more irritating to motorists than educational, and the overzealous exercise of discretionary powers in making arrests for petty violations of codes and statutes in order to look good cheapens and degrades the police profession. One of the most disturbing of police statistics is the tens of thousands of arrests each year in which the accused are never brought before judges or magistrates. These persons, denied the chance to question the merits of the arrests through due process, have been given an indelible arrest record which can haunt them the rest of their lives. And civil rights groups in

Los Angeles and other major cities have repeatedly complained that it is minority persons, the indigent and the ignorant who are the most vulnerable targets for this kind of police practice.

Ever since the race riots in East St. Louis, Chicago and Washington during and after World War I, there have been varying pressures throughout the country for police to be afforded training in human relations. Along with Philadelphia and Detroit, Los Angeles has long included such training as part of its basic instruction. And shortly after he took charge, Parker set up a Community Relations Bureau within the department.

The human relations experiment in Los Angeles has proved a dismal failure, one for which the longtime head of the Community Relations Bureau, James G. Fisk, cannot be held to blame. Fisk, who held the rank of inspector, is an articulate, dedicated man who is, by police standards, sensitive to the problems involved. But under Parker, he was severely limited in his ability to establish a meaningful relationship with the minority community. A dialogue of sorts was entered into with some civil rights groups, but only when those groups properly and formally approached the police department on its terms. And the dialogue was restricted to the Urban League and the NAACP and similar groups. Fisk's bureau was forbidden to have anything to do with militant organizations such as the Black Muslims, CORE and SNCC and indigenous groups springing up in the neighborhoods, as they were not considered "respectable" by police definition. Thus was obviated the chance for attaining a *modus vivendi* at the very level at which it was most sorely needed.

Moreover, this restricted dialogue was further curtailed. As far as Parker was concerned, police brutality simply did not exist, and the subject was not open to discussion. All discussion was subordinated to the chief's outdated version of the law-enforcement mission. In his book, for instance, Negro youth gangs were not the natural result of youth's desire for identification in group activity and hence a potential force for good if channeled into constructive action, but a menacing source of trouble to be harassed and contained and treated as outlaw bands.

As myopic and haughty as this policy was, its glaring inadequacy was covered over by superficial public-relations gimmicks. The department appointed Dodger baseball catcher John Roseboro, a Negro who said he had always wanted to be a policeman, as an off-season "human relations specialist" to work with youth. There were other such gestures. But they were like raindrops on a seething cauldron.

At a workshop in Indianapolis several years ago sponsored by the International Association of Chiefs of Police, Fisk confided to fellow police officials that it was a sickening sight to see Los Angeles police stop a Negro family on the freeway, "pull out the upholstery, find nothing, then leave—the family having to put the car back together." As Fisk put it, "We're very effective, but not very effective with people."

As Watts still smoldered, I hovered over the area in a sheriff's helicopter piloted by Hugh McDonald, then chief of technical services for the Los Angeles County Sheriff's Department. From that height the extent of the devastation was more evident than from the ground; the charred and gutted buildings looked like a Hollywood replica of a town that been hit by Nazi dive bombers. It was a ghastly scene, and I could not help but recall the smug assertions of Mayor Yorty and Chief Parker that it couldn't happen in Los Angeles. "Los Angeles has been the most progressive city in the country in eliminating racial friction," Parker had said in a 1963 speech before the Rotary Club of North Hollywood. "I doubt that Los Angeles will become part of the battleground of the racial conflict that is raging in the United States today," he had told the Sigma Delta Chi journalism fraternity the same year.

On that sweep over Watts, I also recalled an interview I had had with an earnest young white policeman only two weeks before the rioting started. "In that ghetto we walked around being an occupation army in a foreign country," said Michael B. Hannon, a twenty-eight-year-old pink-faced blond patrolman who seven years before had deserted the security of a defense-plant drawing board for the rugged life of a cop.

We talked that late July afternoon in his sparsely furnished cottage across Silver Lake Reservoir from the residence of his chief. We conversed in the law-enforcement cant we both knew so well. The conversation was interrupted several times by the appearance of newspaper and television reporters, for by that time Hannon had been hauled on the departmental carpet for participating in civil rights activity.

His experience in Watts, Hannon said, had awakened his social conscience. "In a white community the Los Angeles police believe they're public servants," he explained, "but in that ghetto it's different—the police make no attempt to understand." The Negro community was seething under oppression, he contended, but Chief Parker responded "with more oppression. He spent $50,000 to buy us helmets, but not a single penny to find out the reasons why."

Profoundly disturbed by conditions in Watts, Hannon had plunged into civil rights activities on his off-duty hours. He became a member of the Congress of Racial Equality and the Democratic Socialists of Norman Thomas. His activities promptly earned him the contempt of his fellow policemen. Insulting epithets appeared on the chalkboard; his ticket books and other chargeable property were stolen; a subscription to the *People's World*, a Communist weekly, was entered in his name and copies began arriving at the station house. When not under harassment, he was given the cold shoulder. His official performance record, previously flawless, began to be marred with such charges as "he creates serious doubts as to his loyalty and engages in controversial political and social activities and creates dessention [*sic*] and dissatisfaction among other officers."

Before long Hannon discovered he was being shadowed by policemen in mufti. One kept showing up at civil rights meetings under the guise of being a sympathizer; Hannon later spotted him in uniform at a station house and learned he had made surreptitious tape recordings of the meetings. Then a barrel-chested type whose gun bulged conspicuously from under a gaudy sport shirt took over—until Hannon confronted him at a civil rights rally.

The department clearly was out to get rid of Hannon but somehow had to circumvent his civil-service protection. "We'll get you in six months," a superior officer warned him. "There are lots of rules." The stage was set by a performance rating signed by his superiors at the Newton Street station, Lt. W. K. Daniels and two sergeants. "In view of the very great doubts and controversies created by his political and social expressions," it summed up, "it is the opinion of the rating supervisors that his continued presence creates a very serious morale and security problem. In this respect it is felt that his overall value to the department is 'unsatisfactory' (lower 10 percent) and that his continued employment poses a grave security threat to the department's plans and responsibilities, to individual officers, and to the national peace and security as well."

One is tempted to speculate on just what plans the department might have to which an officer committed to social progress might pose a threat. And one might comment that the performance rating documents the intolerance and bigotry that dominates the Los Angeles Police Department, whose powers theoretically are delegated by the whole of society. And by labeling Hannon a "security threat," the department stigmatized him with the most ominous label a bureaucracy can apply.

I asked Hannon a rhetorical question: What was the attitude of the department toward the "political and social expressions" of its Bircher members? "What Birchers?" he replied sarcastically. "The chief came on television one night and said he didn't know of any Birchers in the department. Two of them watching in the station house laughed uproariously."

Hannon was formally charged with "conduct unbecoming an officer" for participating in civil rights demonstrations, with sleeping on duty, and with "exposing the identity of an undercover officer"—his barrel-chested shadow. At his departmental trial, Chief Parker took the position that "police participation in public demonstrations of a contentious nature is misconduct per se." One demonstration so deemed by Parker was a 1963 rally in Los Angeles expressing sympathy for the Birmingham civil rights marchers in which Negro author James Baldwin took part.

Before the trial board, Hannon freely admitted the napping incident upon which one count was based. He had taken a catnap in a two-man patrol car, he said, a violation which if uniformly prosecuted would cost most of the force their jobs. But he stoutly defended his right to free public expression in off-duty time, a right which Bircher policemen on the force frequently asserted. The department, he maintained, was a "bastion of bigotry. . . . I believe bigotry means racial intolerance," he testified, "and I believe the overwhelming attitude of members of this department is against the minority. I've ridden in a radio car with an officer where the officer was addressed courteously by a well-dressed Negro and the officer said, 'Hello, nigger.' "

Hannon's harsh indictment of the department was corroborated by the testimony of several Negro officers, one of whom, Norman E. Edelen, affirmed that there was discrimination against Negro officers assigned to his precinct and against Negro citizens served by the precinct. On one occasion, he said, he noticed an anti-Negro epithet scrawled on a picture of Eleanor Roosevelt posted on the division bulletin board. A Negro policeman tore the picture down but a similar one, with the same epithet, was back up the next morning.

The trial board found Hannon guilty and recommended his dismissal. Nettled because the board "did not sustain the department's position that police participation in public demonstrations of a contentious nature is misconduct per se," Parker made a show of perversity by meting out a lighter penalty of six months' suspension without pay. Ordinarily, a protracted period "on the beach" is tantamount to expulsion for a man with a wife and four children. But Hannon stuck it out as a matter of principle, and upon his return a piqued department assigned him to an enclosed guard booth at the city treasurer's office. In the spring of 1966 he resigned to run unsuccessfully for Congress in the Democratic primaries, then, with a law degree obtained in night school, went into private law practice.

The interview with Hannon had been a disquieting one for two reasons. He was bright, intelligent, principled and socially aware, precisely the type of young man the police service desperately needs, but he was being ostracized by that service because he was considered unorthodox. As he himself put it, the department had convicted him of heresy. And his portrait of the typical Los Angeles policeman—courteous and equanimous toward middle-class whites, insolent and rude toward Negroes —revealed a duality that is a surefire formula for trouble.

When Watts exploded, it was the traffic arrest of a young Negro that triggered it. But the gun had been loaded for a long time. A 1950 survey of the department is illuminating on that score. The survey, called "The Social Areas of Los Angeles" and conducted under the auspices of the Hayes Foundation, was started during the regime of Chief Worton. It was based on a demographic study of the Los Angeles area and sampled a representative cross section of the population on their impressions of the police department.

In the category of professional proficiency, 75 percent rated the department as from average to one of the very best; only 10 percent felt it was below standard. In physical appearance, an overwhelming 97 percent thought highly of the department, and an equally favorable response was recorded in the category of "equipment and facilities." It was when the questions shifted to human values that the citizens' esteem for their department tailed off.

Asked whether they felt the police force was careful to protect the innocent, only 22 percent answered in the affirmative, while 45 percent qualified their answer to "only occasionally." Only 31 percent thought the police officers "always respect the constitutional rights of suspected criminals," while 17 percent went so far as to say that officers were often "conscienceless and brutal" in the performance of their duties.

Significantly, the survey detected incipient antagonisms toward the Los Angeles police among minority groups. While 35 percent of the whites interviewed were of the opinion that the department behaved with decorum in its treatment of suspects, only 21 percent of the Mexican-Americans and 12 percent of the Negroes agreed. A whopping 44 percent of the Mexican-Americans and 38 percent of the Negroes felt that officers often acted in a "conscienceless and brutal" manner, compared to only 11 percent of the whites. Among the minority persons polled, the police received a disproportionately high condemnation on such indexes of attitude as "discourteous," "overbearing or superior attitude, and "sarcastic or belligerent." As the police department itself admitted, "the Negro is more inclined than others to view the Los Angeles Police Department with a critical eye."

Over the years the critical eye became a hostile one, and the seeds of hostility can be found in the story told me by a Negro minister of Watts—a story that must be multiplied thousands of times to arrive at the depth of frustration experienced by the people of Watts. A parishioner, a prosperous storeowner, had come to him for counsel. He had witnessed the arrest of a Negro man on a misdemeanor charge. Officers handcuffed the prisoner, although he offered no resistance. They stood him against a wall and beat him on the arms and legs, raising livid welts. When onlookers protested this senseless brutality, the officers warned them to shut up or be arrested themselves. "I was sick at heart," the parishioner told the minister. "I had to pray for the strength not to take the gun I have to protect me against robbers and use it on those cops."

It was the routine indignities that stretched the patience of Watts to the breaking point. Negroes halted for minor traffic infractions often were cowed with drawn guns, frisked, and subjected to an illegal search of their car. "Field interrogations," a euphemism for humiliating street grillings, were common practice. What made these and similar indignities all the more galling is that the offending officers invariably were white —Parker would not permit Negro officers to be especially assigned to Watts because he conceived of it as de facto segregation.

The citizens of Watts knew the futility of petitioning for redress of grievance. There has never been a civilian review board in Los Angeles to process complaints, a task which is handled by the department's own Internal Affairs Division. The method by which police adjudicate complaints against the police has never been a satisfactory one in any big city, including image-conscious Los Angeles. Although the police cite the fact that only 1 out of every 6,000 arrests or interrogations results in a complaint, the low figure seems to be more a manifestation of lack of confidence in the Internal Affairs Division than an indicator of police decorum. In 1964, for example, the division received 122 complaints about excessive force, and sustained only 10.

In the minds of Parker and Mayor Yorty, cause for grievance simply did not exist. "We have the most advanced department in the nation in human relations," Parker insisted to a Los Angeles *Times* columnist on June 25, 1963. "Constant charges of police brutality are usually figments of the imagination," Yorty blandly told the Commonwealth Club of San Francisco on August 13, 1965, as the Watts rioting began. Criticism of the police was categorically written off as Red-inspired, and Negro leaders who tried to lay the facts on the line were put down as demagogues or worse. Negro Councilman Thomas Bradley, a former police officer, said on an NBC television documentary, "The Thin Blue Line," that there is a "great amount of malpractice and abuse," and victims "can't get an adequate hearing," but he was simply ignored.

When Watts finally ignited, it was the sight of the hated police in their neat black uniforms and white helmets that acted as a catalyst accelerating the reaction. Nowhere in the nation's black ghettos are the police kindly regarded, but in Watts the Los Angeles police seemed to provoke an extraordinary fury. As an astonished Parker himself revealed, the rioters "started putting in phony calls to get the police cars in there so that they could pelt them." And pelt them they did: of 103 police cars that penetrated into Watts, 103 were damaged.

Persons I interviewed who had been eyewitnesses to the rioting were shocked at instances of seemingly wanton barbarity by the police. One National Guardsman in a squad assigned to protect a pair of policemen told of the policemen ordering a Negro to stop changing a tire on his car and get off the street. When the man hesitated, the policeman pounced upon him, beat him up, then threw his womenfolk roughly to the ground when they came out of the house to protest. A minister related how a Mexican-American father of four who left his home to investigate the insistent ringing of a burglar alarm on a nearby store was killed outright by a police shotgun blast in the back, fired without warning, as he took down the storeowner's telephone number to report the alarm. Newspaper and magazine accounts of the riots are replete with similar incidents of cruelty.

Watts turned into the biggest riot this nation had witnessed since the nineteenth century—until Detroit. Barely two years before, Parker had said, in a Los Angeles *Times* interview on June 22, 1963: "I doubt if the temper of the Los Angeles Negro community is such that racial demonstrations would reach the intensity of those in the South. But police squads trained in crowd control have undergone refresher training and inventoried equipment, such as helmets and gas masks, and will be ready for any emergency." When the emergency came, the police either willfully or through panic opted for guns and nightsticks instead of conventional riot-control equipment. As a result, the death toll reached thirty-six, six times that of all seven 1964 riots, including the major riots in Harlem and Rochester, New York.

The schism separating American law enforcement and its uncritical supporters on the one side and minority communities on the other was sharply illustrated in the recriminations over Watts. Parker laid the blame on criminal elements and a widespread lack of "respect for the law," a theme he constantly preached. But a placid old man in Watts responded, "Parker and his police don't respect us. They're supposed to represent the law. Why should we respect the law? The law don't show no respect for the Negro." The simple probity of this remark was reinforced in harsher terms by Miriam Makeba, the Negro singer from South Africa. "I don't see the difference between the police here and the police in South Africa," she said. "You hear them saying they shot somebody in self-defense. But like the South African police, they always aim to kill."

Mayor Yorty rose to his chief's defense, saying that indeed "criminal elements" were responsible and that "Communists, dupes and demagogues" were their accomplices. For this bit of demonology, the mayor was acclaimed by the newly sprouted Americans for Law and Order, composed of the right-wing Young Republicans of California and Young Americans for Freedom, a kind of junior auxiliary of the John Birch Society. Not all the supporters of the police and the mayor were extremists: the stolid white community across the freeway from Watts uttered hardly a word of criticism of police conduct.

Reporters who conducted their own inquest among the people of Watts found a consensus running against the police that ranged from anger to quiet appraisal. "Parker is the Hitler of Los Angeles," raged one man to Associated Press reporters James Bacon and Bill Boyarsky. "He runs the police department like Hitler ran the Gestapo." "Maybe the people of Beverly Hills would riot too if they spent most of their life with a cop's club in their face," another man griped to the AP pair. "Or if they had to get out of an automobile with their hands over their head to be questioned for doing nothing at all." Budd Schulberg of the *Times-Post* service listened to a teacher explain: "We live in a police-state atmosphere down here. People who come up from the South feel like they never left home. They are harassed on the street, the kids are constantly being pulled in on 'suspicion,' the whole attitude is they are guilty unless they can prove themselves innocent. The people need some genuine clearinghouse for their charges against the cops —a grievance committee."

The official inquest was conducted by an ad hoc body created by Governor Brown and headed by John A. McCone, a former

Central Intelligence Agency director who is now a Los Angeles industrialist. The McCone Commission, as it was called, was not out to step on toes. In its report it noted that there were "recurring charges" and "bitter criticism" of "police brutality" and abusiveness, and that there existed a "deep and long-standing schism" between the police and the Negro community. Inexplicably, it failed to investigate the truth or falsity of these charges, and concluded its report with the gross contradiction that the police department "serves well this entire community."

The ambivalence of the McCone Commission was taken to task by the California Advisory Committee to the United States Commission on Civil Rights. "The hostility of our chief toward the civil rights movement," said Vice-Chairman Stephen Reinhardt, a Los Angeles labor lawyer, "his refusal to recognize or deal with Negro community leaders, his lack of understanding of the feelings and needs of minority-group members . . . are causes of racial unrest."

Amidst the rubble of Watts, James Fisk of the Community Relations Bureau made an attempt, within the constraints under which he was operating, to project at least a semblance of police empathy. He sent Negro-white police teams into the schools, opened a few workshops for Negro youths, and assigned patrolmen to walk around meeting people and "dispel stereotypes." Parker reacted by buying 700 new shotguns and 300 new helmets, and drilling his men in skirmish tactics borrowed from the Marine Corps. The ghetto continued to simmer, and on May 7, 1966, it almost boiled over again.

On that night Leonard Deadwyler was speeding his pregnant wife, Barbara, to the hospital when police cars took up the pursuit and, after a chase, pulled him to the curb. Officer Jerold M. Bova approached the Deadwyler vehicle from the passenger side, cocked his service revolver, and pointed it in the window. Deadwyler, according to his wife, said, "Officer, will you help me get my wife to the hospital?" They were his last words. Bova's gun discharged, killing Deadwyler instantly.

Again, bitter vengeful crowds swarmed through the streets of Watts. An impromptu "Committee to End Legalized Murder by Cops" sprang up and staged a hysterical rally. There were ugly incidents that threatened to erupt into full-scale rioting, but somehow Watts held its cool, waiting for the inquest.

At the coroner's inquest, Bova testified that the vehicle had lurched forward, throwing him off balance and causing the gun to fire. Barbara Deadwyler gave a conflicting version. The car had come to a complete halt, she said, and Bova had shot her husband without provocation.

The inquest sessions were tumultuous. At the first session, a pushing throng of Negroes took up all the seats in the courtroom, forcing the court officials to call upon a young Black Nationalist to restore order. Then some of the spectators raised pictures showing Sheriff Lawrence Rainey of Neshoba County, Mississippi, laughing during his arraignment for the murder of three civil rights workers; the pictures bore the sarcastic inscription "Support Your Local Police." That night the elite Metropolitan Squad of the police department moved into Watts for a "black beret" operation: four men to a car, armed with shotguns and wearing helmets covered with black cloth to spoil snipers' aim.

When the inquest recessed for the weekend, passions had time to cool. Early the next week, the jury decided the shooting was accidental, and District Attorney Evelle Younger declined to prosecute Bova for involuntary manslaughter. Yet two questions were left unanswered. Why did Bova have his gun out and cocked in the first place? Why didn't the police department hold an administrative hearing to decide the issue of judgment? They were the kinds of questions the department has consistently refused to answer. "If the cops would just say 'Yes, there is a problem,' it would help," a Negro leader told a

Life reporter on July 15, 1966. "But publicly the police act like all these complaints just come from a lot of lying niggers who never could be trusted."

In November 1966 the police, in combination with the sheriff's office, again showed their colors as mercenaries of the power structure. For several years the glitter of Sunset Strip in Hollywood had been attracting increasing numbers of hip teenagers who swarmed exuberantly onto the sidewalks and into nonalcoholic discotheques such as Pandora's Box and The Fifth Estate. Their presence began to affect businesses catering to adults, including the carriage-trade restaurants. For months the Sunset Strip Businessmen's Association pressured the police to do something about the youngsters. The only trouble was, the youngsters had a perfect right to be there—perfect until the police dragged out an old curfew law which prohibited. minors from loitering after 10 P.M. but did not require them to leave the streets.

The police began making arrests of groups of youngsters standing around after the curfew. The tempo picked up, and antagonisms increased on both sides. The climax came on November 27, when a Big Blue Line of 400 club-swinging police and sheriff's deputies drove the youths from the Strip, arrested 100 and issued hundreds of summons. When some 500 youths staged a rally on December 12 to protest the "unjust and unrealistic" curfew, police moved in and jailed 16 on a variety of petty charges, including one of interfering with police questioning leveled against Eason Monroe of the ACLU.

Throughout the turmoil, which continues sporadically even as of this writing, the Los Angeles department has remained implacable. Although a group representing the Sunset Strip teenagers attempted to discuss the situation with the Community Relations Bureau, Inspector Fisk refused, again on the basis that he did not consider the group "responsible."

Since the death of Parker, there has been no drastic shakeup of the department. An interim chief, Thad F. Brown, who was near retirement, served while the police commission decided on a permanent selection. The eligibles included men from the rank of captain on up, and all took a battery of tests, among which was an essay examination on such questions as implementing recent court decisions, cooperation with city government and improving community relations. The commission was to take its pick from the top three scorers.

One of the three was passed over because he was considered too reactionary. The top scorer was James Fisk, who was the choice of minority-group spokesmen for his work with the Community Relations Bureau, but he too failed to get the nod, possibly because he was considered too liberal. The man finally selected was fifty-year-old Thomas J. Reddin, whose twenty-six year record on the force was unblemished by the least bit of controversy. As a compensatory gesture, the commission elevated Fisk to deputy chief in charge of community relations.

A strapping ex-athlete who was forced to drop out of the University of Colorado during the Depression, Reddin served a four-year hitch in the Navy and was working in a gasoline station in 1941 when he heeded suggestions that he join the force. He worked his way up the promotional ladder, and at the time of his appointment as chief was serving as deputy chief in charge of the Bureau of Technical Services, the kind of post that provides little insight into law-enforcement problems.

Some measure of his outlook became clear upon his appointment. Describing Parker as a "great chief," Reddin said he expected to follow his policies but "the difference would be in the public image that I might convey as I articulate those policies." He felt, he said, "that I'm a great deal more people-orientated than Chief Parker was. . . ." Reddin thought that science and systems should take over routine functions, leaving policemen "more time to talk to people."

Reddin ranked his priorities as "crime in the streets," community relations and solving the recruitment problem. Indicators now point to a shift in the basic crime pattern in Los Angeles: in 1966 crime dropped (by 3.8 percent) in only one area, the predominantly Negro Newton Street Division, while it leaped alarmingly in the affluent white West Valley Division. Yet one is inclined to doubt that the department will cope with this crime surge with the same oppressive measures it has used in Watts.

In its recruitment crisis, the department may well be caught in a trap of its own making. The force's manpower is spread as thin as any major force in the country; there are only 1.8 policemen per 1,000 citizens, as compared with 2.5 in Chicago and 3.4 in New York. Parker had contended that a doubled force of 11,000 was needed, yet the department cannot meet its present quota. The low ratio of Negroes on the force— about 4 percent—suggests that, all things being equal, the Negro community would be a fertile source of candidates. But contempt for the Los Angeles force is so deep-rooted in the Negro community that few self-respecting young Negro men care to identify with it.

Although Reddin's regime augers to be an enlightened one compared to Parker's, the new chief does not show an inclination for the radical reform needed. To his credit, he has wasted no time belaboring Supreme Court decisions or uttering platitudes extolling law and order. On the other hand he is adamantly opposed to civilian review boards, and his use of the fear-rousing cliché "crime in the streets" suggests a man anxious to build a reputation as a dragon slayer.

Perhaps Reddin's most outstanding attribute, and the one for which he was selected, is his ability to accommodate himself to his role, which in this case is to create a more progressive image for the department while preserving its essential character. Reddin is glib, convincing, and, according to some who know him, superficial. Almost anything he does will appear, by Parker's lights, rather daring, and he should become a popular chief.

But before Los Angeles can lay claim to having a twentieth-century police department, its essential character must be thoroughly altered. The department is a spit-and-polish outfit—one sees few sloppy-looking cops in Los Angeles—with an elite corps' swagger and an outsized pride in its reputation for cracking criminal cases. As mentioned, it is heavy with men whose Southern and Southeastern heritage does not dispose them to treat the Negro or Mexican-American as a first-class citizen. Officially, it tends to be arrogant, arbitrary and abrupt with individuals or groups who are nonaffluent and nonwhite, or who do not operate from a power base.

Reddin's approbation of the manner in which the police acquitted themselves during President Johnson's visit to Los Angeles on June 23, 1967, strongly indicates that he has no intention of curbing the force's ruthless proclivities. As the President was sitting down to a sumptuous fund-raising dinner in the Century Plaza Hotel, a throng variously estimated at from 7,000 to 15,000 persons marched peacefully down the Avenue of the Stars in front, chanting and singing in protest against the Vietnam war. Police officers circulated through the crowd, handing out copies of an injunction obtained by the hotel prohibiting assembly at its doors. In evident defiance, a few hundred of the marchers sat down in the street. The 1,300 policemen on hand (in addition to a swollen Presidential security guard), outfitted with helmets, guns and nightsticks, became noticeably taut.

When a police captain announced over a loudspeaker that those who did not disperse would be arrested, most of the crowd in front of the hotel began slowly to move on. It was not soon enough for the police, and the charge was on. "I saw a solid wall of white helmets and billy-clubs descending," an attorney told reporter Andrew Kopkind. "I heard the sickening, cracking sound made by a club striking a man's head, and saw men, women and even children fall under the assault of policemen. I saw people injured, bleeding, frightened and crying."

A woman recounted to a Los Angeles *Times* reporter: "The man next to me was moving when a policeman yelled, "You're not moving fast enough, buster," and he clubbed him in the stomach." A parade marshal helping the marchers to keep moving subsequently made a formal statement to the ACLU: "A police officer knocked down two boys on the right and one of them fell in front of me and I fell over him, with my back to the officer. He then hit me on the side of my head with his club and as I arose gasping for breath he hit me with the tip of his billy-club in my abdomen." Motorcycle officers suddenly "fishtailed" their bikes into the crowd, maneuvering so that the rear wheels swung in violent arcs, knocking bystanders to the pavement. Whether the police panicked or became enraged at the marchers is debatable, but as Kopkind put it, there was not "the slightest indication of aggressive intent or action on the part of the demonstrators." The police action, he declared, "produced the most sickening scenes of brutality since the battle of the Selma Bridge two and a half years ago in Alabama."

Reddin had a ready if lame explanation: his men had "inside information" that "agitators" were planning to rush the hotel and, presumably, threaten the President. But in unwitting rebuttal, the *Times* published the full report of an undercover agent who infiltrated the march committee, and there was no mention of any such scheme.

The basic hard-nosed attitude of the Los Angeles police force is further calcified by a politically conservative leaning that is possibly the most extreme in the nation. Trainees and in-service officers attending the Police Academy in Elysian Park are required to view the film *Operation Abolition,* a jaundiced documentary on the San Francisco City Hall riots of 1960 which glosses over police blunders and pins the blame on Communists, and are encouraged to view *Communism on the Map*, a shrill right-wing propaganda film produced at Harding College in Searcy, Arkansas. The Birch-style activism of Los Angeles police will be discussed in a later chapter, but it is appropriate here to mention the almost fanatical degree to which political bias has colored the department's attitudes.

Dr. A. C. Germann, for six years a Los Angeles police officer, is a professor of police science at Long Beach State College, California, and co-author of the authoritative police text *Introduction to Law Enforcement*. In 1959 he wrote an article in *Police* magazine, "The Other Side of the Coin," which looked favorably at the ACLU through police eyes. The article incensed Chief Parker, who had no use for the ACLU, and prompted a policeman, Norman Moore, to try to get Germann ousted from the college faculty. As chairman of the State American Legion Subversive Committee, Moore prevailed upon the Legion to pass a resolution urging that Germann be dismissed. The college administration was not to be intimidated by such tactics, but the implications of the affair are a bit frightening.

On March 4, 1967, I participated in a panel discussion, "Police and the Constitution," sponsored by the law students at the University of California at Berkeley. Acceptances for this panel on eavesdropping had also been received from Henry Ruth of the President's Crime Commission; Sam Dasch, a professor at Georgetown University and author of *The Eavesdroppers*; and Captain Harold Yarnell, head of the Intelligence Division of the Los Angeles Police Department. After the program had been drawn up and the event publicized, Captain Yarnell withdrew without explanation. The student committee called the Los Angeles department, trying to secure permission for Yarnell to appear, for it was too late to find a substitute from another department. They received a curt turndown, without explanation. A sheriff who participated on another panel later told the students what had happened. Police brass had checked the names on the eavesdropping panel and came across my name listed as a former FBI agent and currently a staff writer for *Ramparts* magazine, the rather outspoken liberal monthly. "They made Yarnell withdraw because they said there was a Communist on his panel," the sheriff related.

This is the reaction of a department the McCone Commission, in its post-Watts whitewash, claimed "represented well all of the people." It would be more accurate to say that the Los Angeles Police Department represents well some of the people all of the time.

6

Chicago: A Plateau of Progress

Orlando W. Wilson, Chicago's recently retired sixty-seven-year-old superintendent of police, is one of the few visionaries among the law-enforcement old guard. When he took over the scandal-plagued department in 1960, he instituted reforms that improved the palms-up image of the city's cops, asserted a positive leadership that had been missing in the past, and transformed an operation that smelled strongly of mothballs into a model of cybernetic efficiency. The new Chicago department has been widely hailed in feature articles, and George W. O'Connor, director of professional standards for the International Association of Chiefs of Police, rates it "the best-equipped, best-administered police force in the United States."

The costly renovation (since 1960 the police budget has soared from $73,000,000 to $103,000,000) turned out to be more of a face-lifting than a fundamental reform. During Wilson's regime, venality and malpractice did not cease; they merely went underground. The determined superintendent never was able to freshen the stale attitudes that dominate the precincts, or to de-fuse the time bomb of hostility between the police and the minorities—as the riots of the summer of 1966 confirm. Wilson achieved a plateau of progress beyond which he could not venture.

Wilson's failure is all the more frustrating in view of the considerable promise his efforts at first showed. Prior to 1960 Chicagoans cited one statistic as characteristic of their department: since 1919 there had been 191 gangland slayings, and all but 2 remained unsolved. Police tie-ins with the syndicates were taken for granted, and such spectacles as a police lieutenant taking off for a vacation trip to Europe as the guest of Tony (Big Tuna) Accardo scarcely raised an eyebrow. The cynicism was pervasive: citizens kept a $5 bill clipped to their driver's licenses to pay the expected "fine" levied by the cops' "street courts," and smart burglars carried a roll of bills to "make bond" in an alley if caught in the act.

The traditional alliances between politicians and police rendered the chief of police little more than a figurehead. Officers with political "clout" threw their weight around, secure in the knowledge that complaints against them would be conveniently pigeonholed. ("Forget what they taught you in the academy," was the seasoned cop's standard advice to the rookie; "get yourself a Chinaman [a political sponsor].") Patronage was rife, and the ward healers, not the district captains, called the shots on promotions. Shakedowns were frequent, and racketeers regularly paid a percentage of their gross to police in return for operating unmolested. Chicago was the epitome of police corruption, and probably no force was held in more contempt by its community.

The breaking point came in December 1959. Eight policemen, an informant disclosed, were involved in a burglary ring headed by a professional North Side burglar. The policemen, who were attached to the Summervale Station, allegedly had acted as lookouts and used police cars to haul away the loot. The newspapers had a field day, and a chagrined Mayor Richard J. Daley appointed a five-man civilian committee to select a reform chief for the department.

Passing over an unimpressive list of candidates, the committee finally chose one of its own members, Wilson. The gaunt, tweedish professor was about to retire after a long career in law enforcement and criminology. He had begun in 1924 as a patrolman on the Berkeley, California, force, and after several years as a private detective had been appointed chief in Wichita, Kansas, a post he held for eleven years. During World War II he was an Army colonel and after the war served as chief public safety officer for the military government in Germany. Following a teaching stint at Harvard in 1950, he returned to his alma mater, California, as dean of the department of criminology. His *Police Administration* is regarded as a hallmark text on the subject.

At first Wilson was reluctant to accept the staggering challenge posed by the 10,700-man force, but once committed, he moved with characteristic speed. Armed with a *carte blanche* commission from the mayor, he slashed at the topheavy administrative superstructure and compacted the thirty-eight districts into twenty-one. Then he went after corruption and abuse of authority with the zeal of a circuit rider. "The public has respect for the police to precisely the degree the police have earned it," he declared in setting up a disciplinary apparatus called the Internal Investigation Division. Rather than sitting back and waiting for complaints, the IID sought out infractions. One tactic was to plant fake drunks in jail cells to see if police custodians would roll them.

The notion of police spying on police and employing the same methods as against criminals, however, was too bitter a pill for the rank and file to swallow. The powerful Patrolmen's Benevolent Association called a mass meeting to demand Wilson's ouster, and several thousand officers cheered lustily as one speaker after another chided "the Professor" and his naïve theories. But if the PBA was counting on its customary political support, it was doomed to disappointment. Daley, who had passed the "hands off" signal through the Democratic pipeline, backed his superintendent (Wilson had chosen the title as more modest than chief of police) to the hilt and concurred that the department was justified in "utilizing all investigative procedures and techniques which are legally available to it in ferreting out criminal violations or violations of department regulations by its members." It began to occur to the policemen that the alternative to the IID might well be a civilian review board—civil rights groups in Chicago have long urged one—and the recall movement dwindled away.

Wilson knew as well as anyone that the only real guarantee against malfeasance lies in attracting and keeping men of sound moral character. He substantially hiked the starting pay to $6,228 (after forty-two months a patrolman earns $7,548) and pushed for higher scales in order to become competitive with local industry. More important, he unplugged the promotional bottleneck to enable talented young men to rise more rapidly into command positions. But command positions rarely open up through attrition, and Wilson did nothing to root out the dead wood through forced resignations and retirements or outright firings. This concession to the status quo may have been part of his undoing, for the ranks and line commands have remained relatively inert. The department claims a backlog of applicants well in excess of its turnover, and one measure of the less than dramatic change in its complexion is the fact that there are still only 257 college graduates on the force, a pitifully low 2 percent.

The most complete and obvious transformation wrought by Wilson has been in the department's image. The baroque old headquarters building at 1121 South State Street has been face-lifted and matched by a gleaming new annex. The forbidding foyer of the old building has been replaced by a commodious, brightly lit hall containing exhibits that show the police in action, and visitors are invited to take self-tours of the communications center, data processing section and crime laboratory. "We take pride in the progress we have made," states a printed guide to the self-tour. "We trust that you share this pride with us."

Wilson has deployed electronics in the war against crime on a scale unduplicated by any other department. The data processing section houses batteries of IBM 1410 computers which digest reams of crime data and predict where an outbreak of crimes of a particular category is likely to occur, enabling police strategists to position their patrol forces to best advantage. Once a prisoner is in custody, the time required positively to identify him and ascertain his criminal record, if any, has been cut by one-fifth through a facsimile transmission system called Policefax. In an age when court decisions have forbidden prolonged interrogation before arraignment, a rapid "make" is time gained.

To implement an innovation called "aggressive preventive patrol," Wilson increased the number of vehicles from 1,209 to 1,798 and painted them an eye-fetching pastel blue and white (even the Black Marias are blue and white). The cars dart down side streets and poke into alleys, waging a kind of psychological warfare by creating an impression of omnipresence. Equipped with multichannel radios, the cars can be dispatched within thirty seconds of receipt of a trouble call at headquarters even at peak hours, and where once a Chicagoan in distress might have waited an hour or longer for police to arrive, the wait now is only minutes.

In all, Chicago's new look was somewhat *avant garde* in law enforcement, and Wilson's able public relations director, Mel Mawrence, quickly capitalized on the interest it aroused. A postwar military mayor of Munich and former official in the

Illinois attorney general's office, Mawrence is, like Wilson, a precise, guarded man devoid of flamboyance, but the programs he has concocted have more than a trace of the showman's touch. One is Project Ride-Along, in which selected civic leaders, law students, newsmen and clergymen accompany officers in patrol cars to get the feel of police work. Another is Operation Crime-Stop, which exploits citizens' hidden desires to play detective. Chicagoans are urged to call a special toll-free number, PO 5-1313, whenever they sight a "suspicious person" or suspect a crime is about to be committed. Mawrence likes to tell of one call that resulted in the capture of a bank robbery gang *flagrante delicto*. An elderly woman looked out her window and noticed several men donning masks. When they entered a savings and loan office, she called the Crime-Stop number. Within ninety seconds converging patrol cars had the frustrated robbers in custody.

Crime-Stop seems to have helped the police make arrests. When it was initiated, phone calls spurted, with a collateral increase in the number of "offenses cleared by arrest," a benchmark of police efficacy. The tally for 1965 was over 90,000 citizen calls; police credited the calls with 4,500 additional arrests. Chicago's rate of clearance reached 35.7 percent in 1965, well above the national figure of 24 percent. Coupled with the "aggressive preventive patrol," Crime-Stop apparently had braked Chicago's upward crime curve. In his 1965 annual report, Wilson was able to boast that "serious crimes dropped 11.9 percent following a prior decrease of 3.15 in 1964," this in the face of a nationwide rise. (When the rate started back up in the second half of 1966, however, a police spokesman tentatively blamed the manpower drain required to keep order and the civil rights and anti-Vietnam-war demonstrations.)

While the department is justly proud of its ingenious programs, they have not been carried out without dubious side effects. Chicago has a much higher police-to-citizen ratio than, say, New York or Los Angeles, and the practice of saturating "high crime" areas and conducting massive street "stops" on the slightest suspicion (there were some 250,000 in 1964) creates the oppressive atmosphere of a garrison state. Approximately 75,000 arrests each year, well over one-third of the total, are on the vague charge of disorderly conduct, which seems to have supplanted the now proscripted charge of "suspicion" as a catchall. The arrest total, the department dutifully notes, does not include those persons detained and subsequently released without being formally charged, a shadow area that understandably is not reduced to statistical tabulation.

Some critics argue that the street stops constitute extralegal harassment, since they produce only a handful of prosecutions. Practically all are in fact unprosecutable because, under the Supreme Court's *Mapp* decision in 1961, evidence secured in "fishing expedition" searches is illegal and inadmissible in court. This exclusionary rule, as it is called, sanctions only evidence obtained through the execution of a search warrant in which the evidence is specifically named, or incident to arrest, which requires that the officer have probable cause to believe the subject has committed a crime. Chicago's stops are based on an administrative finding by the department, which admittedly would not stand up should anyone bother to appeal it. But the apparent intent is crime prevention. In 1965, for example, Chicago police illegally confiscated 6,000 hand guns, most through street stops. The weapons are kept for one month in case the owner does go to court to obtain a writ of replevin, then destroyed.

The ostentatious and at times gimmicky "war on crime" distracts from the fact that the Chicago department has scarcely dented the flourishing crime syndicates, which, after all, most seriously affect the population at large. Wilson concedes that progress has been slight, and Virgil Peterson, vener-

THE POLICE ESTABLISHMENT : 114

able head of the privately subsidized Chicago Crime Commission and another frustrated foe of the rackets, told the *National Observer* (September 6, 1965) that "the department hasn't gotten results in breaking up syndicated crime operations. But there was virtually nothing done in this area before Wilson, and at least we can tell they're now trying."

In March 1960, shortly after he became superintendent, Wilson established an intelligence unit to specialize in the war on the syndicates. The unit was directly under the late Joseph E. Morris, whom Wilson had elevated to deputy commissioner. Morris, one of Chicago's toughest cops and a living legend among his colleagues, had commanded the old "Scotland Yard" anti-hoodlum squad that had been inexplicably disbanded following Mayor Daley's first election in 1956.

Morris' nascent unit was bucking obstacles that precluded any climactic success. In order to survive, organized crime must have the indulgence of some politicians and the cooperation of others, and in Chicago the labyrinthine ties are practically impossible to sever. The powerful First Ward is tightly in the grip of the pol-syndicate combine; many state legislators either fear or are friendly to the syndicate czars; and one federal legislator has fondly reminisced about his friendship with Al Capone. Thus the mayor is not much more than the caretaker of a system that long preceded him, and his position vis-à-vis the syndicates is simply that they do not exist.

This situation is not altogether unique to Chicago, it is merely more entrenched there. Joseph D. Lohman, dean of the department of criminology at the University of California and a former Chicago sheriff, pointed out in a recent article in *Focus Midwest* that in many areas "political alliances have made the organized criminal element more powerful than the police." And the interstate scope of syndicate operations has made the problem primarily a federal one. Former Attorney General Robert F. Kennedy sized up the situation by saying that syndicate hoodlums "have become so rich and powerful that they have outgrown local authorities."

As Lohman puts it, "Inroads on this illegal system can only be made if the federal government enters into alliances with honest local officials and helps them clean up." However, the cooperation of the FBI, which has the widest spectrum of federal jurisdiction over the rackets, has always been grudging. In fact, until Kennedy became the FBI's nominal boss in 1961, the bureau had kept a respectful distance from the criminal syndicates and concentrated instead on lesser crimes and criminals. Even after the notorious Apalachin meeting of the nation's top crime executives in 1957, the G-men remained aloof and snubbed the special group set up by the U.S. Attorney General to deal with the problem. The head of the Chicago section of the special group, Richard Ogilvie, had been one of the most resolute foes of the syndicates and the nemesis of Tony Accardo. In a newspaper article he stated: "The FBI is still organized to fight a crime pattern of the 20s and 30s. It is not set up to do battle with the criminal syndicate. . . ." The FBI reacted by branding Ogilvie an "enemy of the bureau." In 1962, Ogilvie, named by *Life* magazine as one of the most outstanding Americans under the age of forty, was elected sheriff of Cook County (Chicago) by a landslide. So the sharpest skirmishes on the organized crime front remain internecine ones among law-enforcement agencies.

In his reign as superintendent, Wilson was not able to work any substantive miracles. The majority of burglars and robbers still do not get caught, and organized crime has emerged almost unscathed. However altruistic his intentions, he was forced to function within the existing structure—to respond to the clamoring of newspapers, the courting of politicians, and the cries of citizens' groups fearful of "violence in the streets" —and consequently could not devote his energies to truly significant crime.

"Too many police departments are too popularity-conscious," Dean Lohman has said in a passage remarkably descriptive of Chicago. "The new look is to look good with 'business methods,' and public relations programs; to buck the blame for crime to the courts and their allegedly inadequate sentences; and to push for more and more arrests."

The "new look" in Chicago has been achieved at tremendous cost, not only in dollars but in progress. It has dignified a police system that is essentially unchanged and has polarized public opinion. Those the police have always served, the "solid citizens," businessmen, pols and blue-collar whites, are lavish in their praise; those the police have always abused, the voiceless minorities, have seen a mantle of respectability draped over the department, and are more despairing than ever.

7

Chicago: The Final Futility

When O. W. Wilson took command of the Chicago department in 1960, one of his first edicts was that the force be integrated in all respects. At present, the Negro complement is between 20 and 25 percent, a ratio that roughly parallels the city's
Negro population and stands in marked contrast to the Los
Angeles and New York ratios. Recently, the height requirement was lowered to make more Puerto Ricans eligible, a step
that breaks with the traditional concept of the cop as a brawny
physical specimen. But these internal adjustments, laudable
as they are, have had practically no impact on the unhealthy relationship between the police in the precincts and the city's
racial and cultural minorities. The alienation had been too
long and too bitter, the basic attitudes on both sides too immutable, for any reconciliation negotiated from the distant ramparts of police headquarters.

Historically, the bitterness traces to the large Negro influx
during and following World War II. As the Negro ghetto over-
flowed and families began to move into white low-income
neighborhoods, white resentment mounted. In July 1953, in
the previously all-white Trumbull Park Housing Project in
the South Deering section, there was open vengence. Over
a prolonged period, white tenants, still in the majority, com-

mitted numerous acts of violence against Negro project dwellers.

In the Negroes' view, the police did not conduct themselves as impartial minions of the law but, rather, sided with the whites. Although the department assigned large numbers of policemen to guard the project—in the course of one twenty-four-hour period some 1,200 were on duty—there were recurring charges that many white officers stood by indifferently while whites openly attacked Negroes. One such incident took place on April 17, 1954. Two Negro women and a small boy driving through the project were hemmed in by the drivers of two other cars, and a cascade of bricks and bottles struck their car. They escaped injury only by ramming through the other cars. Later they said they did not report the incident to the police department because several policemen had witnessed the assault without moving a muscle. A white policeman was quoted by a Negro as saying he was not there "to protect us but to protect the grounds."

In the summer of 1957, Negroes again became the targets of white outrage, this time over the issue of the use of Calument Park in the South Deering section. Again, the police were accused of passivity and refusing to arrest white rock-throwers. Although the department has subsequently tightened its handling of incipient riots, provoked by either side, the pattern of dual enforcement had been too well set to disappear entirely.

The pattern is a familiar one in the nation's ghettos, and varies only with local characteristics. In Chicago, for instance, a convention capital drawing more than 1,500,000 delegates and visitors annually who leave untold millions in the tills of Windy City businesses, the police handle roisterous, inebriated conventioneers with kid gloves, often transporting them back to their hotels in patrol cars. In contrast, the Negro who carries on raucously stands an excellent chance of being booked for "disorderly conduct"—in 1965 36,607 Negroes were arrested on that charge, almost one-fifth of the force's total arrests.

While it is a statistical verity that the incidence of crime is higher among Negroes and that in the ghettos Negro crime is directed against Negroes, the ghetto seems to seethe under Wilson's policy of aggressive preventive patrol. This is at once both baffling and vexing to the police, since their computer, which is colorblind, has told them this is where a rash of crimes occurred in the past and where a new outbreak is most likely to happen.

But the computer, in its total detachment, cannot digitize the deep-seated mistrust and contempt Negroes and police reserve for each other, and thus it is liable to trigger a repetitive cycle of arrest-producing friction. For it deploys into an area masses of police, frequently spearheaded by the crack Task Force, a "Special Forces" kind of squad noted for its blunt tactics, conditioned to the notion that crime is about to happen and ready to challenge anyone on the slightest suspicion. It is axiomatic that in a confrontation such as this, there will be a surge in arrests, if not for the anticipated crimes then for lesser ones. And when the figures are digested by the computers and the answers are disgorged, the nasty cycle of suspicion and arrest starts all over again.

The implacable hostility of the police toward the ghetto inmates is fundamentally a clash of widely separated social strata, one armed with authority, the other charged with despair. It is no different in Chicago than in the other urban centers. The policeman has bridged what sociologists call the cross-cultural gap and achieved a middle-class status whose values stress such superficial virtues as cleanliness, promptness, orderliness and propriety. Having striven and succeeded, he is contemptuous of those left wallowing in poverty and its attendant evils. He is prone to invoke the great American myth that through industry alone man can gain status and security, and thus falls prey to a concomitant myth: that indolence is a racial trait. "My folks came to this country without anything and worked for themselves," a sergeant assigned to the West Side ghetto told a *Newsweek* reporter (June 27, 1966). "Why should these people have special treatment? Who makes a slum? The landlord doesn't make a building into a slum. The people who live in it make it a slum."

Such appallingly presumptive attitudes shut off any chance of empathy between the police and the ghetto. For their part, the people of the ghetto view the police as mercenaries enforcing the social order that has them entrapped. "The words 'police brutality,'" asserts former Chicago Sheriff Lohman, "mean all the double standards and all the indignities police can subject minority people to in an unenlightened community. The police are today in fact less brutal than they have ever been—in terms of physical brutality. But what people are objecting to is that they reinforce a social order that can be more brutal than the worst physical force."

Although the 30,000 Puerto Ricans crowded into the *barrio* bisected by Division Street in the northwest section are mostly newcomers and not as chronically pushed around as the Negroes, they evidently have developed an equally intense anti-police feeling. One catalyst has been the police habit of taunting the volatile Latins with slurs and insults, such as calling their wives or girlfriends *puta*, in the hope of provoking an outburst. (As if with some kind of prescience, Wilson issued General Order 66-9 in the summer of 1966, shortly before rioting broke out in the Puerto Rican section: "Never 'talk down' to any group or individual or engage in the use of derogatory terms such as nigger, boy, spic, wop, kike, chink, shine, burrhead, dago, polack, bohunk and the like.") Another irritant has been the large number of traffic tickets dumped in the section by quota-pressured police acting on the premise that Spanish-speaking people are not likely to contest them.

The hounding of Danny Escobedo has not alleviated the situation. Escobedo is a Chicago Mexican-American whose homicide conviction was voided in a Supreme Court decision that threw into disrepute police interrogation methods. Escobedo became a symbol of mortification to the department, and he has been kept under almost continual scrutiny since, as if he were Dillinger incarnate, and twice arrested on what juries agreed were trumped-up charges. In November 1966 the hapless Escobedo was spotted urinating near a restaurant that had just been burglarized and was promptly arrested for the burglary. As his attorney, Marshall Schwarzbach, complained in court, he is at the top of the department's "most hated person" list.

The lines on both sides were irrevocably drawn by an incident on the late evening of October 26, 1964. With guns drawn and shouting *"Policia, policia,"* off-duty officers Raymond Howard and Thomas DeSutter attempted to arrest two young Puerto Ricans outside a bar. One had a broken beer bottle in his hand. When one of the youths swore at the officers, DeSutter lashed out at him with his gun hand. As he did so, read the opinion of Circuit Judge George N. Leighton, who heard the case, the youth "lifted up his right hand in which he held the broken beer bottle and as a consequence the bottle struck DeSutter in the face." In the ensuing scuffle, Howard's gun accidentally discharged, striking his partner in the leg. DeSutter spent twenty-one days in the hospital recovering from the bullet wound and a deep facial slash.

In a decision that precipitated spasms of outrage, Judge Leighton acquitted the youths, holding that there had not been sufficient grounds for arrest, and that the resisting of "an unlawful arrest with excessive force" was justified under Illinois law. So incensed were Chicago police representatives that they demanded Judge Leighton be transferred to a post "where his obvious prejudice against police officers will not circumvent the laws designed to protect the citizens of our community." Police supporters joined in the chorus.

When the trial transcript was released, however, a curious bit of testimony came to light. Howard had claimed that he and DeSutter were coming out of the police station when a man ran up to them and reported an altercation in progress in the bar in front of which the youths were arrested. Did Howard know the man? Yes, he admitted. Had he seen him since the event? Yes, he had. But for some unknown reason, the prosecution never produced this vital witness who could have corroborated the officers' version and supplied the ingredient of probable cause.*

On the muggy evening of June 12, 1966, the Puerto Rican *barrio* finally exploded. A patrol car responded to a street-fight call at Division and Damen streets. One of the car's occupants chased one of the brawlers and dropped him with a bullet in the leg when he pulled a gun. The sight of the manacled Puerto Rican youth being shoved into the patrol car inflamed the on-lookers, and an angry crowd quickly swarmed around the police vehicle. Then someone tossed kerosene on the car and set it afire. When police dogs were brought in to subdue the crowd, it instead became infuriated and full-scale rioting broke out, lasting into the night.

By the next day tempers had cooled, but they reached the flashpoint again when a police officer apparently tried to run

* Scarcely a year later, Howard and DeSutter were involved in another violent incident. On October 6, 1965, they observed a young Negro couple, the Daniel Morgans, arguing in front of their apartment. Questioned by the officers, the Morgans amicably apologized and started inside, but they were grabbed and placed under arrest. In the patrol car, they said, they were verbally abused and Mrs. Morgan, irate at being called a whore, spat on one of the officers. "At this point," declared the couple's attorney, Mitchell Edelson, Jr., in a letter to O. W. Wilson dated October 11, 1965, "at least one of the police officers seems to have gone insane and clubbed the young lady, beating her unmercifully, until her husband threw himself between the two at which point the officers beat on him until both had been subdued." Edelson charged that while the Morgans were handcuffed, "both officers proceeded to beat, with their fists, rings and I.D. bracelets, upon the face, head and body. . . ."

down a twelve-year-old boy who had tossed a stone at his patrol car. With a shrill cry of *"Venganza!"* from the crowd, the rioting flared anew. Realizing that the police were an inciting agent, Wilson withdrew his men while Puerto Rican leaders attempted to douse overheated tempers. But the truce was broken when a gang of teenagers stormed down Division Street smashing windows, and Wilson responded with a human wave of 500 policemen led by a phalanx of the blue-helmeted Task Force shock troops.

The riots clearly demonstrated that whatever socioeconomic injustices had stirred passions, the tinder had been a latent animus toward the police and the spark a mishandling of a touchy situation by the police. "There was little doubt," reported a *Christian Science Monitor* team, "that the presence of police—and their handling of the Puerto Ricans over a period of several years—was the center of the controversy in this conflict. We heard no other argument or issue in the seven hours we worked the streets." It was the same issue as in Watts, Philadelphia and Harlem.

It was also evident that some police were unable to distinguish between command of the situation and reckless arrogance, a fault that escalated the violence. "Despite careful guidelines," the *Monitor* team continued, "police tactics were not uniformly discreet. One instance took place before we began breaking up the congestion at Division and California. Most of the young men had gone, and we had been thanked by the sergeant on the corner. Suddenly a police captain with a dozen blue-helmeted men stormed across the street . . . the street was virtually clear. The captain and three men pushed into a restaurant where more than fifty people, in family groups, were quietly eating their evening meal. In a loud voice he demanded to see the owner. Moving to the kitchen he demanded that she clear the place and close up. Then he stalked out, shaking his fist and shouting: 'I'll give you fifteen minutes to get everybody out of here, you understand? Fifteen minutes!' Then he slammed the door with such force the storefront windows rattled. In less than a minute, he had changed quietness into anger."

The *Monitor* reporters cited two other incidents in which the police went out of their way looking for trouble. "At 10:50 P.M., only a handful of people were left on the street. A lieutenant and a group of policemen raced to the upper floor of a three-story building on Division Street and hauled out two men who someone said had been seen with crude antipolice signs in a window. Then the police closed a restaurant below where there were a number of young Puerto Ricans. Those in the restaurant scattered as ordered. But two youths, walking slowly a block away, were spotted by a sergeant who cursed them, saying to the lieutenant: 'Those guys were in the restaurant. Let's go get them.' . . . Two police searched one of the youths and then gave him a hard shove that sent him sprawling toward the police wagon. The lieutenant and the sergeant stood on the curb discussing what they could charge the two youths with, since they had only been walking down the street. . . ."

The Rev. Donald Headley, head of the Roman Catholic Cardinal's Committee for the Spanish-Speaking, concurred with the *Monitor's* evaluation. "There is very, very big resentment of the police out there," he told *Time* (June 24, 1966). "The attitude of the policemen to the Puerto Ricans has been very bad." But Mayor Daley, who deflects criticism of Chicago institutions almost reflexively, darkly attributed the disturbances to "outside influences." Wilson, hardly in a position to contradict his boss, quietly integrated police patrols and clamped tight restrictions on the use of dogs.

The last word was had by Mike Royko, the iconoclastic columnist of the Chicago *Daily News*. One of those "outside influences," he wrote, was Daley himself. "He manages to attend many wakes in his part of town. But when the Puerto Ricans invited him to a banquet last week—their biggest social event of the year, except for the riot—he couldn't make it." Nor did Royko, who grew up in Chicago, spare Wilson. "Another outside influence is . . . Wilson," he charged. "He says he has just discovered that his men and the Puerto Ricans don't get along too well. I don't know why the police don't like Puerto Ricans. With all of the shooting they are supposed to have been doing during the rioting, they managed to avoid hitting any policemen while suffering numerous wounds themselves."

As with most tragedies, the riots were not without irony. Only weeks before, in a letter to Daley dated April 2, 1966, Wilson proudly noted that his department in the past year had been able "to cover the city with a greater blanket of aggressive preventive patrol than at any previous time." And, he had added with an almost audible sigh of relief, "a significant highlight of both 1965 and 1964 was Chicago's emergence from the summer periods without serious racial incidents."

As it turned out, the Puerto Rican riots were merely a curtain-raiser to the more destructive Negro riots a month later. The riots started, as so many do, with a seemingly innocuous incident. On the sweltering day of July 12 in the West Side ghetto, children tried to turn on a fire hydrant for relief from the heat but were prevented from doing so by police. A stone was tossed, then another. Soon the police were driven back by a hail of missiles as a group of young Negroes opened the hydrant valve and the water splashed out. Thus, with a show of defiance by the youths, the calamitous disorders started.

The pressures released on July 12 had been building up since spring, when Negroes affronted the monolithic political machine, which had been accustomed to buying their compliance with regular doles, by picketing City Hall in protest against the policies of School Superintendent Benjamin Willis.

Mayor Daley was at first stunned, then annoyed. "Many of the people who are marching are Communist," he alleged, conjuring up the old bugbear used by politicians backed into a corner. "That's been printed. And the police department files show this is true."

Civil rights leaders were outraged at the gratuitous slur. "The mayor has insulted the intelligence and character of many people, including priests, ministers and nuns who have been participating in the current demonstrations," remonstrated a group of Catholic priests. Roy Wilkins, executive director of the NAACP, fired off a telegram to Daley challenging him to either retract his statement "or to produce solid evidence of its truth." In reply, Daley waved an article in the Chicago *American,* a newspaper that habitually detects Reds under all sorts of beds, which declared that several demonstrators were "identified" as Communists or sympathizers by the experts of the police "Red Squad" subversive detail.

Whether Communists or their sympathizers joined the picket lines was not really relevant. It is no dark secret that the handful of genuine Communists in the United States have attempted to exploit the civil rights movement and have swooped down like buzzards on legitimate demonstrations and spontaneous disorders. The movement, for its part, has not found it either practical or necessary to subject everyone who marches to a security screening. But by hanging the Red albatross around the demonstrators' necks and citing the police department as his authority, Daley dodged the real issues and in the process increased the tension between City Hall and the police on the one hand and Chicago's aggrieved Negroes on the other.

Nor did the early summer advent of Dr. Martin Luther King, the Nobel Peace Prize-winning exponent of nonviolence, serve to calm the troubled waters. For his first venture into the ghettos of the urban north, where "keeping the nigger in his place" can be just as effective as but far more subtle than in the Deep South, King had singled out Chicago's walled city of some 900,000 Negroes. Far from gaining hegemony over the city's factionalized Negro groups, however, King merely succeeded in polarizing the antagonists. Understandably, City Hall was cool to his presence, looking upon him as an interloper into local affairs. And most Negroes had long since abandoned hope of meaningful dialogue with City Hall and were prepared instead to exert the doctrine of black power.

When the rioting started two days after his arrival, King took to the streets in a pacification attempt but found himself mocked as a false prophet by young Negro militants. And symbolic of counterattitudes was the experience of a white Lutheran minister, a white Catholic nun, and a black Christian Church minister who set out together from the Shiloah Baptist Church, Dr. King's temporary headquarters, on a peace-urging mission. At Roosevelt Road and Homan Avenue, the *Daily News* reported, the trio encountered a police cordon "sweeping" the sidewalk ahead of them. Before anyone could utter a word, a huge six-foot, six-inch policeman with swinging club and bellowing voice grabbed the Negro minister by the shoulder and in one motion spun him around and sent him reeling back down the sidewalk. "You're only making these people angrier," pleaded the Lutheran minister, "don't you understand?" The policeman, visibly agitated, cut him short. "I don't care!" he cried. "Move out! One more word and you're going. . . ."

Miraculously, the three days of rioting, in which there were prolonged gun battles between snipers and police, claimed only two lives: those of a Negro man and a young pregnant Negro woman whose child was stillborn. Both had been caught in crossfire. In the recriminations that followed, King, the would-be builder of bridges, was hit with a verbal volley from

Daley and Wilson, just as he had been denounced by Los Angeles' twin pillars of power, Yorty and Parker, when he had tried to intercede in Watts.

King had raised official hackles when he accused the police of laxity in protecting post-riot civil rights demonstrators from white attackers who caused more property damage than did the riots proper. "It was clear," King said, "that the police were either unwilling or unable to disperse the riotous mob that so brutally attacked Negroes and whites who had come to the community to seek open housing in compliance with the law." To which Wilson retorted: "I can't see how King has helped the drive for civil rights in Chicago. To the extent he has stirred up hatreds, he has hampered it."

Mayor Daley again blamed "outsiders," a charge contradicted by the fact all those arrested were inhabitants of the West Side ghetto. ("The riots were planned by Communists," a police lieutenant confided to me several months later. When I pressed him for names, he mentioned a member of the then-functioning New York City civilian review board who happened to be in Chicago at the time.) There were outsiders, but they had come to Chicago not to foment the Negro riots but to goad on the whites in the post-riot attack on the demonstrators. There were, for example, George Lincoln Rockwell and his American Nazi cohorts, and Charles Conrad "Connie" Lynch, the peregrinatic Negro-baiter and fundamentalist preacher who had been credited by Florida authorities with spurring mob violence in St. Augustine in 1964 and who headed a Ku Klux Klan parade in Bogalusa, Louisiana, during that city's 1965 racial strife.

It was not so much that Daley perceived a grand design behind the riots as it was expedient that he find one. As D. J. R. Buckner, chief of the Los Angeles *Times* Chicago bureau, put it in his analysis of July 24, 1966: "A number of city officials and police officers . . . are responding to the demands of the white majority in the city, and are looking for a plot or conspiracy, whether it be one concocted by youth gangs or Communist-inspired groups, or by political hotheads. A lot of investigators are scurrying around looking for this alleged plot, and, God help us, they may even find one. Any little old mangy plot, however crazy or ineffectual, will serve very well to salve the conscience of the city."

Chicago, by no means an exception among the nation's cities, prefers to apply analgesics rather than treat directly its grave social ills, of which police-minorities relations are one. Although Wilson undoubtedly would have chosen to reduce the friction, he was neither willing to pay the price in terms of a drastic shakeup of his department, which would have been tantamount to admitting serious police fault, nor able radically to reshape a policy that was not of his own making. As one police insider expressed it, "Daley calls the shots right over Wilson's head."

Consequently the attitudes in the precincts were little changed from the day eight years before when he took over— his attempts at remote control from headquarters were simply ignored. A case in point is the police of the Summerdale Station versus JOIN (Jobs Or Income Now) and United People, two small grass-roots organizations which sought to find job opportunities for chronically unemployed slum dwellers. Both organizations were unsanctioned by the political machine— JOIN was run by liberal ex-students, United People by Presbyterian minister George Morey—and thus were steering a hazardous course in tightly run Chicago. Because of their mutual goals, the two organizations became informally allied.

On July 17, 1966, immediately after the riots, JOIN decided it would attempt to document incidents of police brutality and harassment. Members paired off and started tailing patrol cars on their rounds. On their first tail, Robert Lawson and Ralph Thurman reported, they were eyewitnesses to the beating of a young Puerto Rican lying on the sidewalk. When Lawson started writing down the officers' badge numbers, he and Thurman were arrested for "disorderly conduct."

Shortly afterward a group of some 22 Uptown District residents organized by JOIN and United People staged a march on the Summerdale Station, as it is commonly known, the scene of the 1960 police burglary scandal. The marchers demanded that the station be investigated, that a particularly badge-happy officer be transferred, and that a civilian review board be established. Not unexpectedly, the group left empty-handed. But the officer whose transfer had been demanded, accompanied by several of his police cohorts, went around intimidating some of the march participants and tearing up their JOIN cards. "Guys were told they would be busted [arrested] and beaten if they had anything to do with JOIN," said one member. One man who displayed a JOIN card allegedly was taken to the Summerdale Station and beaten.

Then, on September 1, two weeks after the march on the station, vice squad members raided the offices of JOIN and United People. They were armed with search warrants issued on the sworn testimony of a Richard Traunce (the name was unfamiliar to both organizations) that he had taken narcotics along with others on the JOIN and United People premises. At United People the raiders claimed to have found narcotics and a piece of pornographic literature; Reverend Morey and a man in the office at the time were taken into custody for "possession of narcotics."

The raiders reserved their worst manners for the JOIN office, probably because several JOIN people belonged to the Students for a Democratic Society, identified with the New Left. "About twenty police entered the office," recounted member Richard Rothstein. "They tore down a wall surrounding the bookcase. They scattered all JOIN files, broke chairs, threw furniture into piles, and dumped the mimeograph machine on the floor. I could see them throwing things. I could hear them laughing. They were having a good time." From the shambles the police retrieved, they said, needles, pills, marijuana and, for good measure, "Communist literature." Rothstein and two others in the office were booked for possession of narcotics.

Had the police been seriously concerned about narcotics, the raids were premature, for the cases were thrown out of court for lack of evidence. If, however, the narcotics had been planted to retaliate for the march or discredit the organizations —and the police took the trouble to bring along a friendly newspaper reporter on the raids—the libel had been accomplished. The episode had a revealing sequel. The board of trustees of United People met with the Summerdale commander to discuss the raids. The commander pulled out his dossier on JOIN and passed around photographs he said were taken by the FBI. They were of civil rights activists in the Chicago area, mostly persons associated with a coalition group, the Coordinating Council of Community Organizations. The photographs were mug shots, bore descriptive notations such as height and weight, and were labeled "inclined toward civil disobedience." One of the trustees was perplexed, pointing out that although he admired many of the people in the photographs, none had any connection with JOIN. "It's all part of the same thing," the police commander kept repeating.

One of the thorniest problems related to racial matters is the role of organized youth gangs. In the 1966 Chicago riots it was estimated that most of the damage during the three days was done by a hard core of 300 youths. In dealing with youth gangs who have demonstrated a capacity for maliciousness and violence, the police have adopted a get-tough policy of harassment, containment and arrest on the slightest provocation. There is a body of opinion, however, which holds that the carrot, properly dangled, can divert gang energies into constructive channels. The formula is not unproven. In San Francisco, for example, under the leadership of slum product Orville Luster, the Quaker-sponsored Youth for Service converted gangs of supposedly incorrigible toughs into a force for orderly progress. When the Hunter's Point riots flared in October 1966, for example, Youth for Service members fanned out into the area with the message, "Cool it, man, cool it." The rioters "cooled," and the disorder was short-lived.

In Chicago the police philosophy is the classic "break up the gangs," and the department's one accession to a more enlightened approach ended in a show of bad faith. A "street-savvy" minister, Rev. John Frye of the First Presbyterian Church, started working with the Blackstone Rangers, the city's most notorious Negro youth gang. On July 4, 1966, the Rangers filed into the church and deposited their guns for safekeeping, a concession that may have kept the ensuing riots from taking a worse toll. A few days after the riots, Reverend Frye told Nicholas Von Hoffman of the *Daily News*: "We've got fifty Blackstone Rangers' guns locked up in a church safe because we have an organization that can deal with them and the cops. In return for going light on one of the Rangers' leaders, we got them to hand over their firearms to us."

It sounded as if a vast chasm had been spanned. "The police are really cooperating with us," Reverend Frye enthused. "We sat down with them and told them how to handle themselves in the neighborhood, and we've had our own members out working the blocks day and night. I can't be sure, but I think things are going to hold." It was not long before the police, after tipping off the press, swooped down on the church and confiscated the weapons. The way it was played up in most newspapers, the police had just discovered a dangerous cache of youth-gang weapons. Thus ended one of Chicago's more promising experiments in police-community relations.

In Chicago and other urban centers, it is glaringly obvious

that so long as the police are permitted to set their own standards of conduct and pass judgment on their own adherence to these standards, any *rapprochement* with the minority community is a practical impossibility. A "nigger" humiliated by an unwarranted street stop or a "spic" grossly insulted by a bigoted policeman is not naïve enough to tell his story to a steely-eyed station commander. Nor does an indigent who has been worked over, a prostitute who has been extorted by an officer on the vice squad, or a vulnerable homosexual who has been "rousted around" expect any satisfaction from the vaunted Internal Investigation Division.

IID was formed by Wilson on the recognition that policemen are "frequently exposed to the opportunity for misconduct" and it was charged by him with investigating every complaint and making recommendations. Under IID is an Excessive Force Unit, consisting of a captain and fifteen sergeants, which processes complaints of undue physical force or brutality. The final decision as to disciplinary action rested with Wilson, except that firings or suspensions for more than thirty days must have borne the stamp of approval of the police board. The board, also a Wilson innovation, is composed of five leading members of the Chicago establishment.

In selecting IID's first head, Wilson made a critical mistake. His choice, as mentioned previously, was Lt. Joseph E. Morris, who was elevated to deputy superintendent. Morris had a reputation as an indefatigable nemesis of gangsters and was held in high esteem by his colleagues. But he was a blustery, hard-bitten type who knew how to throw his weight around and was badly miscast as an arbiter of police brutality. On March 5, 1953, Morris himself, along with four other officers of the so-called Scotland Yard Squad, had been found guilty of brutality in extracting a confession from a prisoner. The man had complained that he was blindfolded, stretched across a ladder, and beaten with a plank. Granted a second trial, the policemen were found not guilty, a verdict which prompted State's Attorney John Gutknecht to charge that "brutal and crooked police officers are being protected by the city administration." Morris snapped back that Gutknecht was "fighting the police department and protecting hoodlums," a remark somewhat astray from the brutality issue.

For the record, Wilson insists that IID has fulfilled its intended role. On November 22, 1966, the Chicago *Sun-Times* reported that the superintendent had told a commission exploring police-community relations that as far as excessive force was concerned, "the police Internal Investigation Division has established the ability to deal with cases of this type." As confirmation, the department has pointed out that between October 1965 and August 1966 Harold A. Smith, a law-firm senior partner and past president of the Chicago Bar Association, had examined pending files and concluded (apparently without further probing) that IID was giving "both the complainants and the officers a full and fair hearing."

Such pronouncements stick in the craw of Chicagoans most affected by police malpractice. Dick Gregory, the Negro comedian and civil rights activist who has run the police gauntlet from the Deep South to Watts, calls the Chicago force "the most brutal in the country." Indeed, IID's own figures are not conducive to confidence in its impartiality: in 1965, there were 5,000 complaints, or one for every two men on the force. IID reported that it determined all but 800, or 16 percent, were "discovered to be unwarranted."

Absolving its officers 84 percent of the time has left IID open to charges of whitewash, a possibility the Illinois division of the American Civil Liberties Union decided to test. Under the direction of Jay A. Miller, ACLU attorneys not long ago investigated thirty alleged brutality cases and sorted out twelve considered to be "the most provable factual situations." Two of the selected cases, as synopsized by the ACLU, illustrate the wide range of police malpractice:

> F_____ H_____, white male, was taken into custody at the _____ Station and was there when L_____ X_____ came to arrange bond for him. H_____ and X_____ were beaten at the station. In addtion H_____ alleges a cattle prodder was used on him. Soon after this incident X_____ was found dead in the trunk of a car.

> Police officers came to the G_____ home (Negro) without a warrant and searched for a "John and Jane Doe." The household was terrorized by the officers and the husband was beaten by one officer. The search and arrest took place between 7:00 and 9:00 A.M.

Having determined to its own satisfaction that the twelve cases had merit, the ACLU turned them over to the IID. "Reports were received from the Internal Investigation Division," the ACLU stated, "indicating no misconduct on the part of the police in any of these cases."

IID's *modus operandi,* which may account for its zero-for-twelve batting average, is revealed in a case that started on the late evening of July 12, 1966, in the district of the Summerdale Station. A witness who became a victim of alleged brutality gave this version of the incident:

> Out of 904 W. Wilson two police officers came pushing Michael Alcantar, nineteen years old, out the door and down the steps. Then a third officer came over from the parked squad car. When Alcantar turned to face the two officers pushing him, one of them hit him across the face. Then in the shuffle officer #10859 hit Alcantar with a billy club and knocked him down. As he tried to get up one of the policemen kicked him in the back knocking him to the ground again. During this time Michael did not strike an officer, although he called them names and tried to square off.

> While this was going on . . . other family members came

out of the house. . . . Meantime I was taking notes. An officer asked me who I was and I replied "a concerned citizen." He told me that these guys had thrown a pop bottle at the squad car. He told me that it was none of my concern, but I said that whenever three cops, one with a billy club, beat a man on the streets it is everyone's concern. I started to walk away and about four or five more squad cars pulled up and one cop, whom I didn't see but was later told was Officer _____, Badge 0953, said "Arrest him; he's an agitator." He said, "Against the wall, mother_____." I complied and he frisked me and hand-cuffed me very tightly . . . I also saw them arrest Vincent, age fourteen, who was doing nothing more than asking his mother what he should do.

When we got [to the Summerdale Station] about ten officers crowded into the lockup and taunted us with names and calls such as, "Your mother s_____ d_____" and "I f_____ your mother all the time." Michael began yelling back and telling them they were only big when they had their stars and guns on so one officer took off his badge and gunbelt, took the cuffs off Michael and said something like, "Come on, hot stuff," and Michael said, "You move first and I'll hit back." So the officer hit Michael in the stomach and said, "Come on now." Michael said, "I can't do anything now because I can't breathe."

Then Badge 0953 came up to me and said, "You're the big guy taking notes." Then he grabbed my head and pulled it up and said, "I want you to look at my face, you motherf_____" and then he slammed my head against the steel partition. All this time cops were yelling, "Communist," "motherf_____," or "c_____s_____."

Michael began yelling back so the cop hit him again and then Michael jumped up so he was taken into the back room and beaten up badly. He was pounded up against the wall. He began yelling, "I quit, I quit," and then I heard him getting bounced against the wall. And the officer walked out leaving him back there unconscious.

They processed Vincent and me while Michael lay in the back room passed out. One lockup man kept telling Vincent that he hoped Michael would die. After they processed us, they sent

Vincent to get Michael and Vincent had to half drag Michael, who could hardly move, into the room. When Michael came in his face was all bloody, blood was running from his mouth and his arm was beginning to swell.

They charged me with disorderly conduct and obstructing justice; they charged Michael with aggravated battery, creating a disturbance and disorderly conduct. Michael obviously was in pain but they kept saying it would be better if he died.

When my lawyer came the police said I was too drunk to be released. (I had had nothing to drink). So he demanded to see me and they let him bail me out without any charges for drinking. They told Mrs. Alcantar that she could bond both of her sons out for $25 apiece, but when the lawyer went to get them Michael couldn't get up so he could not be released until he had been treated. So they took him to Ravenswood Hospital and were going to transfer him to Cook County Hospital. Mrs. Alcantar said she wanted him to go to her own hospital and so they told her to go back to Summerdale and pay the bond and she could take him. When she went back the charge had been changed to aggravated assault and he could not be released. So they took him back in the paddy wagon.

What makes this nightmarish story doubling damaging to the police is that there is considerable doubt that Michael Alcantar even threw the bottle that aroused the police ire. Other persons in the Alcantar apartment at the time swear he was sleeping in a bedroom. Another witness, Terry Webb, was among a group of boys in front of the apartment. "Somebody threw a bottle at the police car," he related. "The police officer drew his gun and threatened to blow our heads off. He beat one boy with the gun and chased the boys away." It was then, said Webb, that the police stormed into the Alcantar apartment.

Michael Alcantar was confined to county jail and Bridewell Hospital until August 10, 1966. A broken arm was not set properly and he now suffers from blackouts, nosebleeds and

severe arm and leg pains. The Alcantars did not file a complaint with IID, but a man who heard the story, Jack Korshak,
wrote O. W. Wilson on September 19, 1966, summarizing the
Alcantar version. "I am certain the complete details of this
event and what followed can be determined by you," Korshak
said. "As a former Army Inspector-General I have some experience with investigations and am aware of the ever-present possibility of error in testimony."

On September 26, G. Hobart Reinier, Wilson's executive
assistant, replied, professing deep concern about "any acts of
brutality or disrespect committed by a member of the department" and requesting additional details. Korshak sent the full
details, pointing out that there were "several badge numbers
and squad car numbers." By letter October 7, Reinier informed Korshak that the matter had been turned over to IID,
with the comment that "corrective and/or disciplinary action will be based on the results of this investigation."

In the hands of IID, however, the "investigation" seemed
aimed in the direction of a whitewash. On October 12, Korshak received a telephone call from an IID sergeant who advised that not one bottle, but a case of forty-eight cans had been
hurled at the police car, and that the police did observe from
where it was hurled. No mention was made of the savage conduct attributed to the police, but the sergeant indicated the
inquiry was continuing.

By December 6, Korshak had heard nothing further, so he
dunned Reinier by letter. On December 12 Lt. Charles Siedlecki, head of the complaint section of IID, responded by letter that the Alcantar family, on advice of counsel, had refused
to "properly" identify the accused officers, release medical records, or submit to polygraph examination, thereby thwarting
the investigation. "The department will not condone, nor tolerate the type of conduct ascribed to its personnel in this particular instance," Siedlecki piously declared. "Although this

investigation has been terminated, it will be re-opened, when the complaining witnesses [*sic*] come forth in support of their charges."

The manner in which IID dead-ended the inquiry was a carbon copy of the way the New York department terminated the case of the toppled fruit stand: the battered victims of police brutality did not come forth to seek redress from the police. Anyone familiar with the techniques of criminal investigation might well be uncomfortable with such an explanation. Jack Korshak was. By letter to Reinier December 28, he emphasized that the Alcantars' testimony would be "but one ingredient in any competent investigation." Other neutral witnesses, he said, had reduced their observations to writing as corroborative evidence. The incapacity or death of a victim, or his reluctance to testify, "is no cause for the termination of an investigation where there is a strong desire on the part of the investigative agency to discover the facts." There was no reply. And there, as this is written, the matter rests.

Whatever their desire to eliminate Gestapolike behavior on the part of officers, the police brass in Chicago as well as in other cities face certain inherent problems in dealing with the situation. For one thing, they prefer to try to handle incidents privately rather than publicly admit the existence of brutality, a method that is foredoomed to failure. For another, they must respond instinctively to the attitudes of the town's pols and brahmins—this is their power base—and it is not axiomatic that such civic leaders are dead set against unduly rough tactics. The experience of an attorney who appeared before the Uptown Chicago Commission, a group of the section's leading lights in banking, commerce, business and the professions, suggests those attitudes. The commission had sent a letter to the police department praising the work of the Technical Undercover Force, a roving squad of plainclothesmen that, among other things, prowls for pickpockets and con men at the conventions. The attorney had a story that was anything but complimentary. A TUF man posing as a wino had taunted two teenage boys until one struck him; then nine other members of the elite squad pounced on both boys and severely beat them. When a researcher from a project sponsored by Notre Dame University went to the hospital to take photographs of the boys' injuries, he was arrested for "interfering with an investigation" and "disorderly conduct." In telling the story, the attorney poked a stick into a hornet's nest. The prestigious members of the commission buzzed in outrage—not at the police brutality, but at the attorney for presuming to talk about the police that way.

Another straw in the wind can be found in the account of a City Council finance committee hearing in the *Sun-Times* of November 23, 1966. Alderman Jack Sperling, engaged in a colloquy with O. W. Wilson, "told the Superintendent that in the 1950's the New York City Police had brought youth gangs under control 'by breaking their heads both figuratively and literally.' Wilson asked the alderman, 'Are you suggesting that Chicago policemen go out and break the heads of people?' Sperling replied that he believed the people of Chicago would not be upset if policemen broke the head of an assailant." Later in the hearing the Democratic majority leader on the council shouted at the city's only independent alderman, who had expressed himself in favor of control of police conduct, that the "police brutality lobby" should keep still and let the police do their job.

Since politicians try to tune their antennas to the public mood, it is entirely possible that the majority of the city's voting blocs have no compunction against head-cracking so long as it gets the job done. Certainly proponents of a civilian review board have had as much of a hearing as a piccolo in one of the city's famous windstorms. Mayor Daley himself is firmly opposed to civilian review. When the issue was again raised after the 1966 riots he sidestepped it by appointing a prestigious, unwieldy "citizens committee" of twenty-three to recommend "ways and means of improving the relationship of the police department with the community."

So Wilson, inexorably bound up in the Chicago scheme of things, became a classic tragic figure: the reformer who shoulders an awesome burden and in the end is defeated by its sheer mass. A man of principle, he was forced to play a disingenuous hand. When civil rights leader Albert A. Raby told him, in a private conversation, that there were fifteen men on his force who ought to be fired, he corrected, "No, there are fifty," but publicly he insisted that "discipline is a function of command" and stiffened at the mention of civilian review. And he trod the treacherous patch of ground which holds that vigorous police work and diligent observance of individual rights are mutually exclusive propositions. Contending that Supreme Court decisions were "hampering the police," he rhetorically asked, "Does the law-abiding citizen have more to fear from attacks by robbers, burglars, or other malefactors than he does from encroachments on his civil liberties by the police . . . ?" The answer was yes, but he must have known no.

Paradoxically, when Wilson retired on July 1, 1967, he was a man of the hour in Chicago. While he could not wish away police brutality, tightly control his amorphous blue masses, or cope effectively with syndicated crime, he was widely acclaimed for Operation Crime-Stop, an Officer Friendly program of police visits to the schools, a roving Police Exhibit Cruiser, the installation of modern equipment, and top-level seminars on human relations conducted by the National Council of Christians and Jews. This was the stuff that press agentry was made of, and in 1965 the Publicity Club of Chicago gave the department an award for "distinguished publicity and public relations performance."

In July 1966, during the investigation of the murders of

eight nurses, Wilson stepped before the television cameras with a blown-up mug shot of suspect Richard Speck and flatly declared him "the killer." It was a gesture reminiscent of Dallas authorities after they had apprehended Lee Harvey Oswald, and it could be interpreted by an appeals court as "trial by publicity." Criticized by three Harvard law professors, Wilson tartly shot back, "Well, what are they going to do about it? I saw no reason for withholding this information. He is the killer."

The Professor was playing the publicity game to the hilt. It was a pity, for if anyone could have reformed the Chicago department, O. W. Wilson was the man.

As the long, hot summer of 1967 set in, outsider Wilson called it quits. He was succeeded by a career insider, Deputy Superintendent James B. Conlisk, Jr.

8

San Francisco: The Paradox of Prestige

The chief of the San Francisco Police Department, Thomas J. Cahill, is regarded as one of the brightest stars in the police firmament. He was the only police executive appointed to the President's National Crime Commission, and he has been frequently mentioned as a candidate to succeed J. Edgar Hoover as director of the FBI. Most of Cahill's national reputation rests on his department's model Community Relations Unit, a plainclothes group that has thrown away the book, rolled up its sleeves, and convincingly demonstrated that the police and minorities can work together smoothly in solving their problems.

Although Cahill takes the bows for the unit's success, he originally fought its creation and of late has throttled back its operations, perhaps with the idea of eventually abandoning it. Such a dénouement would be a giant step backward for a department which, with the exception of the unit, has never been at the vanguard of police progress.

Like The Finest in New York, San Francisco's department is rich in Irish tradition. To this day, South of the Slot Irishmen dominate the ranks despite a steady infusion of Italian-Americans from the North Beach section and others from the city's ethnic mix. A practically unbroken string of Gaelic names has adorned the chief's office since James F. Curtis, one-time leader of the unruly Committee of Vigilance, was appointed the first chief in 1856. The ruddy, tousle-haired incumbent still affects the wisp of an Irish brogue and has been known to get his dander up when he or his department is singled out for criticism.

Cahill was named chief in 1958 by Mayor George Christopher upon the death of Francis J. Ahern. When Christopher took office in 1956, he set out to refurbish San Francisco's image as a colorful port city where gambling and vice were viewed benignly as "good for business." He put his holdover chief, George Healy, on notice that the lid was to go on. Apparently Healy did not move fast enough, for when Treasury agents raided six bookmaking joints within a stone's throw of the old Hall of Justice, which housed police headquarters, the mayor decided upon a change. First he installed a new police commission. "It was the practice of some previous administrations," Christopher recalls, "to appoint, for window dressing, one citizen who was above suspicion—'The Airwick,' we used to call him—plus two political henchmen. Thus the mayor controlled the police; he could use them to his own ends." It is a stratagem that is still not extinct in the American police system.

Christopher named three impeccable citizens as commissioners, and they in turn tapped Frank Ahern, an inspector who headed both the homicide and rackets details, as the reform chief. Ahern had proved his incorruptibility and unwillingness to bow to expediency. As a start, he transferred every district captain and 106 of the 206 sergeants in a shakeup that was clearly read by every lax policeman and free-wheeling bookie in town.

But the zealous Ahern did not always know when to stop. His gambling crackdown eventually included such activities as bridge clubs where elderly folks played for insignificant stakes. The mayor had to suggest to him that prosecuting such petty matters might undermine the respect the department was gaining by its success in combatting more serious crime.

When Ahern suddenly died, Cahill, a deputy chief who had teamed with Ahern in the organized-crime investigations of the Kefauver Crime Committee of 1950, was the logical choice as successor. He was tough-minded, straitlaced and uncompromising in his views on strict enforcement. Pointing bleakly to statistics showing a national rise in crime, the new chief immediately launched Operation S (for Saturation), a technique that was the forerunner of O. W. Wilson's aggressive preventive patrol in Chicago. With no preannouncement, police patrols flooded high-incidence crime areas in the hopes of detecting persons committing a crime, about to commit a crime or fleeing a crime. "Attention was to be directed to those persons observed loitering, either on the street or in vehicles, who might be possible burglary or robbery suspects," a departmental publication explains. "Suspicious persons were to be subjected to intelligent interrogation, their identity, residence, destination, reasons for being in these critical areas, etc., ascertained and made a matter of record on the forms. . . ." The form, called the Field Investigation Check, was to be filed with the Bureau of Identification whether or not the person was taken into custody. In this way, certain patterns might develop and if "an individual had been interrogated on numerous occasions under circumstances that would indicate criminal activity, a warrant could be issued for his arrest."

During its first year of operation, the S Squad stopped more than 20,000 persons, filed more than 11,000 Field Investigation Checks, and arrested more than 1,000 persons, some on serious charges. The results, the department declared, "have gone far beyond our initial expectations." However, the operation inevitably began to focus on predominantly Negro neighborhoods, and the recurrent street stops became a source of considerable resentment. And Ernest Besig, executive director of the ACLU of northern California, criticized: "If suspicious circumstances are present, an officer certainly should investigate. But in the absence of probable cause, a policeman has no right to stop anyone. People are never satisfied with a little power—they always try to get more. . . . It's dangerous. If officers are given unlimited authority, we are sowing the seeds of a police state."

Although a slight crime dip coincided with the first months of Operation S, the crime rate subsequently showed a steady rise, hinting once again that massive police action is not a deterrent to a problem rooted deep in socioeconomic conditions. As is general throughout the country, the face of crime has changed appreciably in San Francisco in recent years. Not long ago the city could count on over 200 homicides a year; the 1964 total was 66. The bulk of crimes now fall into the economic category—burglary, petty theft, boosting (shoplifting) and other forms of larceny. Although there has been an increase in muggings and holdups, they constitute a minor part of the total crime picture and hardly justify shouting "crime wave" as the newspapers have a propensity for doing. Possibly the most salient observation about the San Francisco crime situation is that the department has not been particularly adept at crime solution despite the television series *San Francisco Beat*, in which a pair of detectives always track down their man in the picturesque byways of the city.

On Friday, May 13, 1960, the twentieth century caught up with the San Francisco Police Department. Preoccupied with its war against crime, the department was caught napping as the bumptious Congressmen of the House Un-American Activities Committee brought their road show to San Francisco's City Hall and attracted a swarm of angry protestors. As was its custom, the HUAC allotted available seats inside the hearing chamber to superpatriotic groups. The protesters, most of whom were students, were incensed by this favoritism and started boisterous demonstrations. Although fifty-five policemen were on hand, there was not a commissioned officer in sight.

Consequently it was a sergeant, Michael Maguire, who took charge. He ordered a fire hose unreeled and confronted the chanting, clapping, stomping demonstrators. "You want this?" he dared, pointing the nozzle at the crowd. "Go ahead," cried a voice. Maguire barked an order, and a sledge-hammer stream of water struck the crowd. The police charged.

The chaotic scene that ensued was described by reporter George Draper in the San Francisco *Chronicle*:

> I did not see any of the kids actually fighting with police. Their resistance was more passive. They would simply go limp and be manhandled out of the building. At this point it got very rough.
>
> One plump girl was shoved from the top of the stairs and tumbled and slipped down two flights to land like a bundle of clothing at the bottom. . . . The girl started to cry.
>
> I saw one slightly built lad being carried by two husky officers. One held the boy's shirt, the other had him by the feet. He was struggling but he was no match for the two bigger men.
>
> Then from nowhere appeared a third officer. He ran up to the slender boy firmly held by the other two officers and clubbed him three times on the head. You could hear the hollow smack of the club striking. The boy went limp and was carried out.
>
> The stairway above me was crawling with people, police and demonstrators in a milling, struggling, screaming, violent mass.
>
> "Don't push me, don't push me!" several girls shouted as they were roughly manhandled by the police.

Sixty-four persons were arrested and carted off to jail. Charges against all but one were subsequently dismissed by Municipal Judge Albert Axelrod with the comment: "The defendants for the most part are clean-cut American college students who will, within the next few years, enter into the business and professional worlds. . . ." Then the judge addressed a prophetic remark to the demonstrators: "You have achieved a directly opposite result from what you intended."

Indeed, the HUAC and its supporters, made propaganda capital out of the disturbances. When Mayor Christopher, a moderate conservative, regretted that the rioting had cost the city $250,000 and suggested that in the future the committee hold its extravaganza in the Federal Building, HUAC members accused him of being "soft on Communism" and so pusillanimous as to "surrender to Communist-directed violence." It was a harbinger of more to come. The HUAC subpoenaed television films of the rioting and commissioned a private firm to do a documentary movie, *Operation Abolition*. The title was based on the theme that anyone who advocated abolition of the HUAC was either a Communist or a Communist sympathizer. The film was badly slanted—police brutality had been edited out and Communist direction dubbed in. But hundreds of prints of the movie were sold at $100 apiece to American Legion posts, corporations, military groups, chambers of commerce and police departments. The John Birch Society has used it in conjunction with its "Support Your Local Police" program, and the Los Angeles police department, as previously mentioned, shows it to personnel attending the Police Academy.

It is in the last several years that Cahill's formidable personality has fully emerged. He is articulate and, some think, fairly sophisticated. He looks all cop, and he talks in the police cant. An essentially somber man, he is capable of flashes of humor and at times comes off as downright flamboyant. The jut-jawed chief has the avuncular air of a man who knows best, and best is the straight police line. On the 1966 CBS television documentary *Policeman's Lot*, Cahill roasted recent court decisions with the declamation: "In that split second when a police officer apprehends a law-breaker and makes an arrest they expect him to remember every rule and regulation plus recent legislation regarding the crime. To do that he'd have to be God almighty, himself!"

Cahill believes the police dogma with almost religious fervor. I recall a "Law Enforcement Night" at the San Francisco Press Club in April 1966 at which the chief sat on the podium. The featured speaker was James Vorenberg, executive secretary of the President's National Crime Commission; after his speech, as is customary, questions from the floor were entertained. The first question was about civilian review boards. Cahill, who had been listening amiably, leaped to his feet and charged over to the microphone. His face flushed, he delivered a tirade that clearly implied review boards were the work of the devil. "I will not have a civilian review board foisted upon my department," he raged. "When that day comes I will quit." He was perfectly able to handle discipline in his department, he said, and he would deal summarily with any officer found guilty of brutality. He capped this performance with a discursive sermon on patriotism and a declaration of fealty to the President. The audience buzzed in astonishment.

To be sure, Cahill's department bears the reputation as one of the most civilized on the West Coast (as a Catholic prison chaplain expressed it, "San Francisco isn't savage, like Los Angeles and some others in Southern California"). Or it did, until the bloody night of January 10, 1968. Attracted by a speech by Secretary of State Dean Rusk, some 600 war protesters gathered outside the posh Fairmont Hotel atop Nob Hill to chant peace slogans and demonstrate. A phalanx of some 300 policemen, decked out in riot gear, guarded the hotel portals. Inside, Rusk was telling his audience, "This country is committed to free speech and free assembly. We would lose a great deal if these were compromised." Outside, a police bullhorn ordered the assembly to disperse "in the name of the people of California."

When the protesters shouted down the bullhorn with the cry, "We are the people," the police moved foreward in a wall, spraying those who did not move fast enough with Mace, the chemical that "temporarily destroys the will to resist." The area in front of the hotel was quickly cleared, but the police pursued the scattering crowd. Down the hill and out of sight of the genteel hotel surroundings, the steady thud of riot sticks on bodies was punctuated by shrieks of "Gestapo" and "Fascists."

A youth was lying over a girl, trying to protect her from the flailing sticks. A brawny officer clamped his stick under her jaw, yanked her half to her feet, and dragged her down the street while a companion grabbed her hair and twisted every time she screamed. Another girl who had been squirted point-blank in the face with Mace (at close range Mace is in liquid form and causes painful blistering) was advised by police hustling her into a paddy wagon, "Don't worry, just rub your eyes" (which could cause blindess). A young Negro who sought sanctuary in the Wayside Chapel of St. Francis was dragged into the vestibule and clubbed. A well-dressed nondemonstrator who asked an officer for his badge number was summarily arrested and told he could get his answer at the booking desk. In an apparent move to preclude the filing of lawsuits against the police, some of the more battered victims were booked for such felonies as "assaulting a police officer."

The police rampage took place at a time when both the city's newspapers were on strike, so that it went virtually unnoticed. However, reports persisted that the maulings were not spontaneous but planned in accordance with a Department of Defense manual recommendation that violence be initiated in order to deter demonstrations. That this was the case was indicated by the presence of Berkeley police Red Squad members, who pointed out demonstration leaders from the University of California campus to their trans-Bay colleagues. These leaders bore the brunt of the police violence.

The relentless crusade of his department against "smut and obscenity" indicates that Cahill is one of those old-fashioned chiefs who yearn for the return of Victorian standards of morality—and tries to impose those standards on all of the community. In 1964, when Broadway nightclubs introduced topless performers, Cahill's prudish cops arrested the girls and the club owners for "outraging the public decency." As it developed, however, it was the courts who were outraged. At the conclusion of trials at which all defendants were found not guilty, the judges told the police in no uncertain terms that they were not to consider themselves arbiters of the public morals.

This hardly deterred the virtuous lawmen, who see their duty incandescently defined under California's obscenity penal code. The San Francisco Mime Troupe, which does not delete richly descriptive Anglo-Saxon words from its lines, has more than once felt the pinch of police handcuffs. On August 8, 1966, the audience attending a performance of Michael McClure's critically acclaimed *avant-garde* play *The Beard* became aware of a whirring sound. It was a police camera, recording the intimation of a sexual act in the final scene. As the curtain fell, the police arrested the male and female leads. In juxtaposition, the comments of the arrested actress, Billie Dixon, and the arresting officer, Inspector George Rosko, reveal the vast gulf between the police beholder and the performing artist. "All I did was perform the most beautiful play I've ever read in my fourteen years of acting," said Miss Dixon. "They have a certain talent, but certain of their talents shouldn't be shown in public," said the inspector.

Through loss after loss in court, however, the police censors have remained undaunted. In 1966, Cahill set up a two-man

Special Obscenity Squad which busied itself with full-time surveillance of public communications. Composed of Inspector Peter Maloney, formerly with the Juvenile Bureau, and Patrolman Sol Weiner, the squad made the rounds of bookstores and movie houses, casting a critical eye on their offerings. According to Maloney, some 5 percent of the material checked fitted the description of obscenity in the penal code.

When it came, however, the squad's big raid was not on the cheap downtown "girlie" emporiums selling material with obviously prurient appeal, but on two bookstores catering to the hippie trade. On November 15, 1966, Maloney and Weiner raided the Psychedelic Shop in the heart of the Haight-Ashbury hippie district and arrested the owner and a clerk for selling an allegedly obscene book of poetry. The same day they seized a clerk at the City Lights bookstore, in the bohemian area of North Beach, on the same charge. The raids were reminiscent of police actions in the 1950s against the Coexistence Bagel Shop, a North Beach beatnik bistro, which eventually forced it to close.

The poetry in question was the eighty-page *A Love Book* by Lenore Kandel. As far as the police were concerned, the book was "utterly without redeeming social importance." It was indeed replete with the uninhibited language of love-making, but its message that sexual intercourse devoid of the bond of love is meaningless and empty seems to have some importance, if only in the hippie subculture.

Reaction to the *Love Book* raids was mixed. Hippies demonstrated with signs reading "Ban the Bible," an allusion to the unchaste passages that abound in the largest-selling book in the world. Blue-noses were delighted. It was Herb Caen, the noted *Chronicle* columnist, who in his column of November 21, 1966, came up with the most barbed comment:

> To say that a book . . . is capable of "exciting lewd thoughts" is a perversion in itself. Exciting lewd thoughts in

whom—policemen? I'd never heard of "The Love Book," but the attendant publicity excited me into taking a look at it, and it's as I suspected: hard core bore. . . . As the cops walked off with all available copies at the Psychedelic and the City Lights (without paying for them, incidentally), a defender of Law 'n' Order apologized: "They didn't want that book to fall into the hands of children." Stan McNail, watching the police exeunt: "It just did."

The police raids came only a week after the voters of California had emphatically rejected Proposition 16, the so-called CLEAN amendment sponsored by a consortium of right-wing organizations that would have put enforcement of anti-obscenity laws on a virtual vigilante basis.

Although the three booksellers were convicted, ACLU defense lawyers charged that the judge "turned it into a heresy trial instead of an obscenity trial," and appeals are pending.

The department's attitude toward youth activities has been similarly restrictive. The only constructive police response to youthful energies and exuberance has been the Police Athletic League. But as one police officer put it, "Let's face it, not all kids want to play ball."

When entrepreneur Bill Graham endeavored to fill the void by leasing Fillmore Auditorium for various youth events ranging from poetry readings (one featured Russian poet Andrei Voznesensky) and art shows to rock-and-roll dance concerts and a Batman Festival, he ran into a wall of police hostility. Despite the fact that only soft drinks were served and that the events were run in a peaceful and orderly manner, the police took a dim view of Graham's promotions.

The police denied Graham a dance-hall permit. At a hearing before the Board of Permit Appeals, Graham testified that police captain John Cassidy had told him the ban was put into effect because "we don't want your element around here." Although no concrete evidence was produced as a basis for denying the permit, the board, which habitually takes its cue from the police, upheld the denial.

The San Francisco *Chronicle* editorialized on the matter on April 21, 1966: "The police department and the Board of Permit Appeals have displayed a misdirected and highly unfair malevolence toward the innocent and highly popular entertainment now being presented at Fillmore Auditorium. . . . This official hostility is not satisfactorily explained. . . . One suspects that bureaucratic fear, prejudice and instinct for censorship are operating here as they have in somewhat similar situations in the past. . . . Participants are peaceful and well-behaved though they have long hair, and some wear beards, and few adhere to fashions approved by *Esquire, Vogue* or the *Gentleman Tailor.* . . ."

The *Chronicle*'s admonishment fell on deaf ears. The next night, a Friday, police raided the auditorium and arrested thirteen juvenile dancers. Jurisdiction for the raid was an archaic Municipal Police Code which prohibits attendance without an adult chaperone, although many of the juveniles were driven to the dance by their parents and were to be picked up by them. The arrested youngsters were lined up at the side of the paddy wagon and searched like common criminals, then hauled to the Youth Guidance Center, where embarrassed officials subsequently dropped charges. "Do we look like criminals?" demanded one mother of a fourteen-year-old boy. "He likes girls and he likes to dance—so they go ahead and arrest him."

In the matter of narcotics, the police attitude also has been punative and suppressive. The department's most recent "achievement" in this field was its role in the dismissal of Dr. Joel Fort as director of the San Francisco Center for Special Problems. Dr. Fort, who is nationally known for his pace-setting medico-sociological work, had expanded the old alcoholic center to include treatment for homosexuals, drug addicts, prostitutes and others with special problems.

In a 1964 book, *Utopiates,* Dr. Fort distinguished between marijuana and the hallucinatory chemicals and the "hard" narcotics such as heroin and opium. The general ban on marijuana, Dr. Fort wrote, resulted from "hysterical propaganda campaigns led by law-enforcement officials and the sensational press." Publicity about the catastrophic effects of "soft" drugs was unfounded, he contended. In confirmation, he cited the findings of a New York mayor's committee in the early 1940s, identified as the only comprehensive scientific clinical and sociological study of the subject to date. The committee's report stated that marijuana was used extensively by Negroes and Puerto Ricans to create feelings of adequacy but did not lead to addiction, juvenile delinquency or crime. Much of the crime associated with the use of marijuana, said Dr. Fort, is crime by edict or definition rather than antisocial behavior, and reflects the will of the power structure of our society. (A fellow San Franciscan, philosopher Alan Watts, declares that sumptuary laws against drug-taking as well as gambling and wenching require the police to act as "armed preachers.") "Smoking one marijuana cigarette can lead to many years in prison," notes Dr. Fort in pleading for reason, "while the alcohol user drinks with impunity despite the many dangers to himself and society."

Such talk, of course, destroyed the old myths upon which the police and the power structure functioned, and they contrived to get rid of Dr. Fort. Agitation for his ouster came from Lt. Norbert Currie, chief of the police Narcotics Bureau, who represents the obsolete school which holds that addicts are police, not medical, problems. He has insisted, for example, that all members of Synanon, the rehabilitative organization for ex-addicts, register with the police, and that Synanon make its rolls available for police inspection upon demand.

Dr. Fort was finally fired on the flimsy charge of "operating too independently." In the words of one civil-service commissioner, San Francisco had lost "a creative, highly innovative individual," but the police had once again gotten their way. His dismissal was prompted, commented Dr. Fort, because "the San Francisco police and the federal narcotics bureau did not approve of the social approach to the narcotics problem I took."

As the civil rights movement gained momentum in the late 1950s and early 1960s, varying pressures were put on the nation's police departments to create special community relations units which would establish a meaningful dialogue with minorities. The story of the San Francisco Police Department Community Relations Unit dramatically demonstrates that problems between the police and racial and social minorities can be solved at the street level.

At first, Cahill was dead set against a Community Relations Unit and would not even discuss the matter with its proponents, led by Terry Francois of the NAACP (now a city supervisor) and Frank Quinn of the Council for Civic Unity. When the San Francisco *Examiner* came out editorially in favor of the unit, the chief remained adamant. "We are policemen, not sociologists," he maintained. But the newspapers pounded away, and discussions were started. Finally, on March 27, 1962, Cahill announced that the unit would be formed.

Named to head the unit was Lt. Dante Andreotti, a career police officer who once had played baseball in the Boston Red Sox chain. Andreotti traveled to St. Louis to study the prototype community relations bureau there which had been established under Chief Curtis Brostron, whose force is one of the most mechanized and computerized in the nation. "The more people associated with one another under conditions of equality," St. Louis' theory went, "the more they come to share values and norms and the more they come to like one another."

James J. Allman, the husky young blond who headed the St.

Louis Police-Community Relations Unit, stated the police position in these terms:

> The crux of the social dilemma is that there have been many social organizations working in the social arena for a long time which have never been a concern to the police. Only when these organizations are viewed as a potential threat to the peace and tranquility, life and property, or because of the possibility of physical group conflict do they become objects of police concern. I submit that at this stage of development it is too late for the police to be anything more than a temporary arbitrator. The exercising of community leadership by the Police Department is one way to help the community buy time to solve its . . . problems. The Department has the status, the authority and, in the final analysis, the major role if conflict should occur. Also, ironically, if conflict should occur they stand to bear the brunt of criticism from the parties involved. . . . Many organizations lack communication with the Police Department. We need their help and support and they need a contact point. . . . A Police-Community Relations unit can fill this need.

Allman's statement was widely hailed in the police establishment and published in *Police Chief* magazine, and became an exemplar for community relations programs. Close analysis, however, reveals that it advances the forlorn theory that a permanent and viable relationship is impossible and proposes that the police operate from a power position of status and authority with a view toward their own self-interests. In practice, the St. Louis program was in fact rather superficial. It concentrated on formal community councils and a much balley-hooed "Citizens Against Crime" drive, complete with membership cards. Whatever confidence the program managed to achieve in the minority community crumbled in 1966 when Allman resigned to accept a paid position with the John Birch Society. In September, 1966 Negroes demonstrated for six straight nights in protest over the slaying of a Negro robbery suspect by the police; there was sporadic violence, and the demonstrations culminated in a protest march on police headquarters.

In San Francisco, Andreotti wisely dispensed with the trappings of police power. His men, in plainclothes, went out into the hard-core poverty areas where they mingled not only with the indigenous leaders but with just plain people, young militants, and ex-convicts. They talked—and they listened. The accent was not on stiffly formal conferences and meaningless dialogue, but on constructive action. A case history illustrates the unit's *modus operandi*.

A hungry Negro youth ordered a full meal in a restaurant knowing he could not pay. "You'll have to arrest me," he told the owner after finishing. The owner called the police, and a sergeant from the Community Relations Unit responded. The sergeant tried to persuade the owner to let the youth wash dishes to pay for the meal, but the owner pointed out that it was against union rules. "It doesn't matter," the youth interjected. "I have no place to sleep so I'll have to go to jail anyhow."

The next morning the youth appeared before a judge with a unit man at his side. In a move unheard of in pre-unit days, the judge released him on his own recognizance. The unit man took the youth to a local clothier, bought him a suit from the unit's contingency fund, and found him a job through an Oakland plumber's union which is cooperating with the unit. The youth is still working—and staying out of trouble.

The thirteen-man unit reflects the melting-pot composition of the city's population. Eugene Brown and Leroy Jones, who work Negro sections, were University of San Francisco basketball stars during the championship Bill Russell era. Innocente Cisneros and Julio Fernandez are posted to the Mission District, with its large concentration of Spanish-speaking people. No district that has been a source of friction has been overlooked, and the unit members report in the morning not to headquarters but to the district anti-poverty offices. Nor have the social minorities, traditional targets of police harassment, been ignored. In the tough Tenderloin District, the habitat of prostitutes, alcoholics, narcotics addicts and sexual deviates, Officer Elliott Blackstone, a twenty-year veteran of the force, has taken a special course in transexualism and set up open-collar grievance sessions between police patrol officers and homosexuals, "hookers," hermaphrodites and other denizens of the district.

One of the most significant steps undertaken by the unit is its involvement with the Seven Steps Foundation, which helps prison releasees in the difficult transition back into society. The unit has quietly enlisted the help of some San Francisco employers in providing job opportunities for ex-convicts and others whose past difficulties have made finding work difficult. Employer response has been encouraging, although far from unaminous. "I wouldn't hire one of your niggers under any conditions," an industrialist curtly told a unit man. The unit has also tried to dissuade policemen from making cheap and unnecessary arrests, since a record, even without a single conviction, can hound a job-seeker wherever he goes. In a singular departure from the usual adversary stance of the police toward persons under arrest, the unit's monthly newsletter, distributed in the districts, advertised the free legal services for indigents available through the Neighborhood Legal Assistance Foundation.

The no-strings-attached approach of Dan Andreotti's unit has earned it the respect, trust and confidence of even the most militant and police-suspicious elements in the city. For example, the doors of the black nationalist Muslim Temple are always open to the unit's men, a concession probably unique in the country, and the welcome mat is out at the hippie pads despite continuing friction with the uniformed patrol.

Not surprisingly, the unit often finds itself working at cross purposes with the rest of the force. The hippie community, for one, has complained bitterly of police harassment. On January 31, 1967, the ACLU sued Cahill and the department in federal court in order to stop police arrests of residents of the Haight-Ashbury district under the vague "public nuisance" law. The suit was filed on behalf of four hippies, three of whom had been doing nothing more sinister than staging an impromptu sidewalk puppet show, and one of whom claimed he was nabbed by an officer because "your feet are touching the sidewalk." The suit charges the police with "making arrests of persons of whom [they] do not approve, even though these persons are violating no laws." It is still pending as this is written.

Antagonisms were hardly ameliorated by an Easter Week press statement by Chief Cahill that "hippies are no asset to the community." The chief and his officers apparently do not recognize the fact that the hippies *are* a community, albeit an unpopular one with the rooted middle and upper classes. The harassment continues, and one police insider claims knowledge of instances in which some police have planted marijuana on hippies to make narcotics arrests. Haight-Ashbury has become the scene of repeated skirmishes; on February 28, 1967, angry hippies picketed the Park Station, which polices the district, with signs reading "End Police Harassment." Meanwhile the Community Relations Unit was unobtrusively helping some of the hippie community's hard-pressed citizens with food and clothing.*

---

* On the early morning of July 11, 1967, the hippie-psyched police bagged more than their usual quarry in a raid on a Haight-Ashbury pad. Tiring of the high-society parties at which they had been feted during a San Francisco engagement of the Royal Ballet, famed dancers Dame Margot Fonteyn and Rudolf Nureyev accepted a hippie invitation to a party following a performance. According to police, a neighbor complained that the party was too loud. Officer Arthur Fobbs, who responded, later said he only intended to ask the participants to quiet down, but they all scattered when someone cried "It's the fuzz! It's the

It is natural that Cahill, essentially an old-line chief who disclaims the policeman's role as sociologist, should react ambivalently to the unit, publicly backing it and privately regretting it. By proving that police can and should be practicing sociologists, the unit has received nationwide recognition and praise. As chief, Cahill has been the *ex officio* recipient of credit for its success, and he has not been reticent about accepting it. "The only reason there is a Community Relations Unit is because I backed it," he recently boasted. "I run the department and that includes the Community Relations Unit. I've backed it all the way and met every hot spot head-on."

The overweening pronouncement was too much for minority leaders with long memories, among them Dr. Carlton B. Goodlett, Negro physician, publisher and civic leader. "Cahill fought the idea of a Community Relations Unit for three years," Goodlett recalled. "Since its inception, he has become a national police figure—the only chief of police to be selected for the President's Crime Commission. We pushed him into greatness."

Whatever lip service he has paid to the unit, Cahill's cop heart has not been in it. A critical test came on September 27, 1966, when Alvah Johnson, a twenty-four-year veteran of the force, shot and killed one of two Negro boys running from a car "I assumed to be stolen." Johnson said he shouted "Halt!" and fired several "warning shots" before getting off the shot that struck Matthew Johnson, Jr., in the back as he was clambering up a hill in the Negro Hunter's Point housing project. Alvah Johnson, a gun buff who spent many off-duty hours on the police range, was heartsick. But in Hunter's Point there

cops!" With somewhat obscure logic, Fobbs explained, "We had no choice but to call for reinforcements and round them up." Found hiding on the roof was the ballet pair, Dame Margot still in a mink stole. Although the police raiders solemnly reported they had found seven marijuana cigarettes in a search of the pad and booked the pair into city prison for "disorderly conduct" and "being in a place where marijuana was kept," police brass and the district attorney were obviously more embarrassed than impressed. They promptly dropped all charges.

was no mitigating the fact that a boy had been slain for the sake of an already recovered automobile.

An outraged crowd collected at the death scene, then moved menacingly toward the Third Street business section dominated by white merchants. Cahill held back the Community Relations Unit, and three days of rioting followed. "We received more than a dozen reports of responsible Negro leaders who were arrested, beaten or otherwise abused by police out of sheer ignorance," remonstrated Rev. A. Cecil Williams of Citizens Alert, a group formed to contend with police brutality. "Had Lieutenant Andreotti and the Community Relations Unit been brought in immediately, then informed action would have been possible—because they have bothered to learn who these citizens are."

Instead of expanding the unit, Cahill has refused to allot it more men or increase its budget. He has never authorized money for the unit's contingency fund, so that the unit has had to find ways of fund raising. Benefit performances have been one way. The unit can count on actress Diahann Carroll and other show people to donate their services; such sports luminaries as professional basketball players Rick Barry and Nate Thurmond and Roland Lakes, John Thomas and Gary Lewis of the football '49ers are always ready to perform.

In January 1967, in answer to complaints of civil rights leaders that he was diluting the role of the unit, Cahill issued a general order making it mandatory for the entire department to participate in a community relations conference sponsored by the department and the National Conference of Christians and Jews. Since 1964, the conferences have been held annually, although 1967 was the first year attendance was compulsory for all the force. The first conference was marred by ugly incidents. When a white NAACP representative started to speak, a cop voice from the rear heckled, "Nigger lover!" When a Jewish spokesman from the NCCJ began to talk, another voice

yelled, "Christ killer!" A captain of the California Highway
Patrol who had sat in on a classroom session was shocked at the
cops' crude behavior. "You have a bunch of hoodlums in uniform," he told Deputy Chief Al Nelder. The conferences seemingly have had little practical effect. "We just argued 'round
and 'round," one policeman commented to *Chronicle* reporter
Ivan Sharpe after the 1967 sessions. "Each side has its attitude
and they just want to change mine. They can't do it."

Besides a chief who is lukewarm to its existence, the Community Relations Unit has had to contend with sharp opposition from within the ranks. A strong current of racial prejudice
and right-wing extremism runs through the department. Officers sarcastically refer to the unit as the "Commie Relations
Unit" and heap ridicule on its members. Once a picture of
Robert Shelton, Imperial Wizard of the Ku Klux Klan, was
posted on the bulletin board with the notation "Our Hero."
At the height of the Hunter's Point rioting a motorcycle cop
chalked "Take a nigger to lunch today!" on the side of a police
bus bound for the strife-torn area. During the 1966 election
campaign, Cahill had to call a halt to the display of Ronald
Reagan signs on police vehicles.

Immediately after the fatal shooting at Hunter's Point
which precipitated the rioting, Cahill suspended Officer Alvah
Johnson from duty pending a coroner's inquest. The rank and
file took bitter exception, and in a show of solidarity 1,000 off-
duty policemen gathered on the steps of City Hall in what re-
sembled a racist rally. When Johnson was subsequently cleared
of intentional homicide by the coroner's jury, a police captain
exulted, "Well, I guess the coroner got the message."

So evidently did Cahill. After the coroner's verdict, he reinstated Johnson to full duty without holding a departmental
hearing to decide the officer's judgment in shooting under the
circumstances. Like most states, California statute permits an
officer to use deadly force in apprehending a fleeing felon, and

joyriding in a stolen car is technically a felony (although in the Johnson case the car's status as a stolen vehicle is still a matter of doubt). But there are profound moral implications in the taking of a life in such inconsequential matters, and it is at this level that the department deferred examining its conscience.

Not long after the shooting, civil rights leaders met with Cahill and the police commission to discuss the question of deadly force. Although it seems plain that the only morally justifiable grounds for its use is in the defense of the officer's person or the person of another, Cahill and the commissioners would only state that the matter was "under study." It was another rubber-stamp performance by the three commissioners, one of whom is a lawyer handling a number of police divorce cases.*

In 1966, pressures to dissolve the Community Relations Unit have increased. The nine district captains, some of them dyed-in-the-wool reactionaries, petitioned Cahill to put the unit's men in uniform and make community relations the responsibility of each district. The captains nominated district citizens' committees, and at least one nominee is a member of the John Birch Society. Almost simultaneously, the 1966 grand jury police committee issued a report which virtually echoed the captains' petition. The report highly praised the officers and men of the department, and urged that community relations be "placed in the hands of the district commanders. We recommend that the men assigned to Community Relations be put in uniform and assigned to the district where they can be available to perform when needed."

The curious timing of the double-barreled blast at the Community Relations Unit was possibly explained when it was noted that the chairman of the grand jury police committee,

* Most major cities have at least five members, including one or two minority representatives, on their police commissions. In San Francisco, minority groups for years have urged that the police commission be expanded.

Teamsters Union official James Rourke, had joined the police protest rally on the steps of City Hall and was in fact closely aligned with Elijio Morelli, head of the Police Officers Association. The POA had been one of the unit's most persistent critics.

Cahill bent to the pressures and gave the district captains their hegemony over the unit, although the members remained in plainclothes. Andreotti was sorely disappointed, for it was a step backward. Not only were the unit's efforts subject to the dictates of precinct politics, but its fate was in the hands of men who on balance resented its existence. As Andreotti put it, "The philosophy I was trying to engender demanded a central unit. I didn't want the unit to degenerate into a public relations effort."

Reluctantly, the pioneer whose concept was too advanced for the anchor-dragging San Francisco force resigned and moved on to a top consultant's post with the U.S. Department of Justice's Community Relations Service in Washington. In his place, Cahill appointed Lt. Augustus "Gus" Bruneman, a rotund, personable man whose forte, perhaps portentously, is the Police Athletic League. On August 4, 1967, 500 well-wishers—blacks and whites, hippies and homosexuals—crammed into the Third Baptist Church to give Andreotti a rousing send-off. Mayor Thomas Shelley was there, as were minority group leaders; but Cahill and Bruneman were conspicuous by their absence. Andreotti delivered an impassioned attack on racial prejudice in and out of the police department, scoring those who are "anti-Negro, anti-fair housing, anti-everything." A police community relations unit, he declared, "cannot be a rubber stamp. It cannot maintain the status quo—and the status quo stinks!" It was a blunt farewell, and the deafening ovation lasted for a full six minutes.

Whether the unit survives in any semblance of its form under Andreotti remains to be seen, but a bizarre case involving one of its members, Officer Lindsay Crenshaw, suggests that any embarrassment to the unit is a sword in the hands of the brass. On the night of October 8, 1966, Crenshaw, off duty at the time, reported to the Oakland police that his car had been riddled by a shotgun blast fired from a car he had seen earlier at a drive-in restaurant. Crenshaw, a Negro, was reluctant to tell what had precipitated the shooting, and the stories of witnesses were conflicting, but it appears that he had protected a streetwalker he knew who was being threatened by two white men.

When he filed the complaint, an Oakland inspector advised Crenshaw of his constitutional rights. "Am I a complainant or a suspect?" asked Crenshaw, and indeed, the investigation seemed to concentrate not on the shooting but on Crenshaw. Although the Oakland police traced a license number given them by the San Francisco officer and arrested two suspects who admitted they had fired into Crenshaw's car, a felony offense, there was no prosecution. "The allegation of the shooting was discussed with representatives of the office of the district attorney," the Oakland police report asserted, "and there was insufficient evidence to prosecute."

Crenshaw, however, was hauled onto the departmental carpet by Cahill, charged with "conduct unbecoming an officer." The department wanted to fire him. During his hearing before the police commission, an incredible colloquy took place between Crenshaw's attorney and one of the shooting suspects:

ATTORNEY: Where is your .22 caliber?
SUSPECT: It's at home.
ATTORNEY: The police didn't take it from you?
SUSPECT: No.
ATTORNEY: Did they take John's [the other suspect] shotgun?
SUSPECT: No.

[At this point the commission chairman was forced to admonish: "There will be quiet in the room, or we'll have to vacate the room."]

> ATTORNEY: You mean to tell me, you still have—and John still has—the weapon that was used to fire at this man and his automobile on that night?
>
> SUSPECT: Yes.

In the eyes of most of the minority community, an indiscretion on Crenshaw's part, ordinarily punishable by a reprimand and transfer, had been magnified to a cardinal sin in order to put the Community Relations Unit on trial. Editor Robert Simms of the Hunter's Point *Spokesman* said the proceedings "sounded in defamation of one of the most valued community programs and one of the most respected individuals in the police department." Community leader Philip E. Kay wrote Chief Cahill: "For some time many of us have seen and heard of the extremely negative sentiment and resentment held by many persons in the Department against this very unique unit. This is in itself very tragic in light of the great and lasting accomplishment in the field of human relations that has been done by the Community Relations Unit." John Dukes, area director of the Economic Opportunity Council, was even more direct in his statement: "The San Francisco Police Community Relations Unit is the *only* thing that stands between us and a direct confrontation."

As the hearing was in progress Crenshaw suddenly resigned from the department, but shortly thereafter sought to withdraw his resignation. Cahill would have none of it. The police department is "strongly opposed to the withdrawal of Lindsay Crenshaw's resignation," he wrote the police commission chairman, "and requests your commission take the necessary steps to make his resignation . . . final." The commission obliged.

Cahill is a sincere man, and a righteous one, but very likely he would prefer to have been chief in the days when the white-gloved ranks of lads in blue swung smartly up Market Street to martial airs as the proudest of the proud in the St. Patrick's Day parade. There were no hippies then, nor was there a Hunter's Point, and the Supreme Court was a mystical body a continent away. As it is, the nostalgic chief represents the paradox of prestige. His national prestige is based upon the glowing success of the Community Relations Unit, yet he has been gradually sabotaging it. He has a reputation as a progressive, yet as a member of the President's National Crime Commission he opposed practically every progressive measure considered. He teamed with J. Edgar Hoover (who was not a member of the Crime Commission but wields influence wherever law-enforcement topics are discussed) to beat down the ombudsman proposal, which was to be recommended as a means of fairly processing citizen grievances against the police. He sided with the harsh traditionalists against the abolition of capital punishment, the legalization of marijuana, and liberalization of court procedures, and for legalized wiretapping and bugging.

9

Oakland and Berkeley: Two Sides of the "Berlin Wall"

On the eastern littoral of San Francisco Bay, a seven-mile drive across the Bay Bridge, are Oakland, a sprawling, nondescript industrial city, and Berkeley, a grown-up university town that has reached full city status. On October 15, 1965, at the border between the two cities, the Oakland police stood massed in full battle regalia to form the famous "Berlin Wall" blocking peace marchers from the territory of Oakland. It was one of the most frightening uses of police power ever in a free nation, and it marked the Oakland force as one of the most reactionary in the country. On the same day that Oakland threw up its barricade, the same kind of peaceful, well-organized protest march moved unmolested down Fifth Avenue in New York under the protective eyes of The Finest, and down the streets of 100 other American cities.

In one way, the emergence of the Oakland Police Department from its neolithic age into a functionally modern force is the story of Chicago, of Los Angeles, or any number of other departments which are public-relations success stories. Once riddled with corruption, the department was cleaned up,

THE POLICE ESTABLISHMENT : 170

computerized, and held up as a model of efficiency. But Oakland, beneath the image, retains the truncheon mentality.

In the 1940s, the Oakland department was one of the most corrupt and brutal in the nation. Policemen rolled drunks openly in the streets and beat Negro prisoners as a matter of routine. The excesses became so notorious that the California state legislature launched a probe of the department, with the result that the chief resigned under fire and one officer was sent to San Quentin Prison.

A reform chief, Wyman W. Vernon, cut the roots from under the department. He was incorruptible and laid down the law to his men. He professionalized the force, showing a genuine concern for civil liberties and civil rights in the process. It was during his administration that the nation's first planning and research unit was established. O. W. Wilson, then dean of the Department of Criminology at the next-door University of California, originated the idea of a special unit that would research the genesis of police problems, apply modern technology to their solution, and plan for the future. A program was worked out whereby Wilson's criminology students would be employed by Vernon's department in the Planning and Research Unit, an arrangement that continues between the two institutions to this day. Many of Oakland's bright young criminologists are now with the International Association of Chiefs of Police in Washington, acting as consultants to problem-ridden departments throughout the country.

In 1959 Vernon retired and was succeeded by Edward M. Toothman, who had started as a patrolman in 1941 and bore credentials as a traffic specialist from the famed Northwestern University Traffic Institute. By this time the Oakland force was being singled out by the press as a paragon of police prowess. For example, an article entitled "Wanted: Good Cops" in *Look* (July 3, 1962) focused on Oakland. The article noted that the pay, starting at substantially over $7,000, was superior, that high I.Q.s and college degrees were highly prized by the department, and that officers were encouraged to further their education at the University of California by tuition grants from the City of Oakland. "We select our men for twenty-five years of service," Toothman was quoted, "so we pick them with great care. Out of 1,049 who applied in 1960, we took only 8." An Oakland recruiting team scoured the campuses of universities which had criminology schools, such as Michigan State, Washington State and Florida State, seeking the cream of the crop. By 1965, the department was able to boast that over 40 percent of its sworn personnel had one or more years of college, and 9 percent had four or more years, inordinately high ratios for police organizations.

This rosy personnel picture coupled with a reputation for technological progress gave Oakland its glossy image, which was neatly packaged in a gleaming new ten-story headquarters in downtown Oakland. In 1965, the department became the first user of the Police Information Network, an electronic data retrieval system that within a minute or two can advise an officer in a radio car whether a license number is listed to a stolen car from anywhere in California, and whether the registered owner is a fugitive or has a criminal record. The network, now expanded to the entire Bay Area, has reduced the backlog of unserved warrants, helped in stolen-car recovery, and added an ingredient of safety to warn officers when a driver may be dangerous.

But under the patina of progress lies an essentially antiquated force. In January 1966 I talked with Chief Toothman in his modernistic office affording a sweeping view of his domain. Toothman is a stern-looking man, with a creased face offset by basset-hound bags under his eyes. He is so scrupulously honest his men refer to him as "The Fang." He takes a dim view of modern permissiveness, so much so that he once banned an issue of *Playboy* magazine from the newsstands. He spoke slowly, diffidently, with the air of a man who had seen his duty and done it, yet somehow had fallen short.

The department was having manpower trouble, for one thing. Despite the optimistic picture in *Look*, the 650-man force had sagged well below its authorized strength, and the prospect was for things to get worse. (According to a survey conducted by the San Francisco *Examiner* about this time, the force was 40 men under its quota, and Lieutenant Earl Rueter, personnel officer, predicted the shortage would triple over the next two years because of retirements and service-connected injuries; the *Examiner*'s independent inquiries "revealed that a high percentage [of the men recruited from Eastern universities] soon leave the force for other employment.") Toothman blamed the crisis on the berating and abuse that nowadays goes with the police job.

The chief looked with a jaundiced eye on the activities of the student democratic left on the Berkeley campus. Months before the "Berlin Wall" confrontation, he had instructed his intelligence unit to infiltrate the Vietnam Day Committee, which staged the march. He had been plainly disgruntled when a federal judge ordered the city of Oakland to permit a previous antiwar march to traverse Oakland streets, despite traffic expert Toothman's plea that it would seriously disrupt traffic. The judge's decision, he had complained, was "undemocratic" because the marchers were prohibited from entering the federal Oakland Army Terminal yet allowed to use the city's streets.

Toothman's eyes narrowed as he talked of the session he had had with the student leaders of the Vietnam Day Committee. "Those students sat right there," he said, pointing to a row of chairs on one side of his expansive desk. "They were antagonistic, unyielding and had no leadership. What they proposed was not practical—not even if it had been the Veterans of Foreign Wars." As an alternative to a march through Oakland, which he claimed would be an "arbitrary imposition upon the community" and would be a nuisance to motorists and shoppers, the chief had proposed to contain the protesters in Bushrod or DeFremery parks, small city parks close to the Berkeley border.

Since the objective of the march was to hold a rally in front of the Oakland Army Terminal, at the other end of town, the student leaders were not to be dissuaded. Exasperated, Toothman had accused them of wanting to instigate a riot that would be "more bloody than Watts." When the committee applied to the city manager for a parade permit, he denied it on the advice of Toothman and downtown commercial interests. Meanwhile, the Berkeley Police Department, which is empowered unilaterally to issue permits, readily gave the committee a permit to assemble and march through its bailiwick. The Berkeley force is a cut above Oakland in its appreciation of society's pluralism, and in granting the permit it commented that it had found the committee responsible, their plans well organized, and their right to march well founded.

Any treatment of law enforcement in the Oakland area is incomplete without bringing into perspective the Alameda County district attorney's office and its perennially incumbent D.A., J. Frank Coakley, who prosecutes Oakland's cases. In an article on the Oakland municipal monolith in its February 1966 issue, *Ramparts* magazine described the diminutive, feisty D.A. this way:

> Gangbusters. That is Alameda County District Attorney J. Frank Coakley. He is gangbusters against the Red Menace; gangbusters against murderers, armed robbers and dope addicts. But he is not so gangbusters against civil rights violations. Or the crimes of corporations. Or police brutality. A hanging D.A. whenever he can be, Coakley believes in stiff punishment for ordinary criminals; he knows nothing of the sociology of crime. A prototype of the tough D.A. so favored in American

cities, he is an honest, tough man who is hipped, lately, on two things: anti-communism and the young radicals at the University of California.

In 1944 Coakley was a legal officer in the Navy when a munitions ship blew up in an East Bay shipyard, killing 300 people, most of them Negroes. Fifty Negro survivors refused to go on loading ammunition, and Coakley prosecuted them for mutiny. There was an organized conspiracy, he charged, and he subjected the terrified seamen to a merciless cross-examination. "Don't you know you're guilty of insubordination for not having called me sir?" he browbeat one defendant. In summation he pronounced: "Any man so depraved as to be afraid to load ammunition deserves no leniency." The defendants got none, receiving sentences ranging up to fifteen years' imprisonment.

To Coakley, means do not seem important. When antiwar leaflets recently were dropped from a small plane over East Bay military installations, he pored through the statute books and finally prosecuted the offenders as litterbugs. When his office struggled through three trials in an unsuccessful effort to get a conviction that would stick against an eighteen-year-old Negro shoeshine boy accused of slaying a white pharmacist and his Negro assistant, it was revealed that the D.A. had planted a hidden microphone in the jail visiting room to overhear the defendant's conversations. "That mike was put there for the entirely legal purpose of helping to solve one of the worst crimes in the history of the state," Coakley proclaimed.

When the Free Speech Movement developed on the Berkeley campus in 1964, Coakley saw Red. He launched a vendetta against the FSM, determined to prove it had a Communist base, but came away empty-handed. Then when the big Sproul Hall sit-ins occurred, civil liberties attorney Robert Truehaft was on hand at the behest of the FSM. "Somebody is here who is not a member of the press," boomed a deputy sheriff. "Well, that makes two of us," fired back Truehaft, who was placed under arrest. Coakley had the pleasure of prosecuting an old antagonist who has pressed numerous brutality cases against the Oakland police, and in the doing he may have scored half a political point.

When the stage was set for the massive Vietnam Day march —the march committee decided to proceed through Oakland without a parade permit—Coakley proceeded to escalate matters. He attacked what he termed the "seditious and treasonous" interests of the marchers, and tried in vain to obtain a federal court order denying the marchers their right of assembly. He made allusions to Berkeley officials "conspiring" with the march committee, referred ominously to the U.S. Code on sedition, and in general helped create a climate of crisis that intimidated Governor Edmund Brown into putting the National Guard on alert and assemble an army of 3,200 lawmen in Berkeley.

When the 8,000 Vietnam Day marchers reached the Oakland border they were blocked by a wall of blue-uniformed Oakland police, tear-gas guns and nightsticks at the ready. The marchers halted, and suddenly there was trouble. The Oakland police had somehow let a band of Hell's Angels motorcyclists slip around their flank, and the rowdy Angels baited and shoved the marchers. The police still made no move. "Those guys got their constitutional rights, too," answered a police official when marchers complained. The Angels challenged the marchers to fight, then ripped a loudspeaker from a rented truck leading the march. "There were fistfights and an incipient riot," Toothman told me, "so finally we had to move thirty-five feet into Berkeley and smother the riots." An Oakland officer privately told me that the general reaction of the police was, "Yea for the Hell's Angels."

Although the Oakland force has yet to be accused of using cattle prods, it is one of the most racist outside the South. It is 97 percent Caucasian in a city with a 25 percent Negro population. Ordinarily, such a large Negro manpower reservoir should provide relief for a personnel drought, but the reputation of the department is so Jim Crow that self-respecting Negroes fear to join it.

The department's version is that it has attempted to recruit Negroes but has not found men with the "right qualifications." The qualifications apparently include indifference to the civil rights movement. One Negro rookie who did join the force was discovered to be a member of CORE, and was terminated for a minor mistake before his probationary period was up. For the complaisant Negro who does make it on the force, the odds are stacked against promotion. There is one Negro captain, and the chief was in the habit of taking him along whenever he had to meet with Negro groups. There is one Negro sergeant, and that is it. Moreover, Negroes are systematically excluded from the choice assignments. None have made it to Personnel and Training or the Internal Affairs Section. At one time the Homicide Squad showcased a Negro officer, but he remained a patrolman in rank. The Vice Squad used Negro officers as undercover "stoolies," but none have made the grade as full-fledged members of the squad.

One of the most sought-after assignments is the Motorcycle Squad, and it also has remained inviolate. At one time the squad had a crack motorcycle drill team which traveled around the country giving performances; Negroes were then excluded because Florida and other segregationist states were on the itinerary. When the drill team was disbanded about six years ago, several Negroes put in for the squad but did not make it, although vacancies were being filled by whites. When some questions were asked, the captain in charge polled the squad and they voted not to let Negroes join. The Negro applicants were gently told that they could not be considered because on the Motorcycle Squad they would be more likely to come in contact with white people and cause friction. The explanation was consistent with the department's long-standing policy of confining Negroes to Negro areas.

Like many departments, Oakland has its own social and fraternal club, called La Société de la Camaraderie. Meeting notices are approved for posting on departmental bulletin boards, and the department's property clerk collects members' dues. A representative of La Société personally contacts every member of rookie classes at the police academy urging them to join. Every member, that is, except Negroes—La Société is an all-white club. On several occasions Negro police officers have tried to make application but gotten no further than polite excuses.

The bulletin boards in the department frequently become sounding boards for police prejudices. Racially scurrilous material pops up often. One hate sheet posted after a Negro tried to apply for La Société was a mock "Application for Membership in the NAACP." Its items included: "Use All Names You Has Went By," "Name of Mutha," "Number of Children Claimed on Relief," "Number of Children Legitimate (if any)," "Marital Status: Check—Common Law, Shacked Up, [or] Deserted," "List Your Greatest Desire in Life (Other than a white girl)." There followed a pledge: "I believe in equality, that Niggers is better than white folks is, and that white folks should pay more taxes than us Niggers should, and us Niggers should have more and more welfare, and now that we have the Supreme Court and the U.S. Army on our side, the laws should not be changed no more, no how! . . ."

The department has its share of Bircher cops. One was trying to proselytize members by distributing a tract "proving" that Governor Brown was part Communist because one of his wife's relatives was Jewish. Despite a rule that material with religious or political content cannot be posted, watch commanders have approved for posting on the bulletin boards such notices as a Birch Society event featuring Robert Welch and an anti-Communism speech "From Cuba to Watts" by a former Batista air force officer.

The force's political and racial bias shows in its eagerness to take sides. "When we were being briefed on what to do at the university sit-ins," reports one Oakland officer, "the captain kept referring to the students as 'those sons-of-bitches.' And the brass were so proud to rush the motorcycle troopers onto the campus." In May 1967, when racial disturbances erupted at a San Francisco amusement park—police answering a petty-theft call had stuck guns to the heads of the young Negro suspects, arousing the ire of Negro onlookers—the Oakland department canceled all leave, mobilized its men, and volunteered to come to San Francisco to help quell the trouble. On April 12, 1967, when the police radio announced that Negro cop-killer Aaron Mitchell had been executed at San Quentin—the first execution in California in four years—the men in the squad cars burst forth with such appreciative remarks as: "Hear, hear!" and "It's about time."

A swagger outfit, the Oakland police have been under steady fire on the brutality issue. Symbolic was the bent old Negro who picketed Municipal Court in 1966 with a sign declaring: "On April 8 my family and I were victims of police brutality. Oakland must have a police review board now." In Oakland the thus far fruitless struggle for a review board has been led by anti-poverty groups, who contend that police harassment, not outright brutality, is the principal complaint. A white Oakland officer told me one way it is quite legally done. An officer spots a car he wants to shake down. He pulls a wire on its electrical system, then stops it for defective tail lights. He taunts the driver into reacting, then arrests him for battery and searches the car incidental to arrest.

In the fall of 1965 pro-review-board pickets showed up at Chief Toothman's home in the solidly white Oakland hills. Toothman conferred briefly with them, his faithful Negro captain at his side, but grew indignant and stormed into the house with the words, "I won't be intimidated by you people." He called headquarters and summoned forty-five cops with gas masks. Three months later the chief retired prematurely, fed up, he told friends, with the civil rights and peace movement activities. He put his house up for sale with a "Caucasians only" tag attached.

Named as new chief was Robert J. Preston, dour career officer with a hard-nose reputation. Preston immediately vetoed the idea of a review board, declaring that his two-man Internal Affairs Section was entirely capable of dealing impartially with complaints. In a speech before the Lions Club, Capt. Palmer Stinson asserted that "nearly all critics of police are from the radical left." Sgt. Sam Mullins, president of the Police Welfare Association, belligerently vowed that police would not cooperate with any review board and "will go to the courts if necessary." The police need not have worried, for the powers-that-be in Oakland are not of a mind to sanction a review board. The City Council twice has turned down proposals by eight-to-one margins, the lone dissident being the only Negro councilman. And the Oakland *Tribune*, run by the archconservative Knowland family, backed the council with the stand that a review board "would inevitably be a long step toward weakening the authority, undermining the morale, and destroying the effectiveness of the Police Department in . . . protecting us from those who would prey on us."

As a consequence of the inflexible posture of the police and power structure, tension has reached the breaking point. On August 29, 1966, two policemen brandishing a riot gun roughly ejected two teenagers from a public park in the East Oakland ghetto. That night six Negro youths ordered one soft drink and six straws in a hamburger restaurant patronized by whites. The owner called the police, and six officers responded. When one made a threatening gesture, thirty Negroes appeared and jumped the police, disarmed them, and beat two so badly they had to be hospitalized. Police cars swarmed into East Oakland, snatching Negroes off the streets and booking them on whatever petty charges were convenient. For three days intermittent rioting went on, but it was unreported in the *Tribune*.

A 1966 U.S. government study of Oakland concluded that the racial situation was incendiary and that communication between the police and minorities had "broken down completely." It was against this backdrop that a member of the Lawyers' Committee on Civil Rights of the staid American Bar Association visited Preston. Upon being invited by a local ABA member, the committee offers its services in cities where police-minority liaison has been retarded (it had previously been invited to Atlanta, Seattle and Detroit). Preston was recalcitrant. "We have no problem here," he officiously told the committee member. "Who invited you?" The committee member named a moderate Republican lawyer. "Oh," Preston said knowingly, "he's a pinko."

Behind the bombast, however, Oakland knows it has serious problems. In rejecting negotiation, it has relied on preparations for force. After Watts, a group of high-ranking Oakland officers met with Thomas Reddin, now chief in Los Angeles, to discuss how Oakland could cope with its own inevitable Watts. Reddin advised his northern colleagues to get portable jails to transport prisoners away from the riot scene and thereby leave policemen on the scene to make more arrests. Also discussed were extra-hard rifle butts, special colored helmets to identify ranking police officers in the swirl of battle, and the number of National Guardsmen to be called in.

The force tried out its new weaponry at a demonstration in front of the Oakland armed forces induction center on October 17, 1967. A crowd of 2,500 war protesters had gathered, some forming a human barricade which prevented the day's inductees from entering. Intending to remain passive, the protesters expected that at worst they would be hauled off in paddy wagons. What happened made Selma look tame by comparison.

From a command post across the street a police bullhorn ordered the protesters to disperse. They shouted it down. With no further warning, the police, 250 strong and backed by hundreds of sheriff's deputies and California Highway Patrol officers, charged. Ex-Marine Charles Howe, military editor of the San Francisco *Chronicle,* wrote this account:

> Police—ten lines deep—made their attack shortly after 7 A.M., beating their way through a thin, running line of frightened demonstrators.
>
> Charging down Clay Street, officers squirted liquid Mace—a tear gas—and rattled clubs against anyone who didn't move out of their way fast enough. Newsmen, ordinarily exempt from police clubs, were pushed, kicked or otherwise shoved aside. . . .

When the police wave came to the human barricade, there was a momentary pause, then:

> [Officers] suddenly surged down the street, their hard wooden sticks mechanically flailing up and down, like peasants mowing down wheat.
>
> Demonstrators who tried to get to their feet and move on were struck, kicked, knocked down and gassed.
>
> Bodies began to pile up at the 14th street entrance and the cries of women could be heard as the clubs thudded into them.
>
> "I went to an injured woman," said Dr. Norman Marcus, a physician at Mt. Zion Hospital here. "A policeman struck me in my chest as I tried to help her. I asked for his badge number; he smiled and hit me again."

Dr. Marcus noticed the alternating fear and sadism so often exhibited by police squads in moments of stress: "I saw people beaten and dragged through the streets, and the policemen who weren't frightened were laughing." The Rev. Mark Sullivan, a Roman Catholic priest of the Rochester, New York, diocese, recounted that when he tried to shield a woman who was being clubbed: "An officer said this was an unlawful assembly; then I was hit in the stomach and knocked to the ground." A paratroop veteran of World War II and Korea, Dr. Donald L. Gerber of Chico, California, disgustedly told Howe: "The cops came at a little girl who was scared to death. My God, these were Americans they beat up today. . . . I've never seen anything like this in my life."

Probably incensed that their savageness was being recorded, the police turned on newsmen. Don Brice of KPIX television charged that attacks on newsmen "not only were unprovoked but it appeared to reporters on the scene that some members of the Oakland police department were deliberately selecting news people as targets for this treatment." Ralph Mayher, a cameraman for ABC television, cried out, "They're trying to kill me," as he was knocked down, kicked, and beaten. Jerry Jensen of KRON television, who commented that the protesters "just couldn't get out of the way of the police fast enough," was squirted in both eyes with the chemical Mace "by a cop who knew damn well I wasn't a demonstrator." Paul Gorman of UPI, prominent with his camera, reported he was knocked to the ground and clubbed. "They also kicked me in the head. I kept hollering I was with the press, but they didn't listen."

In an unprecedented move, the news media sought and obtained a federal court injunction forbidding the police from further attacks on newsmen covering the demonstrations. The demonstrators, of course, had no redress; the futility of lodging complaints with the department itself was suggested by the smug pronouncement of Chief of Police Charles Gain that their demonstration was an "illegal assembly" and that his

minions' use of force was "necessary to restore peace." * And
California Governor Ronald Reagan, a knee-jerk champion of
police rights, declared that the police had displayed "excep-
tional ability" which was "in the finest tradition of California's
law enforcement agencies."

On the other side of the border, the Berkeley Police Department stands in marked contrast with Oakland. The tradition of
August Vollmer, the first chief (in 1905) and one of the few
authentic police visionaries, still lingers. He instituted a rigid
code of conduct and ethics, and in an era when third-degree
methods were winked at by most police chiefs, Vollmer insisted that his men abide by civilized standards. The kid-glove
approach did not detract from efficacy, for Vollmer pioneered
in scientific aids and his men compiled an enviable record of
crime solution. The department was the first to apply blood,
fiber and soil analysis to forensic use, the first to use radio-
equipped patrol cars (1928), and the first to employ the lie
detector—the Keeler polygraph was developed by Lenard
Keeler in conjunction with the Berkeley department.

In 1916, Vollmer established a school of criminology on the
Berkeley campus and made his men attend. The "college cops"
precedent has endured, and today Berkeley requires entering
patrolmen to have at least two years of college and spend an
average of 260 hours in classes during the first year. To screen
out misfits, inductees are subjected to a stiff psychiatric examination. Berkeley has always paid well, and current scales—
a sergeant starts at $862 a month—are among the highest in

---

* Gain had been appointed chief following the sudden death of Robert Preston
at a police convention in Kansas City in August 1967. The Texas native had
joined the Oakland force in 1947 and climbed steadily up the ladder to deputy
chief in charge of the Bureau of Services, which included under its wing the
almost inert Community Relations Section. Gain was a familiar speaker on the
Bay Area right-wing banquet circuit.

the nation. Two distinguished "alumni" of this "class" department are O. W. Wilson and Chief Justice Earl Warren.

Since most of its officers have studied on the Berkeley campus, the anti-intellectualism and hostility to unorthodoxy that is so pronounced in other departments is minimal on Berkeley's. During the mass arrests of Sproul Hall sit-ins in 1964, most complaints of undue force were directed at other agencies, and the force's skillful handling of the 1965 peace march earned it the plaudits of the marchers themselves. Physical brutality is not an issue in Berkeley. Mrs. Frankie Jones, a local NAACP leader, told *Time* magazine (February 18, 1966): "I have seen police at work all over, and there's not a police department in the United States that excels this one."

Berkeley's long-time chief, Addison H. Fording, who retired in 1966, wasted little time bemoaning court decisions. "Certainly court decisions have imposed increasing limitations," he remarked to *Time*. "Our job now is to live within the framework that the court has set up." Fording made his officers do their homework on the new guidelines and was a stickler for thorough preparation for court presentation, with the result that the department has a high conviction rate and rarely is embarrassed by having cases overturned on appeal.

But even in Berkeley enlightenment has its limits. In 1965 Fording bought two enrollments in sessions of Dr. Fred Schwarz's Christian Anti-Communism Crusade school when it came to Berkeley. The chief awarded college credit to officers who wished to attain the standing of "senior patrolman" with an equivalent raise in pay. Fording, whose tolerance apparently was exhausted by the Free Speech Movement, defended his action by saying, "It lets you learn a great deal about Communists and Communist tactics in a relatively short period of time." But the patriotic chief showed little wisdom in his choice of a teacher, for Dr. Schwarz dispenses a brand of anti-Communism that is as radical on the right wing as the FSM was radical on the left wing.

In the last months of Fording's regime, relations with the Berkeley offbeat community worsened, and they have not grown better under the new chief, William P. Beall, Jr., a California alumnus who spent two wartime years as an FBI agent. On the night of April 12, 1966, a violent fist- and club-swinging melee broke out in downtown Berkeley when police tried to seize an amplifier being used by antiwar demonstrators; eight were arrested for fighting with the police. Two months later the police released statistics purporting to show "skyrocketing" crime in the Telegraph Avenue district, sometimes called the "left bank of America." When the department used the statistics as a reason to saturate the district with uniformed officers, students and Telegraph Avenue businessmen formed the "Better Berkeley Committee" to keep an eye on the police. The "crime wave," the BBC charged, was not confined to the Telegraph Avenue district but was general throughout the city. Furthermore, the saturation technique had failed to stem the increase in major crimes but had resulted in a rash of petty arrests for such offenses as jaywalking—the targets inevitably being "beatnik types." Fording fumed, counteralleging that the police themselves were being harassed by the "avenue people."

Then, early in 1967, Chief Beall announced that the department had arrested 474 persons in the year's period on drug charges, a jump of 220 percent over the year before. Beall evidently was using a "pot wave" to rouse public opinion against student marijuana smokers, for he decried the publicity attendant upon the use of marijuana as contributing to "the illusion of a pioneering trend toward general usage and social acceptance," a concept that is anathema to the police. But the validity of the statistics was cast in doubt when it was discovered that there were only 74 court convictions, and that 57 of the persons convicted had been granted probation. What happened in the other 400 cases was a matter Beall declined to reveal.

So East Bay law enforcement shows little promise. Berkeley's bright portends have slightly dimmed. Oakland remains notoriously old-guard. And the Alameda County District Attorney's Office has the musty scent of a frontier museum.

10

Dallas and New Orleans: The Dissimilar South

For reasons it would prefer to forget, the Dallas Police Department is known around the world. The abortive attempt to transfer Lee Harvey Oswald from the police jail to the county jail some blocks away was witnessed by press representatives from all over the world and by millions of Americans on television. The fiasco subjected the force to ridicule of a degree seldom if ever accorded a law-enforcement body. It had been a whirlwind hero-to-goat transition. Fewer than forty-eight hours before, the Dallas police had been acclaimed for their swift capture of accused Presidential assassin Oswald. Ironically, the precipitious tumble into ignominy had been preceded by years of encomiums, for the department had been regarded, by the ofttimes eccentric standards of law enforcement, as a model of efficiency.

Writing in *Fortune* magazine in 1949, Holland McCombs, an intimate of the Dallas scene, described the city as one of the "best policed" in the country. I can recall that in law-enforcement circles Dallas was regarded as one of the top agencies in the Southwest. In fact, the director of the Police-Community Relations Institute at Michigan State University declared in 1962 that "the Dallas department has enjoyed for many years a nationwide reputation for outstanding efficiency."

This was the legend, but the facts were not as glossy. During the late thirties and early forties, gambling, although illegal, was going full force under the tolerant eye of police on the take. To lend the appearance of enforcement, the police raided gambling joints, but the raids came at slack hours, and the operators agreeably paid the nominal fines before returning to business as usual. As Warren Leslie put it in *Dallas Public and Private*, "By the time the Texas Centennial opened in 1936, you could find a dice game or a bookmaker up almost any stairway in the city of Dallas."

The two top gambling figures during this lush era were Benny "Cowboy" Binion and Herbert Noble. At one time close associates, they had a falling out when one of Binion's henchmen killed a Noble man. The ensuing feud was monumental. Binion wound up transplanting his operation to Las Vegas, Nevada, but distance did not deter Noble from his dreams of revenge. Rigging an airplane with a bomb rack, he intended to dive-bomb Binion in his Las Vegas home. As the story goes, a lieutenant of the Dallas police got wind of Noble's bizarre scheme and talked him out of it. Not long after, Noble's wife was blown to bits when she stepped on the starter of the family car in front of their Oak Cliff district home. Noble himself was finally killed some months later when a bomb planted in his mailbox exploded as he reached for his mail.

In the mid-forties the Chicago syndicate made its inevitable grab for a piece of the Dallas action. A mob emissary named Paul Rolland Jones approached Sheriff Steve Guthrie and, oddly, an obscure lieutenant of the Dallas police, George Butler. Guthrie and Butler played along, recording the negotiations with hidden microphones and eventually securing indictments against Jones for attempted bribery. Butler became a hero of sorts. When Senator Estes Kefauver started his organized crime hearings, Butler was tapped as the Dallas expert on the subject. But years later, when he was interviewed by the

FBI regarding his friendship with Jack Ruby, Jones claimed he believed Butler was at first in earnest and wanted a payoff, desisting only when he learned the Texas Rangers were wise to the negotiations.

While the episode firmly established the Dallas police in the public mind as scrupulously honest, it also acted to keep outside hands off the Dallas rackets. From the volumes of the Warren Report on the assassination of President Kennedy, a picture of behind-the-scene Dallas can be drawn which indicates that the rackets are still autonomous. In February of 1964, as the background of Jack Ruby began to take shape, two staff members of the commission wrote in an interagency memorandum: "Ruby has very carefully cultivated friendships with police officers and other public officials. . . . At the same time, he was peripherally, if not directly, connected with members of the underworld. . . . Ruby also is rumored to have been the tip-off man between the Dallas police and the Dallas underworld. . . . Ruby operated his business on a cash basis, keeping no record whatsoever—a strong indication that Ruby himself was involved in illicit operations of some sort. . . . His primary technique in avoiding prosecution was the maintenance of friendship with police officers, public officials, and other influential persons in the Dallas community."

The volumes are replete with instances in which Ruby went out of his way to ingratiate himself with the police; he gave them free meals and drinks at his Carousel Club and did them favors whenever possible. An admitted gambler, Jack Hardee, told the FBI that Ruby was the man to see in Dallas vis-à-vis starting any racket activity, presumably because he could make the proper arrangements with key police officers. On the other side of the law, Ruby was well acquainted with Paul Rolland Jones, Las Vegas gambler Lewis McWillie, and other rackets figures.

Although tie-ins with the underworld are not unique to the

Dallas force, Holland McCombs in his *Fortune* article contends that the department tends to emphasize regulatory duties instead of serious crime prevention and solution. "I used to be surprised," McCombs said, "by the number of policemen Exchange Park could get out to supervise parking in a new plant. In my job, I had to know that a good deal of violent crime was taking place in the city, and here were all these officers steering people into the right parking places. I remember that I always used to think that the Dallas police were tougher on jaywalkers than on murderers—to coin a phrase."

Dallas annually runs one-two with Houston in the national homicide-rate derby, yet the police are not particularly distinguished by their skill in handling complex investigations or by their familiarity with modern crime-detection techniques. The investigation of the President's assassination supplies several illustrations. It took them forty-five minutes after the shots were fired to find the alleged assassination rifle on the sixth floor of the Texas School Book Depository Building, and in their crime-scene search they overlooked a brown paper bag at the sixth-floor window where the ejected shells were found that supposedly had been there all the time. Much of the physical evidence was so pawed, presumably by its police custodians, that possibly significant latent prints were obliterated. Dr. Vincent Guinn, an outstanding authority on nuclear activation analysis, the recently developed supersensitive process that actually detected traces of arsenic in a relic of Napoleon's hair, alleged that the Dallas police bungled in using the obsolete chemical tests for the presence of gunpowder residue on Oswald's hands and right cheek.

Lt. J. C. Day, the Dallas department's crime-scene search "expert," rather glumly admitted to the Warren Commission that he had only a limited education and virtually no formal training in the collection, preservation and processing of physical evidence. And for all the hours that prime suspect Oswald was grilled by Capt. Will Fritz of the Homicide Bureau, with representatives of federal agencies sitting in, the historic sessions were not preserved by either an electronic recording or a stenographer's transcript.

But these deficiencies in its lawmen Dallas does not view with concern, for the city has a character all its own. "Like everything else in Dallas," ventures ex-reporter Warren Leslie, "the police force is management-orientated." The city is ruled by an oligarchy of business executives called the Citizens Council (not to be confused with the racist White Citizens Council), which tightly controls the operations of all phases of city government, including the police department. The chief reports, in matters of consequence, not to his nominal superior, the mayor, but to the council.

For example, it is common knowledge in Dallas that Jesse E. Curry, chief at the time of the assassination, was not summarily fired after the abortive transfer of Oswald and its humiliation of a prideful city because it was a member of the council, not Curry, who ordered the transfer in the first place. But by early 1966, "pressures resulting from the assassination" had forced the premature retirement of Curry. One of the pressures was a rift with the FBI. Lt. Jack Revill of the Criminal Intelligence Section of the police department filed an affidavit quoting FBI agent James P. Hosty as saying, "We knew he [Oswald] was capable of assassinating the President," an incriminating remark hotly denied by Hosty and J. Edgar Hoover. Curry backed his own officer and, while he was chief, the FBI would not invite Dallas officers to its prestigious FBI National Academy. By its pragmatic lights, the council saw no advantage in a continuing estrangement from the FBI, and Curry's successor, Charles Batchelor, made his peace with Hoover. Curry was not completely discarded—he was accorded a niche in Dallas' private industry.

In the minds of the Citizens Council, "business as usual" is the main objective, and the manner in which integration came to Dallas exemplifies this philosophy. For all its pseudosophistication and burgeoning population (now at nearly one million in the greater Dallas area), Dallas is a frontier town. It is fundamentally white Anglo-Saxon, and the doctrine of white supremacy is still very much alive. But when the integration handwriting was on the wall, the Citizens Council did not wait for picket lines, street violence and federal intercession, as did Little Rock, Birmingham and other cities of the Deep South. A pro forma integration was worked out behind the closed doors of executive conference suites, taking the initiative out of the hands of the civil rights movement. The businessmen of Dallas simply decided that it was inevitable and had best be accomplished with the least disruption. It would have been inconceivable, they reasoned, for a city that revered law and order to clash with federal authorities—and besides it would be bad for business.

In compliance, Curry set in motion the wheels of integration within his department. By the time of the assassination in 1963, there were a few Negro police officers. On December 4, 1963, the Dallas *Times-Herald* reported that the police were quietly admitting Negro civilian employees. Two Negro girls had been hired the previous summer, it said, and on December 1 a Negro girl became the first to work in the detective bureau as a civilian.

In a book that coincided with Dallas' measured integration, Curry, a thickset former truckdriver, turned author to express his views on *Race Tensions and the Police*. Published by a police-science house and done in collaboration with Capt. Glen King, the department's public relations officer, the book was billed as a timely text on the problems generated by the Supreme Court's ruling (some years before) that "equal but separate facilities" were a thing of the past.

In the style of the Citizens Council, Curry and King revealed themselves as realists. The police officer who understands the nature of racial differences, they declared, "will be in a better position to bring his own prejudices under control. If the officer knows the source of his prejudices, he can more ably cope with them and prevent them from influencing his official action." This bit of advice was followed by a pedagogic discourse on anthropology and its law-enforcement ramifications.

Dallas officers are not always able to submerge their prejudices, however. In November 1964, as an example, a Negro youth was stopped for having a loud muffler on his car, taken to the Trinity River bottom that separates Dallas proper from its more unseemly sections to the south, and thoroughly beaten. As a final insult, the officers tore up his valid driver's license. The incident was reported, and the officers were indefinitely suspended.

Unlike their brothers in Watts, Harlem and Chicago, Dallas Negroes are not constantly harassed by the police—as long as they confine themselves to the company of other Negroes in the Negro slum areas. But should they venture obtrusively into white neighborhoods, they are liable to be stopped, checked, and told to move out of the area. The point is, and few Negroes fail to heed it, in Dallas everything and everybody has his place.

It is possibly one manifestation of Dallas' obsession with property rights that the police have devised what is called the "jack-in-the-box" technique—special squads that lie in wait in buildings and warehouses likely to burglarized to blast would-be burglars with sawed-off shotguns. On December 19, 1963, the Dallas *Times-Herald* proudly recounted the technique's success: "Police initiated the use of shotgun squads in 1961 and the tactic proved effective. Police shotguns roared almost by the time the special squads were first placed on duty. A squad hiding in a South Dallas drive-in surprised two Negro hi-jackers [a colloquialism for burglars] and felled both with buckshot. Neither lived to reach the hospital."

The shocking spectacle of police executing men on the spot for a crime against property is probably some kind of a hangover from frontier justice, when a horse thief was strung up from the nearest tree. Yet it does not seem coincidental that practically all the victims of the "jack-in-the-box" squad have been Negroes or Mexican-Americans. Tom Howard, Jack Ruby's first defense attorney, blustered to the press that the killing of Oswald was "just another nigger killing." In the South, crimes involving Negro victims are treated as inconsequential—the death of a Negro (or of Oswald) is not the same as the death of a white citizen.

In its degree of right-wing extremism, the Dallas department mirrors the political bias of the city itself. Dallas is a city of Bircher oil magnates, of General Walker, Dan Smoot, H. L. Hunt and the National Indignation Committee. It is where then Senate Majority Leader Lyndon Johnson and his wife were booed, hissed and spat upon in front of the Adolphus Hotel in 1960, and where Adlai Stevenson was jostled and reviled shortly before the assassination. While the majority of the people of Dallas are not extremists, extremism of the right is respectable.

Dallas journalists tell me that the police department is heavily loaded with Birchers, and one police official is reputed to be the number-two man in Dallas in the Minutemen, the superpatriotic paramilitary group that believes the country has already gone Communistic. When I was in Dallas in 1963 covering the aftermath of the assassination—it was my first trip to Dallas—I was somewhat startled to see a number of detectives in their lounge engrossed in copies of *Life Line*, a radical right-wing newsletter published under the patronage of H. L. Hunt, the oil billionaire.

Hunt, a powerful figure in behind-the-scenes Dallas, is usually escorted to his public engagements around town by a Dallas officer, ordinarily Lieutenant George Butler of the Kefauver Crime Committee fame. It was Lt. Butler (who is assigned, oddly enough, to the Juvenile Bureau) who was in overall charge of the transfer of Oswald on November 24 and who gave the "all clear" to bring the prisoner into the basement—and to his death at the hands of Jack Ruby. Penn Jones, Jr., the scrappy editor of the Midlothian, Texas, *Mirror*, recounts that Butler was in town in 1961 to give an anti-Communism speech and dropped in the *Mirror* office. "He offered me the job of printing a regional newspaper under the auspices of the Ku Klux Klan," says Jones. "He told me that half of the Dallas police were members of the KKK."

Despite the fact that it is not a physically impressive force, the Dallas police have almost a fetish for polished, outsized silver belt buckles, shiny guns, Masonic rings and pins—the accouterments of the law-enforcement cult. Nor is the force impressive by mental standards. A large number of officers do not even have a high-school diploma; few have had any university-level training. Most Dallas police are former oil-field workers or otherwise unskilled, or have worked in the non-unionized trades, and have joined the force for the security and fringe benefits it offers. Recruiting posters distributed all over the Dallas area announce: "You can be part of an honored profession." The advantages listed are steady employment, free training, merit advancement, and college opportunities.

Nevertheless the force has a manpower crisis. In 1966, a survey showed that of 1,033 applicants for the police position, only 375 passed the written examination, and only 127 of these passed the physical examination. After the background check, the number was reduced to 29; most of those rejected had a previous arrest record, a bad driving record or a poor credit rating. In the meantime, the resignation rate remained high.

Lt. Thurber T. Lord, president of the Dallas Police Association, said that an exhaustive study by his organization showed that a lack of training, poor job opportunity and low salaries had resulted in rock-bottom morale conditions. Lord pointed to two newspaper ads running side by side in which the city offered a higher starting salary to bus drivers than to policemen.

Dallas' salaries, under $6,000, hardly qualify the police position as an "honored profession." Officer Jefferson Davis Tippitt, who allegedly was killed by Oswald, had been eight years on the force without a promotion, and he was forced to moonlight at Austin's Barbecue in Oak Cliff to make ends meet. The restaurant, incidentally, is a meeting place for many of the Bircher policemen.

It is highly paradoxical that in affluent Dallas, where political conservatism is a way of life, the Birch Society slogan "Support Your Local Police" is empty demagoguery, and the police remain ill-paid pariahs in the midst of one of the highest per-capita income areas in the nation.

Some 400 miles to the southeast of Dallas is the colorful port city of New Orleans, where Old South attitudes blend uneasily with the cosmopolitan character of a modern metropolis. The city's ambivalence is mirrored by the 800-man police force.

The New Orleans Police Department, whose patrol cars sport the Crescent City emblem, is located on the ground floor of a massive graystone edifice at 2700 Tulane Avenue which houses practically all the components of criminal justice in the city: the sheriff's office, the district attorney's office, the municipal and superior courts, the grand jury room, the coroner's office and, at the rear, the Orleans Parish (county) jail. Until recently, the police department was as dated as the post-World War I building on Tulane. It has moved haltingly forward un-

der the guidance of the current superintendent, Joseph I. Giarrusso.

A rotund, laconic man in his late forties, Giarrusso has cop-
ied, on a smaller scale, the popular trends in national law enforcement. The department has worked out a program in conjunction with Loyola University of New Orleans that aims
eventually to give every man on the force at least some college
training. Giarrusso has been able to wheedle modest salary increases for his men from a grudging city government and in
return has taken steps to upgrade the efficiency and morale of
the force. As one move he has ordered his men to act dignified
and refrain from using such self-deprecating nicknames as
"Slow Motion," "Heavy Belly," "Skeeter" and "Mr. Wonder-
ful." As part of a revamped public-relations program, New
Orleans officers have distributed 25,000 coloring books with
a police motif to schoolchildren in grades one through three.

Beneath the patina, however, the department is little more
than an agent of the status quo. Despite Supreme Court decisions which have chipped away at segregation, New Orleans
retains a large degree of de facto discrimination, and the police
have not lacked zeal in enforcing this philosophy. The August
1964 raid on the Quorum Club attests to their zealousness.

The Quorum Club, a coffeehouse on the fringe of the
famous French Quarter, had invited noted Negro blues musician "Babe" Stovall to perform. He accepted gratefully, for he
was ineligible to join the Jim Crow musician's union local and
was performing sporadically for whatever he could pick up.
On opening night Stovall proudly brought along his grown
daughter and nephew. Since the ground rules in New Orleans
permit a Negro to perform for whites but prohibit the mixing
of races in the audience, they ordinarily would have had to
stand in the doorway; the management instead seated them
in the audience. It was not the first time the Quorum

Club had violated the rules, a fact which had not escaped the racist White Citizens Council. A few months previously, the council had put out a circular letter denouncing the club's "integration" policies, and the New Orleans police had taken note.

Two Negro police undercover men had been assigned to watch the club; they played their roles so well they even improvised poetry and recited it at one of the regular Sunday evening readings. As "Babe" Stovall began to sing and play a Negro spiritual ("Time, time is a-windin' up, Destruction on the land, God gon' lift His hand . . ."), one of the undercover men mounted the stage and announced, "This is a raid. Everybody line up against the wall." About a dozen uniformed officers stormed in, herding all seventy-three persons in the audience into paddy wagons. The bag included two Louisiana State University faculty members, a pregnant white woman, an attorney, several married couples who had left their children at home with babysitters, and three elderly ladies. It was one of the most massive roundups in New Orleans police history.

The arrested persons were booked for "creating a disturbance," a charge even an incorrigible racist would have to prefer tongue-in-cheek. A municipal judge before whom they were arraigned that night set bonds at $100 cash, an unusually high rate for such a nominally trivial offense. Most of the seventy-three settled down for at least a night (some stayed two) on the cement floors of the cells into which they were crammed. The white women were obscenely reviled by the police raiding party and jail custodians for presumed sexual intimacy with Negroes. A prominent New Orleans attorney explained the underlying police rationale: "The police of New Orleans, reasoning perhaps from their own habits and proclivities, cannot envisage whites and Negroes coming together for any other purpose than to copulate."

Recently a hippie colony has sprung up in the French Quarter, and Giarrusso, like his colleague Cahill in San Francisco, has taken a dim view of what he calls the "transient beatniks." Traditionally the police have left unmolested the large group of oddly assorted artists who set up their easels in Jackson Square, the heart of the historic Vieux Carré; they contributed to the quaintness of the scene and were considered a tourism asset. But early in 1967, as the nonartist element proliferated, police bemusement ended. A group of Bohemian types who had been playing guitars and singing in the square were arrested under an ordinance prohibiting "loungers using Jackson Square on a daily basis."

Then, acting on what he claimed were numerous complaints from merchants and tourists, Giarrusso assigned two Vice Squad undercover men to "ingratiate" themselves with this "undesirable element," a not overly difficult feat with the unsuspicious hippies. "The officers were successful in being accepted by this group and were able to determine first hand their conduct, which was most reprehensible," declared Giarrusso primly in announcing the arrests of thirteen persons, among them a fifteen-year-old boy and the hapless "Babe" Stovall. "We don't arrest people because of the way they choose to dress or wear their hair," commented Vice Squad Detective Sergeant Jerry Lankford almost apologetically. "We arrested individuals who had violated the law."

In sharp contrast to the prejudice-laden penny-ante enforcement of the police is the office of District Attorney Jim Garrison, which has tackled cases most prosecutors would studiously avoid. Since February 1967, when New Orleans newspapers broke the news of Garrison's probe into the assassination of President Kennedy, the D.A.'s office has been the subject of national controversy centering on the methods and merits of its investigation. For his pains, Garrison has been one of the few *prosecutors* of recent times to undergo "trial by newspaper"; an overwhelming segment of the press has depicted him as a ruthless politician driven by high ambition to parlay the death of a President into personal gain. As is so often the case, Garrison's bad press is without basis in fact. His record shows that he has a history of taking on politically disadvantageous causes, which is the only realistic category into which his assassination probe can be placed.

First elected in 1962 (and reelected in 1966) on a reform platform, Garrison quickly served notice that he meant to carry out his campaign promises. In the New Orleans area the crime syndicate has headquarters across the Mississippi River in Gretna, Jefferson Parish, a wide-open town often called "the Cicero of the South," but it has cast covetous eyes on New Orleans proper, where in recent years relatively clean law enforcement has kept the lid on. An emissary of the mob lost no time in approaching a Garrison aide with a deal no venal politician could turn down. The D.A. was supposed to bring a test case against slot machines designed to eventuate in the machines being declared legal; in return for the "favor" he would get ten dollars per machine per week, which, with the installation of 300 machines anticipated, would amount to a slice of $3,000 a week. The answer was a booming "No."

Garrison emphasized his rebuff by padlocking mob-backed strip joints on Bourbon Street and scattering the B-girls who were playing tourists for suckers, often drugging their drinks and rolling them. He reformed the bail bond system under which petty offenders had been held for exorbitant bail. When the police vice squad tried to sweep James Baldwin's *Another Country* from bookstore shelves, he refused to prosecute ("How can you define obscenity?") and denounced the action in stinging terms, thus incurring the wrath of the White Citizens Council. And in a wholly impolitic move, he chastized local judges for holding too brief court sessions and taking too long vacations; the judges collectively sued for defamation, and Garrison had to go all the way to the Supreme Court to win the point.

The only point of comparison between Garrison and his Dallas opposite number, Henry Wade, is that both are former FBI agents. Where the unimaginative Wade performs routinely within the rigid Dallas structure, aided by his truculent right-wing assistant Bill Alexander, Garrison and his urbane number-one-man, Charles Ward, have brought a new scope and dimension to the district attorney's office. Standing six and a half feet tall, speaking in a measured, confident baritone, Garrison is one of the breed of "investigating district attorneys." Several police detectives, including Chief Investigator Louis Ivon, are posted to his office, and his staff of able young attorneys, all nonpolitical appointees, double as field sleuths.

In June 1967 I spent four hectic days with Garrison inside the press-besieged battlements of his office. His desk is cluttered with papers stacked in order of priority, for in addition to the intricate assassination investigation there is the normal workload of the office. On a table next to his desk is a litter of books, articles, photographs and tape recordings dealing with the assassination, plus a set of the twenty-six volumes of the Warren Report. On the rich walnut-paneled walls of his office, alongside a Master of Law diploma from Tulane University, are blown-up photographs of Dealey Plaza, the assassination site, and several items of evidence crucial to the case. A handsome inlaid chess table stands alone on one side of the spacious, comfortable office; Garrison is one of New Orleans' more formidable chess masters.

After prolonged exposure to Garrison, one tends to reject the press myths about him. He is unusually intellectual for his profession, possessing a profound grasp of history and reading tastes that range from Graham Greene to Ayn Rand. He views capital punishment as futile and inhumane and abhors violence. Both former G-men, we were studying a somewhat blurred photograph of a Dallas police officer in front of the Texas School Book Depository Building on November 22, 1963, holding aloft a rifle or shotgun.

"What kind of weapon do you think it is?" Garrison asked.

"I can't make it out," I replied, "and besides I hate guns."

"So do I," he said, grinning. "In the Bureau they had to give me special training in order to qualify on the practical pistol course."

Well regarded in professional circles, Garrison in 1965 was given the honor of writing the foreword to *Crime, Law and Corrections*, a criminology volume whose contributors compose a galaxy of the most illustrious names in the field. Garrison had come upon Dachau with the advancing Allied Armies in 1945 (he is presently a lieutenant colonel in the Louisiana National Guard), and the vestiges of horror he witnessed there left him with an indelible impression. "Earth was a fairly peaceful place back in the halcyon days when Tyrannosaurus was king," he wrote. "Avarice and guile were unknown. There were no dungeons, no leg irons and no thumbscrews. Justice had not yet been discovered, so there were no hangings. . . . The more irrational an idea has been the more firmly man has embraced it. When the idea has been sufficiently inane and destitute of merit, millions of people have united in their devotion to it. One of the most popular perversions of intellectuality was German National Socialism with its glorification of hatred, its belief in the right of the strong to rule the weak, its contempt for individual rights and its mystical nationalism."

In his foreword, Garrison perceived in the murder of Kitty Genovese in New York, when thirty-eight apartment dwellers refused her cries for help, the same strain of apathy and indifference that was responsible for the studied cruelties of Dachau, Auschwitz and Treblinka. It took a Jim Garrison in New Orleans to investigate and prosecute the tragedy of Dallas. It was a task which less committed law-enforcement officers had defaulted.

11

Philadelphia:
The Noble Experiment

Since 1958 the Philadelphia Police Department has been under the continual scrutiny of the nation's first civilian review board. That the city fathers saw fit to establish the board does not imply that law enforcement in the City of Brotherly Love is more barbaric than elsewhere; in some respects it is more enlightened. But the board, annoying as it is to the police and despite its sharply limited powers, has amply demonstrated that a civilian hand on the police shoulder can measurably lessen police-minority frictions.

The Police Advisory Board, as Philadelphia's review board is called, keeps an eye on a 6,975-man force headquartered in a double-circular concrete structure that resembles two huge military pillboxes. Although the police problems faced by the department are similar to those in most Northern urban centers, the fact that Philadelphia's Negro population stands at 38 percent and is rising accentuates the need for judicious police-community relations.

Under former Commissioner Howard Leary, the department came up with several innovations. One is the Stake-Out Unit, a squad that tries to anticipate where holdups are likely to occur and be there when they do. The squad's specially trained plainclothesmen lurk in the backs of stores, banks, loan offices, etc., and may even pose as bank tellers. They are instructed to shoot to kill only if the suspect displays a weapon and indicates he will resist arrest, and only if there is no risk to bystanders. So far about half the suspects surprised in the act of armed robbery have resisted or attempted to flee, and several have been mortally wounded. The Stake-Out Unit has been widely advertised in the hope it will prove to be a deterrent to robbery.

Another innovation is the Civil Disobedience Squad, which is designed to bring as much order as possible to civil disobedience demonstrations while protecting the demonstrators' constitutional rights. The C.D. Squad maintains liaison with civil rights, antiwar and other protest groups. By knowing in advance what they have planned—most groups cooperate with the squad—the police can deploy their men with maximum economy and strategic advantage. C.D. members are chosen for their even temperament and maturity (the average age is thirty-eight) and are required to study sociology and attend lectures on civil rights by University of Pennsylvania law professors.

In a city apt to produce a demonstration protesting anything from strict divorce laws and lax rape laws to the Vietnam war and white power, the squad is indispensable. During the protracted seven-month picket line in 1966 at Girard College, whose endower had stipulated that only white orphans could be admitted, C.D. responded to demonstrators' jibes and epithets with perpetual grins. During a July 4th antiwar demonstration at Independence Hall in 1966, C.D. doused the fury of a swarm of military veterans by giving instant lectures on the rule of law.

This does not mean that the squad is sympathetic to the demonstrators; the laws are on the books and must be enforced. The historical validity of passive resistance is irrelevant to them. But in one form or another, passive resistance appears among the ancient Greeks, in medieval German thought, in early Scandinavian law, and in the chronicles of India. In essence it can be described as honoring the structure of the law while violating a particular law regarded as immoral. Civil disobedience as defined by Gandhi held that every citizen is responsible for every act of his government, but Gandhi also counseled that a citizen must qualify by prior obedience to the laws of the state to exercise on rare occasions his duty to violate an unjust law. Martin Buber drew from the Torah a mandate for the people to challenge the theocracy and thus force a dialogue, and he saw this principle as extended to the civil relationship between the people and the state. Most present acts of civil disobedience are directed not at immoral laws but at immoral social conditions or government policies, to which the laws broken are immaterial. But they remain in effect a nonviolent confrontation of the will of the governed with the will of the state.

Not only are the police paid agents of the state, they are usually neither intellectually equipped to consider the principle involved nor politically disposed to indulgence. In fact, civil-disobedience depends upon the intervention of the police to dramatize the immorality of the law, conditions or policies. The more vigorous and physical the police intervention, the more dramatic the effect. Philadelphia's C.D. Squad minimizes the dramatic impact by making arrests in the most genteel manner possible. A typical arrest may go like this: "You are interfering with the free movement of vehicles and pedestrians. Please move." Then, "Will you move?" As the resister remains in place, the C.D. man informs him that his act violates Section 406 of the Pennsylvania penal code in that it constitutes disorderly conduct. Again he asks, "Will you move?" After a pause, the C.D. man pronounces: "You are now under arrest. Will you walk to the patrol wagon?" If the resister declines, he is warned: "The additional charge of resisting arrest will be placed against you."

In an article in *Police Chief* magazine January 1967, Chief Inspector Harry G. Fox of the Philadelphia department pointed out that the kid-gloves treatment will favorably affect "public reaction to the use of police powers." As a result of his training, said the chief inspector, the C.D. man "refuses to act as judge or jury no matter what the provocation"—a delimitation not uniformly observed by the police as a whole.

Yet behind the sophisticated approach to the civil-disobedience problem, the Philadelphia role is still laden with hypocrisy. A proliferation of misdemeanor laws is on the books— statutes or ordinances that prohibit such acts as jaywalking, expectorating on the sidewalk, drinking in public and disorderly conduct—that can only be selectively enforced. The sometimes boisterous antics of Knights of Columbus, Shrine and American Legion conventioneers, for instance, frequently annoy and embarrass casual passersby and constitute disorderly conduct, but arrests are rare. The police buff with a Fraternal Order of Police sticker on his windshield is not as likely to be stopped for a technical traffic infraction as the Negro in a dilapidated car. Moreover the police themselves, as in their indiscriminate use of electronic "bugs" or wiretaps, display a cavalier attitude toward the law in enforcing the law. In this light the sanctimonious arrests of nonviolent demonstrators become somewhat Pharisaical.

It is the issue of the Police Advisory Board that has focused attention on the Philadelphia law-enforcement scene. Because the department is fairly representative of the character of the American police system, Philadelphia is a suitable laboratory for the analysis of the civilian review concept. That the city is typical of others is shown by the statement of former Commissioner Leary, echoed by a succeeding commissioner, Edward J. Bell, that the trend of court decisions is "making sophisti-

cated law for an unsophisticated society." Also typically, Philadelphia is plagued by police corruption. For example, the Internal Security Squad recently has been conducting an intensive secret investigation into reputed liaisons between some
two dozen officers assigned to West Philadelphia and known
underworld figures.

The department also has its paradoxes. While educational
requirements are low (many policemen have only a grade-
school education), its rate of crime solution averages nearly
40 percent, well above the national average of about 25 percent. And while the proportion of Negro officers at close to 25
percent adequately reflects the city's makeup, the force has
been disrupted by the outbreak of Birchism in the ranks.

For some years prior to 1958 there had been agitation for
an independent police review tribunal in Philadelphia, but
the creation of the Police Advisory Board was triggered by
alleged police mistreatment of John Archer, a Negro, and a
subsequent whitewash of the charges by the Internal Security
Squad. Archer was arrested by Patrolman William Leader in
his grocery store for reasons still vague and was tossed into a
patrol car, where Leader allegedly manhandled him so
roughly that a rib was broken. At the station house, Leader
threw a punch at a police lieutenant. He was tried by a police
board of inquiry for being intoxicated on duty, for striking a
superior officer, and for using excessive force against Archer.
When he was found guilty only of hitting a superior officer,
demands for an impartial review body were renewed. Armed
with an ACLU compilation of statistics on specific complaints
that demonstrated the inadequacy of police internal procedures, Mayor Richardson Dilworth empowered the Police
Advisory Board to process citizen complaints about "brutality,
false arrest, racial, religious or ethnic discrimination or other
wrongful conduct of police personnel toward citizens." In its
formal and open hearings, the board would observe due proc-

ess by providing counsel for both sides and affording the opportunity for cross-examination. However, the board was given no punative powers; its recommendations were to be acted upon by the mayor and the police commissioner, who would make the final decision.

The need for such a tribunal in Philadelphia and elsewhere is clear, since it is too much to expect the police to police themselves. The existence of police malpractice is thoroughly documented. A 1961 report of the U.S. Commission on Civil Rights declared that "police brutality is still a serious problem throughout the United States. . . ." Charlotte Epstein, social scientist and consultant to the Philadelphia Police Department, is quoted in the ACLU pamphlet "Police Power and Citizens' Rights" as saying: "Policemen are more suspicious of Negroes than whites, because there are such misconceptions . . . they stop more Negroes without probable cause than whites . . . given these prejudices, hostility, the policeman's authoritarian personality, limited training and ignorance of the law, there has to be police malpractice."

In *The American Journal of Sociology* of July 1953, William A. Westley explains the illegal use of violence by the police in terms of the policeman's need for recognition, which in turn goes a long way toward clarifying the almost pathological hostility of the police to civilian review:

> The analysis of [police] use of brutality in dealing with sexual deviants and felons shows that it is a result of their desire to defend and improve their social status in the absence of effective legal means. This desire in turn is directly related to and makes sense in terms of the low status of the police in the community, which results in a driving need on the part of policemen to assert and improve their status. Their general legitimation of the use of violence *primarily* in terms of coercing respect and making a "good pinch" clearly points out the existence of occupational goals, which are independent of and take precedence over their legal mandate.

One argument advanced by the police against review boards, which on the face of it seems cogent, is that an aggrieved citizen can seek redress through the courts. But the impracticality of this method was well exposed in "Police Power and Citizens' Rights":

> Both criminal and civil court proceedings against police are forbidding and unknown complexities to the poor, the minority groups and the social outcasts who are so often the complainants. Arrayed against the resourceless and friendless is the interlocking chain of the law enforcement "establishment." For instance in criminal court proceedings, the district attorney can hardly be expected to drive hard against the very police officer whose help he needs to get evidence for convictions in the day-to-day work of his department.

Civilian review boards in their present form would not be able to bring criminal justice to brutes and bullies with badges, nor could they directly discipline them. But they could exert strong leverage on the wheels of justice, as Spencer Coxe of the ACLU in Philadelphia observes: "The police commissioner can ignore the recommendation of the board only at the greatest peril to public relations; therefore, the board's lack of actual punative authority is of little practical disadvantage. . . ."

The true value of civilian review lies in its ability to resolve nonlegal grievances. When a policeman hurls a deprecating epithet at a person, he may start a riot but he is not committing a crime per se. And when he exercises his prejudices by routinely stopping interracial couples for questioning, as did Philadelphia police until five years ago, he is safely within the law. This is the kind of malpractice that the review board is best equipped to halt.

A major objection to review boards raised by police is that police work is so complex and unique that civilians could not possibly make sound judgments about the correctness of po-

lice action in a given situation. The argument is based on the
faulty assumption that the police are masters of their profession, but according to a 1961 survey by the International Association of Chiefs of Police, over one half of the nation's larger
departments could afford recruits only a smattering of classroom instruction before turning them loose with nightstick,
gun and badge. The argument also assigns an unwarranted
complexity to the simple decision as to whether an officer has
conducted himself according to civilized standards.

Perhaps the most specious police polemic is that outside review invites crime by making the police hesitant to enforce the
law vigorously for fear of sanction by "outsiders." Coupled
with the warning that overcautious law enforcement may cause
you the citizen to be the victim of a crime, the police have used
the "handcuffed" argument with great emotional impact on
the public. But the implications of the argument are shocking.
It admits that the police are willfully shirking their duty as
they see it because they do not wish to be encumbered with
civilian checks on the manner in which they use their powers.
It fallaciously implies that vigorous law enforcement cannot
be accomplished in a lawful manner. The police position is
rebutted by FBI statistics: after four years of the Police Advisory Board, the FBI Uniform Crime Report showed that Philadelphia had the lowest crime rate per 100,000 population of
the five major cities in the United States—and the highest rate
of arrests for crimes committed.

Underlying the almost rabid police hostility to civilian review are latent police prejudices. The prominent citizens usually appointed to the boards represent a broad spectrum of the
community. The charter members of the Police Advisory
Board, for example, included Dr. Clarence Pickett, a Nobel
Peace Prize-winner, and Dr. Thorsten Sellin, a University of
Pennsylvania professor internationally known as a sociologist.
Current members include a respected businessman, a Puerto

Rican minister, and a representative of organized labor. But since the police are historically anti-intellectual, racially bigoted to a degree, and adverse to the labor movement, an attitude dating from the days when they were frequently used as strikebreakers, the businessman is probably the only member above suspicion in the eyes of the police.

Thus it is not only an inherent distrust of outsiders that stirs police phobia over review boards, but an absolute fear of the type of individuals appointed to the boards and the egalitarian ideas they profess. The topic is so heinous to police they cannot discuss it rationally; the discussion inevitably degenerates into an imputation of members' motives and intent. Police Chief Daniel S. C. Liu of Honolulu, who has archly described review boards as "a secret weapon of a foreign ideology," warned his colleagues of the International Association of Chiefs of Police in a 1964 speech, "We must continue to speak out against meddlers who would hamstring the police with civilian review boards. . . ." In its issue of November 1960, the *California Peace Officer* magazine flatly declared: "Police review boards . . . are a page out of the Communist manual. . . ." Inspector Edward M. Davis of the Los Angeles department, speaking before the California League of Cities October 23, 1962, insinuated: "If you cooperate with the executive director of your review board, you will probably get the full support of at least one vocal element of our press—*The People's World.* . . . Why are we such prime targets of the darlings of *The People's World?*"

Such hysteria suggests the emotional depths to which the subject of civilian review drives the police. In a more measured but equally unequivocal stand, the International Association of Chiefs of Police has contended that review boards are merely "politically expedient" and the problem must be attacked from the other end by upgrading police personnel and training. Most police groups are less reasoned in their opposition. The Fraternal Order of Police, by far the nation's largest line organization with over 90,000 members and 600 chapters from Baltimore to Alaska, has zeroed in on the Philadelphia Police Advisory Board, which has become symbolic of the review-board menace. In 1965 Philadelphia Police Sergeant John J. Harrington was elected national president of the FOP by virtue of his implacable opposition to the Police Advisory Board.

The fifty-five-year-old Harrington, a brawny man with a brush cut, retired from the force shortly after his election to devote full time to his FOP duties. His wood-paneled office in the graystone, *circa* 1920 building housing FOP Lodge 4 on Spring Garden Street is cluttered with memorabilia accumulated during his police career and FOP travels, including a desk-mounted pistol, a plaque designating him an Honorary Kentucky Colonel, and a framed slogan: "Respect Law Enforcement." In many ways Harrington is the stereotype of the policeman. He once unhesitatingly paid the $50 hospital bill of a destitute Puerto Rican woman after some of the city's best ladies' clubs had declined. He admires the anti-Communism stance of the John Birch Society and says he would join if he had the time. "A lot of Catholic priests are members," he told me, "and I figure they know what they're doing." He talks straight from the shoulder, as for example his explanation of why Sunday mornings are the quietest part of the police week: "The drunks are sleeping it off, the good people are in church, and the niggers are out in the suburbs looking for houses."

Harrington preaches the straight police line. On October 30, 1966, in Providence, Rhode Island, he labeled recent court decisions on the rights of suspects "idiotic," maintaining there was "too much crying for the criminals and nobody is weeping for the victims." But the main fire of Harrington and the FOP is aimed at civilian review; his arguments are the standard ones, and he adds a few personal fillips. "The boards are instigated by people who don't trust anyone—the police, the courts or the FBI," he alleges. "And the members don't know anything about police work. In Philadelphia we've got a housewife, a rag man and a minister not long over from Europe." Like most policemen, Harrington perceives the specter of Communist conspiracy behind the review-board movement. Of a member of the now-defunct New York review board he says, "If ever there was a Communist, he was it." A member of Philadelphia's board is also suspect in Harrington's view because he once collected money for the Committee to Abolish HUAC. "I told him to his face," recounts the FOP president, "a pink is too yellow to be Red."

Harrington decries review boards as convenient forums for pathological cop-haters and devices for persons who want to get their arrest record expunged. He also feels the boards are grossly unfair to the police. For one thing, he asserts, they constitute a form of double jeopardy—the accused officer can later be brought into criminal court.* For another, officers risk being falsely accused by persons who have it in for them. "There was one case in which officers were accused of breaking into a party and shoving one guy down the stairs," Harrington recalls. "The guy identified Red Smith, who is pretty well known, as the one who shoved him. Red was out of town on vacation at the time." (The Police Advisory Board record shows that Officer Smith was exonerated and his record completely cleared; in pre-Advisory Board days the accusation might have remained a permanent black mark in his personnel file.) So adamant on the topic of outside review is Harrington that he sees no merit in the ombudsman concept, which allows citizens to present their grievances against all branches of city government.

Harrington cites the rioting that took place in Philadelphia

---

* Civilian review is an administrative procedure, not legal; it is no more a matter of double jeopardy than is the internal discipline of the police themselves.

in August 1964 as a prime example of how the onus of a review board handicaps the police. During the looting the police stood idly by because they were afraid to use force. "You saw the pictures of the cannibals coming out of the stores with television sets on their heads," he said. "If it hadn't been for the Police Advisory Board, we would have grabbed them and, if they resisted, hit them with our blackjacks." He explained that the use of blackjacks had previously been made mandatory by a departmental general order because too many officers were going on extended sick leave with fractured hands suffered in pummeling resisting suspects into submission. But blackjacks drew blood, the police reasoned, and blood attracted the sharks of the Advisory Board. Not until word came down that the mayor would issue a proclamation invoking the old Riot Act and temporarily suspending the jurisdiction of the Advisory Board did the police go into action. "When word came," Harrington said, grinning, "we really went out and 'proclamated' them, and the rioting was over in four hours."

In the summer of 1964, Rochester, New York, Harlem and six other locales were rocked by racial violence. An inquest of sorts was conducted by the FBI, which concluded, contrary to the gratuitous statements of a number of police spokesmen that Communists or "professional agitators" were behind the disturbances, that they had not been systematically planned. But the FBI report, which went to the President of the United States and received widespread publicity, took the police side in the civilian-review dispute:

> The investigations also revealed that where there is an outside review board the restraint of the police was so great that effective action against the rioters appeared to be impossible. This restraint was well known in the community and the rioters thereby were emboldened to resist and completely defy the efforts of the police to restore order. In short, the police were so careful to avoid accusations of improper conduct that they were virtually paralyzed. . . .

This stagy sulking of the police, an incredibly bold abrogation of their sworn duty to uphold the law, apparently failed to affront the FBI's reputed dedication to professionalism in law enforcement. Nor did the G-men, who ordinarily detect the slightest conspiracy, seem to notice that police passiveness was more organized than spontaneous.

An additional passage in the FBI report heaped insult on injury as far as review-board proponents were concerned:

> Interviews with individual policemen from patrolmen to high-ranking officers revealed a general feeling that if they take action deemed to be necessary in such situations they will be pilloried by civilians unfamiliar with the necessities of mob control, or even ordinary police action, and may lose their posts and their pensions.

The publication of such one-sided pulings by the prestigious FBI did immeasurable harm to the review-board cause and provoked at least one prominent Philadelphian, attorney Henry W. Sawyer, III, to take J. Edgar Hoover to task. Sawyer's remonstration, in the form of a letter dated September 29, 1964, is worth presenting in full not because it courageously challenges an almost mythical public figure, but because it delivers an eloquent exposition of the civilian-review principle:

Dear Mr. Hoover:

> As the author and original legislative sponsor, when I was a member of the City Council of Philadelphia, of the Police Advisory Board of Philadelphia, I read with incredulity the attack on the Board which was contained in your report on the riots. I am unaware of a single responsible person or agency in the Philadelphia community who would agree with your report or who even actually seeks the abolishment of this excellent Philadelphia institution. To speak of this Board of distinguished citizens "pillorying" policemen or operating in any fashion which could give rise to any legitimate fear on the part

of policemen borders on the absurd. To state as you do that policemen fear the loss of their jobs or pensions through the activities of this Board indicates that you are totally uniformed as to its powers and duties. The Board, as its name might have suggested, is advisory only.

One is also puzzled by the idea which your statement conveys that civilian review of police activities is something novel conjured up through the creation of these boards. I am sure that as a lifelong police officer you do not need to be reminded that police action is and always has been subject to "civilian review,"—namely by the judiciary. This is an essential and indeed a characteristic aspect of a democratic society. An advisory civilian board such as operates in Philadelphia therefore simply provides a form for the hearing of complaints and grievances, real or imaginary, without the necessity of bringing court action.

The thing that is, however, so surprising to those of us here who have had something to do with the establishment of this Board is that you would lend the prestige of your position to an attack upon a community institution which has performed its role with discretion and understanding, is not even opposed by the highest officials of the police department, has received appropriations yearly from the City Council on the basis of recommendations from the Mayor, and which has come under attack from no source other than via the anonymous phone call propaganda of the John Birch Society.

Very truly yours,
(signed) HENRY W. SAWYER, III

Sawyer's statements are borne out by the record itself. Since the inception of the Police Advisory Board in 1958, a total of 704 complaints have been received (as of January 1, 1966), of which only 38 have resulted in recommendations for disciplinary action against police officers. Surprisingly enough, the police commissioner and the two chief inspectors who receive the recommendations and act on them concurred in every case, and in one increased the recommended penalty. A large proportion of the complaints, 320, have been settled without a hearing, either by the complainant's failing to pursue the matter or by an amicable concord between the complainant and the accused officer, with the board acting as intermediary.

In reality it is the board, not the police, that is handcuffed. It has no decisive power, only the grant to recommend. It does not have its own investigators and must rely on police reports. It is understaffed and bogged down by a backlog of cases. It has been forced to spend an inordinate amount of time defending itself against the FOP's attacks, especially two legal actions. The first, filed in 1960, was a suit for an injunction which was withdrawn when the board agreed to changes in procedure. The second, in 1965, seeks an injunction to prevent the board from operating, and as of this writing is still pending.

The board is also crippled by rules which prevent its obtaining all the information necessary. One rule denies it access to police records in homicide cases, which, as two recent cases show, effectively bars the board from considering the most serious kind of malpractice possible: that which results in death. A week after the 1964 riots, while tensions were still high, a white driver and his Negro passenger were signaled to a halt by a police patrol car for a minor traffic violation. Because the car was borrowed and they did not have the ownership papers, the pair fled. After a high-speed chase, they were halted at a barricade. The driver, emerging from the car with his hands up, was summarily shot in the head and killed by a sergeant. The Negro passenger was soundly beaten by the sergeant's partner. A coroner's jury ruled the case justifiable homicide on the grounds the law permits the use of deadly force against fleeing felons, even though the victim was in the act of surrendering. The board could not get the records and hence was powerless to reckon with the fitness of the officers to wear the police badge.

A complaint form filed with the board by Mrs. Lilly Davis

bears mute testimony to the frustrations of the board. On July 6, 1966, her son Isaiah M. Davis, age nineteen, and another Negro teenager, William Rainey, stole an automobile and took a brief joyride. When they returned the car to the theft scene they were accosted by its owner, off-duty patrolman John W. Boyd, Jr. Although a number of witnesses agreed that the youths offered no resistance, Boyd pistol-whipped them and shot Davis, who died in a hospital the next morning. A coroner's inquest bound the case over to the grand jury, which failed to return a criminal indictment against Boyd. He remained on active duty, shielded from any action by the board by the peculiar clause in its charter.

That the board is severely limited in its authority is realized by most victims of police malpractice, and they consequently have little stomach for lodging formal complaints and leaving themselves open to further police abuse. A case in point happened in the Richard Allen Homes, a low-income housing project that is overwhelmingly Negro. Because the police chronically crash into apartments without warrants and terrorize the occupants, residents of the project have dubbed it the "Torture Pit." Recently, two policemen tried to break into an apartment but were barred by a young Negro serviceman home on furlough from Vietnam. Infuriated, the officers forced the door. One slugged the youth, and when he tried to defend himself the other laid into him with a nightstick. At the hospital where he was being treated for multiple fractures, the young man told Clarence Farmer, executive secretary of the Police Advisory Board, that he preferred not to sign a complaint against the police. His mother likewise declined with the comment, "We have to live there."

Despite its helplessness in homicide cases, the board serves a generally useful purpose as a means of catharsis for indigent and illiterate slum dwellers who bear the brunt of police maliciousness. "Most complainants are not vindictive," Clarence

Farmer advises. "They realize the officer probably has a family and they don't want him punished. But they think someone ought to know what happened, and often the matter is settled without a hearing. There's a great need for this kind of thing."

The actual role of the board was described by its first chairman, the late Dr. Clarence E. Pickett: "We know that on the whole the police don't like us and haven't wanted us but they cooperate very well with us. The police represent the strong arm of the city. We represent citizen concern—for common decency to be observed in the community. . . ." In hearings on the FOP injunction against the board, Maurice B. Fagan, chairman of the Philadelphia Fellowship Commission, sounded a positive note with the observation that "there has been a tremendous improvement in respect for the police; there are far fewer wild rumors flying."

In effect the board has served as a pyschological deterrent to extremists of both sides. Yet, despite the fact that the board is carefully circumscribed, the FOP and Philadelphia's rank and file seem determined to get rid of it, a course that is emblematic of police absolutism. "Totally negative police opposition to review boards is both wrong in principle and strategically foolish," stated Professor Herbert L. Packer of the Stanford University Law School in April 1966. "To reject it categorically and in advance seems to deny that the police are part of society . . . the sensible strategy for police is to accept it, to domesticate it, and make it their own. . . ."

Yet the police are dead set on totally negative opposition. The climactic battle over the nascent New York City civilian review board in 1966 makes it abundantly clear that there will be no compromise.

12

The Great Battle of the New York Review Board

It was, it seemed, the battle at Armaggedon that was fought on the sidewalks of New York City during November 1966. The warring factions had been building their forces since the previous June, when Mayor John V. Lindsay installed a civilian-dominated review board to watch over the conduct of The Finest. The board was the fulfillment of a promise made in May 1965 during the election campaign. "It is time, then, for police procedures to be strengthened in accordance with our traditions [of due process]," Lindsay had proclaimed. "It is time for independent review to be joined with professional knowledge." But the appointment of a majority of civilians to the already existing board had touched a raw nerve with the police. Commissioner Vincent J. Broderick had left after a bitter exchange with the mayor. The appointment of Howard Leary, who had "learned to live with civilian review" in Philadelphia, did little to still the petulant rank and file. In an unprecedented move, the powerful Patrolmen's Benevolent Association plunged openly into politics by suing to have the issue put to a referendum on the November 8 ballot. The suit was successful, and civilian review became Question 1 on the ballot and the most hotly debated issue of the campaign.

The pressures for a civilian review board in New York had been mounting for some time. The Marchi State Senate Committee had held hearings on the subject, and bills to install civilian review had been introduced intermittently in the City Council. The Weiss Bill sponsored by Councilman Theodore S. Weiss was opened to hearings in 1964 and 1965. The bill had been impelled by the killing of two Puerto Ricans in police custody on November 15, 1963. According to the police version (the only version, since there were no witnesses), the Puerto Ricans were arrested for public intoxication and placed in the back seat of the patrol car. The police decided to return to the 24th Precinct by way of the West Side Highway to avoid traffic. At the West Side Underpass, one of the Puerto Ricans whipped out a gun and fired, striking the dashboard. The police returned the fire, killing both prisoners. A grand jury had no choice but to return a no bill, since there was no evidence to contradict the police version. But even conceding that one of the handcuffed prisoners did manage to produce a gun and fire it, there was no reason to kill both, and certainly no excuse for the gross negligence in failing to search the prisoners at the time of arrest.

The civilian-review movement was given further impetus by the series of incidents of undue force that culminated in the Harlem riots in the summer of 1964. About this time the Committee on Civil Rights of the New York County Lawyers Association offered a compromise plan which, if accepted by the police, might have blunted their opponents' drive. The plan called for the addition of one or two "outside civilians" to the existing departmental board, which consisted of three non-sworn deputy commissioners and was misleadingly called the Civilian Complaint Review Board. To placate the police, the plan proposed that the additional member or members be former judges or others with experience in weighing evidence rather than representatives of so-called pressure groups. Mild as the plan was—it would have left the department with the upper hand—it failed to evoke a conciliatory attitude on the part of the police. Then Commissioner Michael Murphy rejected it out of hand with the supercilious statement that he could see "no valid, logical or practical reason" for permitting civilians on the board.

The clamor for civilian review was renewed. In April 1965 a delegation of thirty Puerto Rican leaders told Mayor Robert Wagner at a City Hall conference that their community's relations with the police department was "at its lowest ebb." Since the two Puerto Ricans had been fatally shot in the police car, they charged, there had been nine deaths and six "maimings" of their people; during February and March 1965, four Puerto Ricans had been found hanged in police precinct cells. Gilberto Gerena Valentin, president of the National Association for Puerto Rican Civil Rights, bluntly told Wagner that "every single case that has been brought up to be investigated and and/or prosecuted by the police intra-trials has been whitewashed."

On June 29, 1965, the police and their supporters were given the chance to present their case against civilian review at the Weiss hearings. The scene at City Hall that day was one that few New Yorkers who saw it will soon forget. Thousands of off-duty policemen in uniform, with service revolvers strapped on and wearing PBA buttons (the buttons were later removed at the request of the police commissioner) tightly ringed City Hall and packed its corridors. Many carried signs with such slogans as "WHAT ABOUT CIVIL RIGHTS FOR COPS," "DON'T TIE OUR HANDS," "SUPPORT THE POLICE DEPT., and "DON'T LET THE REDS FRAME THE POLICE." Adding to the spectacle were dozens of American Nazis and John Birch Society members toting American flags and shouting encouragement to the police. Some of the police pickets yelled at a quiet group of CORE counterpickets, "Go home, finks," "Send 'em to Vietnam where they belong," "Wave a bar of soap at them and they'll all run," and other epithets and obscenities. Over the police radio crackled unauthorized messages urging as many police as possible to join the demonstration; one anonymous voice sang off-key the civil rights song "We Shall Overcome," at the conclusion of which another remarked sourly, "They already have."

Inside in the City Council chambers, the PBA's rough-hewn president, John J. Cassese, in an echo of Senator McCarthy's celebrated bluff with a "list" of numerous Communists in the State Department, was declaiming that a "black book" at police headquarters contained the names of many prominent proponents of civilian review—all Communists or Communist sympathizers. Pressed for names, Cassese feebly named Roger Baldwin, the old warhorse of the ACLU.

The choleric police performance, frightening in its implications, dramatically illustrated the urgent need for civilian control of police conduct. Rev. Dr. Gardner C. Taylor, a former member of the Board of Education and pastor of Brooklyn's largest Protestant church, fired off telegrams to Wagner and other city officials contending that "screaming racial insults by armed police pickets . . . and seizure of police radio network for bigoted messages . . . raise serious questions among Negroes and Puerto Ricans as to whether New York City police are able or willing to protect minorities. . . ." His call for an "immediate investigation of racism among New York police" was seconded by James Farmer, national director of CORE, who had been denounced by police pickets as a "fink."

There was no investigation; Commissioner Broderick attempted to draw off some of the heat by promising certain changes in the departmental board's procedures. An office was to be set up outside the forbidding confines of police headquarters where department personnel in civilian clothes would take complaints and where hearings would be held. In addition, complainants were to be notified in writing of the disposition of their cases. These were minor changes in form, and prompted CORE's Farmer to reply: "The Broderick plan is no more than a beefed-up internal police review and misses the essential element of outside adjudication of police behavior by civilians. No military organization in the nation is allowed to function without civilian review. Why then is the New York police force, a paramilitary organization of 27,000 men, exempt from a procedure so essential to a democratic society?"

The review board as finally appointed by Lindsay on July 7, 1966, did not exclude the police; it was civilian-dominated by a four-to-three margin. Its chairman was Algernon D. Black of the New York Society for Ethical Culture and a director of the NAACP. Civilian members were Dr. Walter I. Murray, a professor of education at Brooklyn College; Manuel Diaz, a leader of the Puerto Rican Community Development Project; and Thomas R. Farrell, an attorney specializing in corporate law who was active in the Catholic Interracial Council. The police representatives were Edward J. McCabe, Deputy Commissioner of Licenses; Deputy Inspector Pearse P. Meagher, a twenty-five-year veteran of the department; and Franklin A. Thomas, Deputy Commissioner of Legal Matters. The board set up offices at 201 Park Avenue South.

"Contrary to expectations," reported Thomas during an appearance at the University of California on March 3, 1967, "the board was not divided along police-civilian lines. There were many unanimous decisions." Yet to the police rank and file, the very existence of the board was catastrophic, and without giving it a chance to prove itself the PBA went all out to destroy it. A petition was filed with the city clerk to place the issue on the November ballot, but it was turned down on the grounds that the board was properly an administrative decision of the mayor and not a political matter. Whereupon the

PBA filed suit in the State Supreme Court (in New York actually the lower court) and won its point. "It is completely within the prerogative of the electorate," opined Justice Irving H. Saypol, the ex-federal prosecutor who sent Julius and Ethel Rosenberg to the electric chair, "to initiate legislation in this area." Thus the PBA, which was to use the slogan "Keep Politics Out of Police Work" in its campaign against the board, plunged deep into the political swim.

At the same time, the Conservative party of New York obtained a qualification to bring the issue of the board to a referendum. The Conservatives, who nominated William F. Buckley, publisher of the *National Review*, as their candidate for mayor in 1965, were using the theme "Support Your Local Police" as a political rallying cry. Not wishing to split the antiboard vote with two referendums, the Conservatives withdrew their action and threw their weight behind the PBA. The police review-board issue was a tailor-made cause for ultraconservatives around the nation; from Dallas, for instance, oil millionaire H. L. Hunt reportedly contributed $10,000 to the PBA campaign.

The campaign turned into one of the most acrid in the turbulent history of New York politics. The PBA side was managed by Norman Frank & Associates, for nine years the policemen's "public relations counsel." Frank, whose posh office suite at 800 Madison Avenue blossomed with anti-review-board literature, is a natty, urbane man with a flair for high-powered publicity techniques. His program to "sell" the PBA's antiboard "product" was budgeted at half a million dollars, and there was a million and a half more in reserve, pledged from the PBA treasury.

Frank's strategy was to conduct a "class" campaign aimed personally at every New Yorker who had ever felt a tremor of fear over street violence. First PBA President Cassese, whose antics such as the "black book" affair at the Weiss Bill hearings were considered a liability, was put under wraps for the duration. Then the ad hoc New York Independent Citizens Committee Against Civilian Review Boards, composed of distinguished New Yorkers, was formed to lend dignity to the occasion. A co-chairman was Barry Gray, the radio personality. "If the police are intimidated," warned Gray on accepting the post, "we're going to have an asphalt jungle."

It was precisely to citizens' latent apprehension over an "asphalt jungle" that Norman Frank keyed his pitch, which pounded on the theme that police cowed by civilian review could not effectively stem the rampage of street crime. "Don't tie the strong arm of the LAW!" exhorted one pamphlet whose cover depicted a policeman with his right arm hogtied behind his back (the pamphlet was withdrawn when it proved to be too "camp" for sophisticated New York). One poster showed looted stores and a rubble-strewn sidewalk, and bore the caption, "This is the aftermath of a riot in a city that *had* a civilian review board." The text carried J. Edgar Hoover's statement that police in cities with review boards were "virtually paralyzed" and a charge by the FOP's John Harrington that the opprobrium of the Police Advisory Board had prevented police from aggressively quelling the 1964 Philadelphia riots. (Unmentioned, of course, was the fact that the worst riots occurred in Los Angeles and other cities that *did not* have review boards.)

Another poster depicted an empty chair and asked: "Why did the minister resign from Philadelphia's civilian review board?" The answer was a quote from Reverend W. Carter Merbrier, a former member, that "most cases involved criminal elements bringing in policemen in an attempt to have their records expunged . . . a lot of people came before the board almost with a sense of revenge . . . I believe sincerely in my heart that the review board was accomplishing nothing." Coupled with this appraisal was the claim of six disgruntled policemen that the presence of the board made them think twice about performing their duty.

The most grabby poster of all showed a young white girl emerging apprehensively from a subway onto a dark street. "The Civilian Review Board must be stopped!" read the caption. "Her life . . . your life . . . may depend on it." The poster was so lifelike one could almost hear the approaching thug's footfalls. "With a Civilian Review Board, it may be the police officer who hesitates, not the criminal." The poster was run in full-page ads in the New York *Times*, and its theme repeated incessantly on radio and television spots and by sound trucks.

Besides using mass-media propaganda, Frank organized a vigorous grass-roots campaign to carry the police message from door to door. At PBA campaign headquarters in the Sheraton-Atlantic Hotel, volunteers manned telephones to solicit neighborhood workers, who were mailed "Abolish the Review Board" kits containing buttons, bumper strips and instructions for a doorbell-ringing drive. Sub-headquarters were set up in the five boroughs and thirty-five storefront operations. The PBA's Conservative party allies were particularly helpful in this phase of the campaign.

All was not solidarity in the police camp, however. For some time the 1,360 members of the Guardians Association of Negro policemen had been on record in favor of civilian review. On June 1, 1965, the membership voted to urge the formation of a board. Reporting on the voting meeting, the weekly *Amsterdam News* of Harlem said several Guardian members complained that "even Negro police officers suffer injustices at the hands of white superiors within the department which they cannot openly discuss because of rigid departmental policies." And, the *News* reported, there was "a growing fear by Negro policemen over the rise of John Birch Society attitudes on the part of many white policemen while on duty."

On November 4, 1966, four days before the election, the Guardians, who also are members of the PBA, filed suit against the PBA for allegedly illegally spending members' dues in its political campaign to quash the review board. "They have taken the money of Negro and Puerto Rican policemen," said President William Johnson, "and engaged themselves in a racist and divisive campaign." The suit charged that PBA President Cassese not only refused to consult with the Guardians but "has publicly accused petitioners of having put their race ahead of their jobs as policemen." The respondents had until after the election to reply, and the matter is still in litigation.

The forces opposing the PBA were not as organized and well financed. Coalesced into a group known as FAIR (Federated Associations for Impartial Review), the review-board partisans took space in the aging Governor Clinton Hotel and launched an austere campaign of distributing literature, giving telephone pitches, and making speeches before neighborhood groups. The effort was directed by an irrepressible, rumpled man named David L. Garth, a professional press agent who had assisted in the radio and television phases of the Lindsay mayoral campaign. This time Garth's meager budget could stand little in the way of media presentation.

The largest single group behind FAIR was the Anti-Defamation League of B'nai Brith. When the question of a referendum first arose, Arnold Forster, general counsel to the ADL, announced that his organization "legally and substantively opposes efforts by the Patrolmen's Benevolent Association and the Conservative party to bring the matter of a police review board to a referendum on the November ballot." Seymour Graubard, the ADL's New York chairman, declared that police opposition to civilian participation "tends to increase minority group-police department frictions."

Among those supporting FAIR were Mayor Lindsay, U.S. Senators Jacob Javits and Robert F. Kennedy, former U.S. Attorney General Herbert Brownell, and columnist Jimmy Breslin, who noted that he himself came from a "cop family." After viewing the PBA's videotape commercials, which showed marching youth gangs, the aftermath of a riot, and the frightened girl of poster fame, Lindsay angrily commented, "These commercials spread all over New York City by the PBA and the Conservative party are base and false and deeply insulting to the intelligence of a free people."

The high-tension campaign produced cries of extremism on both sides. PBA supporters implied that because the New York Communist party had favored the board, the entire FAIR organization had been infiltrated by Communists. Treading on factually sounder ground, FAIR partisans charged that the PBA campaign was being cynically exploited by right-wing extremists. In a joint statement on October 26, 1966, Senators Javits and Kennedy said: "We believe it is significant also that the John Birch Society by its own statements has made it clear that it sees this campaign and similar efforts across the country as a guise behind which it can broaden its influence and openly expand its membership." The society admittedly has given high priority to the recruitment of police officers, and the anti-review-board stand was one more lure in the "Support Your Local Police" program.

Toward the windup of the campaign, a new issue was injected that for a time overshadowed the issue of civilian review. It revolved around a "sleeper clause" in the PBA referendum which forbade any city official, the mayor included, in any way to authorize action against the police department upon civilian complaints. As interpreted broadly, the clause would shield the department from outside investigation of graft, corruption, bribery and tie-ins with organized crime. "It will isolate the police department in a way that is unequaled in any other part of the United States," warned Robert Kennedy. "It's a most dangerous precedent." Lindsay saw the clause as an attempt "to totally insulate the biggest department in the City of New York from any performance control, inspection and investigation."

Perhaps the most remarkable feature of the campaign was the avid and unabashed campaigning of the police themselves —a performance so bold and partisan that it underscored Lindsay's fears of police defiance of civilian authority. Bluecoats buttonholed pedestrians on Manhattan sidewalks, giving them the anti-review-board message and handing out literature. Patrol cars were converted into rolling billboards decrying civilian review. Police used their citation powers discriminately: automobiles bearing pro-review-board signs were ticketed at the slightest real or imagined infraction, while those with anti-review-board signs were indulged to the point of absurdity. It became an "in" game to fasten an "anti" sticker on one's bumper and park all day in a meter zone.

The abuse of police discretionary power was graphically demonstrated in an incident on the West Side. On October 24, 1966, a young man whom we shall call Richard Berle was walking on 72nd Street when he encountered a group of Young Conservatives passing out leaflets condemning the review board. He hied himself to a nearby Reform Democratic Club, obtained a supply of pro-review-board literature, and began handing it out from a position near the Young Conservatives. Before long a police lieutenant and two patrolmen arrived and ordered him to stop distributing on the grounds that he was creating a disturbance. Standing on his legal right to distribute, the young man disengaged himself from the police and continued to hand out the literature. Thereupon the lieutenant ordered his arrest, and when two bystanders protested they were also arrested—for "disorderly conduct." The three were hauled off to the 20th Precinct station.

At the station, Berle recounted, "they asked me who I was representing, whether I was being paid, and whether I was a

Communist." After bombarding him with such intimidating questions for half an hour, the police called pro-review-board headquarters to advise them of the arrests. Two assemblymen went to the station to secure Berle's release, but the police stalled. Finally, they reached State Supreme Court Justice Harry Frank at home. Frank called the desk sergeant and told him to release the men. The sergeant refused, saying he did not know the judge's voice and could not be sure of his identity. At 3 A.M. a written order signed by Justice Frank arrived at the station. Still the sergeant balked, contending he could not be sure it was the judge's signature. The three remained in cells while the Young Conservatives presumably were home in bed after a night of unmolested campaigning.

Incidents of this nature marked the campaign. A citizen who admonished occupants of a patrol wagon for displaying "Stop the Civilian Review Board" signs was gruffly challenged, "You looking for trouble, Mac?" and arrested for "disorderly conduct" when he insisted that the signs were not proper. Two Lower East Side residents who objected to anti-review-board stickers on a patrol car were booked for "disturbing the peace." A sixteen-year-old boy of Brooklyn lodged a complaint with the review board that on October 21, 1966, he was carrying literature he intended to distribute in an apartment house when he was accosted by a policeman. "He asked me what I was carrying," the youth reported, "and I told him, 'It's for the civilian review board.'" The policeman accused him of loitering, so he began to walk away. The policeman then called to a gang of youths, "Take him to the back and burn the papers." The gang hustled him to the back of a store, the youth said, and grabbed his literature. His story was corroborated by a Department of Corrections employee who witnessed the incident.

This kind of muscle-flexing intimidated many. For example, the Council of Citywide Small Business Organizations, representing 25,000 businessmen, announced it was endorsing the review board but not actively participating in the campaign. "We've found many storeowners support the board," explained Louis Powsner, the council's co-chairman, "but are just afraid of putting up posters because they don't want any police harassment."

On November 8 the police won a resounding victory at the polls. As the tally wiping out the civilian review board soared, the PBA's John Cassese emerged from the background and, blinking under the harsh television lights, crowed, "I say tonight there are eight million winners. Thank God we saved this city."

There were a number of contributing factors to the review board's defeat. The right-wing vote was surprisingly strong, as evidenced by the unexpected showing of William Buckley in the mayoralty race the previous year. John Garabedian in the New York *Post* November 10 diagnosed the vote as "dividing voters along racial lines, except in Manhattan, where many predominantly white neighborhoods provided the board with its strongest support." There was also an economic stratification to the vote: relatively well-off minority neighborhoods whose middle-class status helped to minimize police malpractice delivered a heavy vote for abolishment. But the crushing margin of almost two to one could be explained only by the publicity *coup* sprung by the PBA. Its slick, emotion-packed campaign had bamboozled the average citizen into believing that safe streets and civilian supervision of the police could not coexist.

Following the review board's defeat, the *Post* recorded the voices of despair from the ghetto. "Now that the board's defeated, the cops are arrogant," said Jesse Gray. "They're going to be more vicious than ever. The PBA is led by a racist, and they think we are asking to much to be partly free." Salvator Cruz sounded a common complaint that the police often ignore trouble calls from the ghetto: "When the police hear the sound of my broken English they don't come when I call. It was bad; now it will be terrible." A middle-aged East Harlem storekeeper predicted: "Even with the board there was brutality. Now there'll be more. I know. I have this business. The police come around asking for free drinks. What can I do?"

The New York PBA, flushed with victory in its first all-out venture into politics, has made rumbles about a strike unless its demands are met. Ironically, the PBA quoted extensively during the campaign from J. Edgar Hoover's denouncements of review boards, including the statement, "One of the major weaknesses of these boards is their inherent political overtone. . . . If there is one thing career police executives have learned over the years, it is that politics have no place in effective law enforcement." Having savored the heady aroma of political victory, the PBA bids well to incorporate politics into law enforcement as a means to realizing its ambitions and preserving the status quo. Success is infectious, and the political means may well spread throughout the law-enforcement body.

The tremendous din over civilian review boards has distracted from the fact that they represent merely a civilian foot in the police door, and that stronger measures are needed to fling the door wide open. As we have seen, the Police Advisory Board in Philadelphia is so circumscribed as to be ineffective in dealing with major abuses. The Rochester, New York, review board, set up in 1963, has been described by former Public Safety Commissioner Harper Sibley, Jr., as playing a valuable symbolic role in easing fears of police mistreatment, but it has been crippled by a series of police attacks. The police-oriented Locust Club, abetted by affidavits sworn to by half the force that the presence of the board inhibits them from their duty, has obtained a court injunction prohibiting the board from functioning while its constitutionality is being tested in the New York courts.

In Washington, D. C., the Complaint Review Board also is

limping along with little real authority. In his column "Potomac Watch" in the Washington *Post* of September 19, 1966, William Raspberry noted the common problem that "the people most likely to need its services have little confidence in it. That is an especially troublesome problem in this city where if any policeman has ever been disciplined for improper actions against a citizen the case does not come readily to mind." The only other civilian review board in a major city, Detroit, Michigan, has just begun to function and it is too early to tell how effective it will be. In Los Angeles and Atlanta, there have been proposals for modified boards that would award complainants up to $500 damages for police abuse yet leave the disciplinary aspect in the hands of the department; reasonable as they are, these proposals have been fought tooth and nail by the police.

One substitute for review boards that has been increasingly advocated is the ombudsman concept, a system used in some European countries and New Zealand to receive and investigate civilian complaints against all branches of city government. Former New York Commissioner Vincent Broderick, who was ousted because of his opposition to civilian review, is amenable to the idea. "I suspect that the police officers here would not object to the ombudsman," he told the *Post* on October 19, 1966, before testifying before the State Senate Committee on City Affairs, "because it applies to all civil servants and would not single them out." At first the PBA, basking in the glow of its win at the polls, was not inclined to oppose the ombudsman. But shortly after, the PBA bowed to a deluge of protest from its affiliates across the country and announced that it would in fact strenuously contest the ombudsman proposal.

The President's National Crime Commission in its report sidestepped the contentious issue of civilian review. "In view of the extreme claims made for and against civilian review boards," it said, "the commission has been struck by how little is known in fact about their successes and failures." After due deliberation, the commission proposed to advocate instead a version of the ombudsman. A first draft of the report acknowledged that there must be "an effective administrative procedure for reviewing the complaints of citizens who are not satisfied that they have been treated fairly within the police department" and placed the problem as "part of the larger problem of dealing with complaints against official agencies generally. . . . It seems unreasonable to single out complaints against the police as the only complaints that should be reviewed," the draft conceded. "The treatment of citizens by housing, sanitation, health or welfare officials should be subject to public scrutiny." But even this watered-down version was unacceptable to the police protagonists, and in the end the commission backed down from fully endorsing the ombudsman.

No matter; the ombudsman still leaves unanswered the ancient question posed by the Roman poet Juvenal: *"Quis custodiet ipsos custodes?"* ("Who shall guard the guards themselves?") The police are not housing inspectors, garbage collectors or welfare caseworkers. They possess a unique grant of power from the state: to use deadly force, to deprive a person of his liberty, and to use discretionary powers in applying the law. All other agencies must rely upon persuasion, public opinion, request or the legal and judicial process. Because of their extraordinary powers, the police must be subject to extraordinary scrutiny.

A debilitating flaw in outside review procedures designed thus far is that action to control the police is initiated only upon the receipt of a specific complaint, leaving unattended the more sweeping abuses of power that accompany police policies. One example is the 1966 police "clean-up campaign" waged in Times Square and Greenwich Village. As one phase of the campaign Tactical Patrol Force men dressed in tight pants, sneakers and polo sweaters loitered in those areas, arresting homosexuals who allegedly solicited them. The ruse posed a substantial legal question of whether the police were crossing the fine line dividing legitimate investigation from entrapment, but the question was never resolved because of the vulnerability of homosexuals. Although Chief Inspector Sanford Garelik expressed the hope that instances in which police tricked homosexuals into breaking the law in order to arrest them would be reported, a spokesman for the Mattachine Society of New York, an organization which provides information on legal and medical services available to homosexuals, scoffed at Garelik's naïveté. "The last thing homosexuals are going to do is complain about something," the spokesman was quoted in the *Times*, April 2, 1966. "They'll just sit there like a possum, they're so afraid of their families' finding out, or losing their jobs."

Another illustration of the need for a self-starting body to monitor police activity is the 1966 Gallashaw case in Brooklyn. On a hot August day police moved in to break up a skirmish between Negro youths and young whites belonging to a group with the taunting name SPONGE—the Society for the Prevention of Negroes Getting Everything. Suddenly eleven-year-old Eric Dean, a Negro bystander, fell dead with a bullet in his chest. Police denied firing a shot, but the Negro community was up in arms, certain that either the police or whites were responsible. A week later, when detectives arrested a flashy, street-wise youth for the murder, all but the diehards sadly agreed on how the investigation was running. For the suspect was Ernest Gallashaw, a Negro and the possessor of an arrest record; two witnesses had reported seeing him climb onto a roof, point a pistol at a police officer, and hit the boy instead.

But Gallashaw steadfastly denied guilt, and when an unusual decision to free him on bail drew suspicion to the arrest, the *Times* sent a team of reporters onto the streets. They learned that the Gallashaw indictment was based solely upon stories told by an emotionally disturbed fourteen-year-old and an eleven-year-old later adjudged incompetent to testify under oath. Both were Negroes, and they recanted their signed statements to the reporters. Moreover, the reporters discovered that the police had chosen to ignore the testimony of another young Negro that he had seen a white boy fire the fatal shot. As the *Times* series of articles unfolded, District Attorney Aaron Koota agreed to an early trial. After hearing the state's flimsy case, a jury acquitted Gallashaw.

A statement issued by CORE charged that the affair was "a cynical scheme to relieve tensions in the East New York area by sacrificing the life of a young black man and the peace and tranquillity of his family." At best it had been a shoddy exhibition of police work, and were it not for the "meddling" of the *Times* "outsiders" a tragic miscarriage of justice would probably have occurred. The case demonstrates the desirability of having an independent body to continually watch over the entire range of police activity.

Such a body, I believe, would most practically take the form of a compact agency composed of experienced investigators empowered to probe specific complaints and, on their own initiative, the general conduct of police business as it relates to proper and ethical methods. On a panel forum, "the Police and the Constitution," sponsored by the University of California Law School on March 4, 1967, I proposed that a federal "truth squad" responsible only to the President or a designated Cabinet member—other than the Attorney General, because of the conflict in interest in being the federal prosecutor—be created to check constantly on the manner in which the federal police agencies discharge their public trust.

As an example of the need for such a squad, I cited the FBI's promiscuous use of wiretaps and "bugs" that has recently come to light and the inability of anyone outside the bureau to plumb the true extent to which these practices are used. The squad would have unrestricted access to agency files, *carte blanche* authority to question agency personnel, and the prerogative to conduct spot checks of all phases of the agency's operation. The squad would be staffed by men intimately acquainted with law-enforcement problems yet far enough removed from law enforcement itself to have a broader perspective; and there are in fact many former law-enforcement officers, disillusioned with the present state of affairs, who could be co-opted into such a squad. It was my opinion that the squad would upgrade federal enforcement by deterring personal misconduct, ferreting out inept, illegal or unethical practices, and bringing a new perspective to old problems.

On the local level, a counterpart to the squad could be established to report directly to the mayor's office. In too many cities mayors have shirked their responsibilities vis-à-vis the police department by adopting a hands-off policy in accord with the old myth that the police must be divorced from politics. The police have never been free of external or internal politics; they have been inexorably bound up in the political authority which delegates them their powers. That this authority should not be exercised in the conduct of police affairs is sheer folly.

Shattering as the idea may be to the police mystique, a firm civilian hand on the police shoulder is one of our best guarantees of effective and ethical law enforcement in a democratic society.

13

The Police Versus the Courts

At 2 A.M. on a December morning in 1964, a Negro postal employee was rudely awakened by the crashing of the door of his Baltimore home. Four armed raiders toting shotguns burst in, shining flashlights in his face and the faces of six children. The raiders identified themselves to the frightened man as Baltimore police officers. Earlier, a schoolteacher was showing slides to a Bible class in her home when six armed men swept in while eight others outside barred her hysterical mother from entry. They too were Baltimore policemen. When a seventy-two-year-old woman refused to answer the insistent pounding on her door, she was arrested by a band of police along with her mentally retarded grandson and grilled for two hours on the pretext of "investigation, suspected of assault and shooting." At a Negro pool hall, officers wearing bulletproof vests and brandishing machine guns held patrons at bay while their partners searched each one.

The police reign of terror was an effort to capture Negro brothers Sam and Earl Veney, who allegedly had killed one policeman and gravely wounded another while escaping from a liquor-store holdup on Christmas Eve, 1964. In a blindly indiscriminate manhunt, a flying squad of some fifty officers, acting on anonymous and unverified tips, spent nineteen days on round-the-clock raids on more than three hundred houses in Negro neighborhoods of Baltimore. Ironically, the suspects were later apprehended without fuss by the FBI in New York City.

So wanton and reckless was the police disregard for the Fourth Amendment that in July 1966 the U.S. Court of Appeals for the Fourth Circuit, in a unanimous decision, branded the raids "the most flagrant invasions of privacy ever to come under the scrutiny of a federal court." Although the department had issued an order after the raids that its officers must have "probable cause to believe the accused person to be on the premises to be searched," the court was not satisfied. Judge Simon Sobeloff, speaking for the court, pointed out that the police "repentance" came only after it became "manifest" that the suspects had skipped town. "The determination of what constitutes probable cause is still left to the policeman," commented the judge on the department's order. The court handed down a singular order that Baltimore police can no longer stage raids solely on anonymous tips.

In his opinion, Judge Sobeloff made two cogent points. "Lack of respect for the police is conceded to be one of the factors generating violent outbursts in Negro communities," he chided. And he quoted the warning of the late Justice Louis D. Brandeis: "Crime is contagious. If the government becomes a lawbreaker, it breeds contempt for law; it invites every man to become a law unto himself; it invites anarchy."

In their loud and sustained protest over the trend of recent court decisions about the treatment of suspects and the obtaining of evidence, the police look upon themselves as guardians of law and order rather than potential anarchists. Yet the inescapable fact remains—and the Baltimore fiasco is a graphic example—that these court decisions stem from police abuse of power or flouting of the law.

The tandem *Escobedo* and *Miranda* decisions concerning the right of a suspect to remain silent and to have legal counsel have brought the controversy into sharp focus. Until these decisions by the Supreme Court, "Let's go downtown" was one of the more familiar phrases in the police lexicon. It was an invitation to a grilling that most suspects were not really free to decline. Hustled to a bare cubicle in the bowels of the police station known as the "squeal room," alone among strange and menacing antagonists, he was subjected to a protracted verbal battering by relays of cops. It was an ordeal from which few suspects, guilty or innocent, emerged unscathed. More often than not the police got what they wanted—a signed confession.

It was against this backdrop that the high court in 1964 delivered the landmark *Escobedo* decision. Danny Escobedo was a young laborer who wound up in a Chicago police squeal room as a suspect in the slaying of his brother-in-law. After a marathon interrogation, during which his lawyer was in the front room of the station trying unavailingly to see him, he gave the sought-after confession. Afterward he recanted the confession, saying it was obtained under duress. In toppling the conviction, the Supreme Court carefully limited its edict: "We hold only that when the process shifts from investigatory to accusatory—when its focus is on the accused and its purpose is to elicit a confession—our adversary system begins to operate, and, under the circumstances here, the accused must be permitted to consult his lawyer."

In the 1966 *Miranda* decision (Ernesto Miranda was convicted of rape in Arizona) the court further defined the *Escobedo* principle and the constitutional guarantee against self-incrimination. Whenever a person is "deprived of his freedom of action in any significant way," the court ruled, he must be "warned prior to any questioning that he has the right to remain silent, and that anything he says can be used against him in a court of law, that he has the right to the presence of an attorney, and that if he cannot afford an attorney one will be appointed for him prior to any questioning, if he so desires."

This meant that when a police officer in effect says, "Let's go downtown," it is the point in time when the suspect must be advised of the rights he has possessed since the Bill of Rights was written. The thrust of the two decisions is to extend the umbrella of the Bill of Rights to the uneducated, the mentally limited, the ignorant, the gullible, the fearful and the timid. It put indigents, misfits, human tumbleweeds and those entangled for the first time in the relentless machinery of the law on a par with the professional criminal, the white-collar culprit, and the czars of organized crime who have always known their rights and asserted them. "A guy who has been through the mill before is not going to talk anyway," commented Chief of Police Thomas O'Brien of Somerville, Massachusetts, in *Time* magazine August 5, 1966. "Anyone who has had half an education knows his rights, and anyone connected with organized crime isn't going to talk either. So the only people this really protects are the ignorant, and that's not a bad thing."

O'Brien is one of the rare police executives who perceive the wisdom behind court decisions. The day after *Miranda* was handed down I sat in the office of Chief of Police Clarence P. Kelley of Kansas City, a former FBI field official with whom I had once served. Kelley had just returned from a statewide meeting of Missouri peace officers over which the news had broken. "They were stunned," he reported. "One even fired off a telegram to President Johnson in protest." Kelley was at a loss to fathom the despair. "In the FBI we always advised suspects of their rights," he said, "and we didn't seem to have any difficulty getting confessions."

Throughout the police community a furor arose. "The emphasis of the court's decision is on individual rights and the public be damned," fumed Minneapolis' Chief Calvin Hawkinson, one of the court's most persistent critics, in a *Newsweek* interview (June 27, 1966). The ruling "puts the police . . . out of business," mourned Philadelphia's Detective Captain Clarence Ferguson. The police and public are dismayed, wrote Quinn Tamm, executive director of the International Association of Chiefs of Police in a *Police Chief* article entitled "Police Must Be More Free" (May 1966), "that a culprit is allowed to go free because law enforcement officers, through alleged overzealousness, possible errors in judgment, or because of lack of familiarity with the complex restrictions placed upon them sometimes err in dealing with a prisoner and evidence." And Justice Byron R. White, a Kennedy appointee who has emerged as one of the most moss-backed members of the court, bitingly dissented: "In some unknown number of cases the court's rule will return a killer, a rapist or other criminal to the streets . . . to repeat his crime whenever it pleases him."

Justice White's emotional plea is the kind politicians have used to prey on the fears of the citizenry, but in point of fact the courts in upsetting convictions do not necessarily turn criminals loose to victimize society again. After his conviction was reversed, Miranda never saw the outside of prison; he was retried without the tainted evidence, convicted, and sentenced to thirty years. Since the decisions originate in police malpractice, the burden is on the police, not the courts, to mend their ways.

What the Supreme Court has done in *Escobedo* and *Miranda* is not create new laws but lay down ground rules for interrogation based on the long-standing "civilized conduct" yardstick. The rules were long overdue. In England, for instance, the Judges' Rules have since 1918 afforded basically the same guidance to British police. The rulings do not proscript the police from making normal and proper inquiries during the course of an investigation; they merely insist that when the police point the legal juggernaut in the direction of a suspect, they remind him that he can elect to oppose it.

The courts would not have had to step in at all had not police annals been replete with instances of confessions obtained through brutal or subtle extortion. The so-called third degree, a grilling session accompanied by threats, beatings, arm-twisting and other forms of physical and mental torture, is not a storyteller's fiction nor as yet wholly extinct. Many times when I was interrogating a suspect about a crime in which there was both federal and local jurisdiction, he would practically beg to be prosecuted by federal authorities rather than go through the local police mill again. In *The Innocents*, a book dealing with miscarriage of justice, Edward D. Radin correctly observes: "While police brutality in questioning suspects to force a confession is not as prevalent as it once was, it still crops up in the best of police departments, and in some sections of the country this practice has never been abandoned, particularly with suspects who are of minority groups."

In the more sophisticated police circles, physical duress has been supplanted by techniques of bluff, ruse and deception, the use of which has not been found unpalatable by most courts. The hoariest ploy is the tough guy–nice guy rotation: a gruff interrogator who warns he will "throw the book" at the suspect is superseded by a mild-mannered, sympathetic questioner who gradually coaxes an admission. Another technique is to wave a fake telegram at the suspect, telling him police in another city have captured his companion and obtained a confession implicating him. Still another is to have a coached witness "identify" the suspect in the hope that he will be demoralized into confessing; a variation is to have a bogus witness connect him with imaginary crimes, the idea being that he will become rattled and confess to the real crime in order to shed the false accusations.

The common notion that scientific evidence is infallible can be exploited, as is recommended by former New York City Detective Charles E. O'Hara in his police text *Fundamentals of Criminal Investigation*. ". . . the detective can mix pseudoscience in his statements," says O'Hara. "In a hit-and-run case, for example, the interrogator can suggest that blood has been found on the car and that the laboratory experts have determined it to be the victim's blood."

Emotional appeals and tricks failing, O'Hara continues, the investigator "must rely on an oppressive atmosphere of dogged persistence. He must interrogate steadily and without relent, leaving the subject no prospect of surcease. He must dominate his subject and overwhelm him with his inexorable will to obtain the truth. He should interrogate for a spell of several hours pausing only for the subject's necessities in acknowledgment of the need to avoid a charge of duress that can be technically substantiated."

Another widely used police manual, *Criminal Interrogation and Confessions*, is coauthored by Fred E. Inbau, a Northwestern University law professor regarded as a foremost expert on interrogation. It is Inbau's contention that police should be given a "reasonable opportunity" to interrogate suspects before arraignment—without a lawyer present. His manual, termed "the police interrogator's Bible," is heavy on psychological advantage. The interrogator is depicted as "a hunter stalking his game," and his preserve is a small, bare, windowless room that affords absolute privacy. "Display an air of confidence in the subject's guilt," the manual instructs; appear to have "all the time in the world."

In the interrogation proper, Inbau advises that the suspect be shorn of status by being addressed familiarly rather than by the title "Mister." The interrogator should gradually move his chair "closer, so that, ultimately, one of the subject's knees is just in between the interrogator's two knees." He asks rhetorically, "Your mouth's very dry, isn't it?"

The practical application of this kind of theory was illustrated before the Senate Judiciary Subcommittee in 1966 hearings. The case involved the 1962 mugging of an elderly woman, who later died. The suspect, John F. Biron, age eighteen, of Minneapolis, was put through a lengthly verbal wringer; the Senators listened to it on a police tape recording accidentally discovered by the boy's attorney. *"You're* the fella's gonna determine how long you're gonna be buried," came the rasping voice of the detective. *"You* got the shovel. *You're* diggin' the hole." Then the switch: "It's just like you go to confession . . . I'm a Catholic myself." Interspersed throughout the tape were repeated lies that Biron would be handled in juvenile court, even though he was legally an adult. When he finally "spilled his guts," as the police phrased it, he was charged with murder in adult court. After hearing the same tape, the Minnesota Supreme Court threw out the confession and overturned the conviction. Interestingly enough, Biron was subsequently reconvicted on independent evidence the police had all along.

The Kafkaesque climate of the squeal room apparently appalled Chief Justice Earl Warren, for he devoted six pages of his majority opinion in *Miranda* to quoting from police interrogation manuals, including O'Hara's, and summed up: "This atmosphere carries its own badge of intimidation. . . . The . . . practice of incommunicado interrogation is at odds with one of our nation's most cherished principles—that the individual may not be compelled to incriminate himself."

As the leader of a court that has been increasingly firm in curbing police abuse of power, Warren has been the main target of police sniping and the object of an "Impeach Earl Warren" campaign by the John Birch Society. Ironically, he has been accused of being blind to police problems, yet the Chief Justice, unlike many of his critics, has had substantial experience in law enforcement, both as a patrolman on the Berkeley

force during his college days and later as District Attorney
of populous Alameda County, California.

Escobedo and *Miranda* promise to put a crimp in the back-
room shenanigans, not only because they have removed the
profit from illicit interrogation but also because many more
suspects will be able to avail themselves of attorneys' services.
Until the decisions, some 60 percent of criminal defendants
were too impoverished to afford an attorney and had to rely
on the tender mercies of the police. Thus the de facto economic discrimination that has prevailed will all but disappear, and the platitude "equality under the law" will take on
new meaning. Dean Joseph Lohman of the University of California Department of Criminology and a founder of the Southern Police Institute put it succinctly on the *Playboy* "Crisis in
Law Enforcement" panel: "It is precisely to protect the liberties of the weak and indigent that these new court decisions
are being made. . . . Up to now, the police have acted toward
submerged sections of the population without the same re-
straint that they've shown toward the more articulate and ad-
vantaged citizens who have long held power—and enjoyed
the benefits of counsel as a matter of course." Famed attorney
Melvin Belli framed the same thought in less elegant terms:
"We're just damned lucky that we live in a country where the
Supreme Court protects the stumblebum sleeping under the
railroad bridge as zealously as it does the president of the railroad sleeping in his private car."

The police counterargument is founded on the usual pragmatic philosophy: that, as the late Justice Robert Jackson expressed it, "any lawyer worth his salt will tell the suspect in no
uncertain terms to make no statement to police under any
circumstances." Most lawyers will indeed give such advice,
and at first glance the decisions seem to make obsolete the confession as readily obtainable evidence—evidence that many police regard as the *sine qua non* of case investigation. Juries tend

THE POLICE ESTABLISHMENT : 248

to accept inculpatory words from the lips of the accused as the most persuasive kind of evidence, and, even more important from the police viewpoint, the majority of suspects who furnish signed statements wind up pleading guilty—in some jurisdictions the rate runs as high as 90 percent—thus sparing them the trouble of a trial. As *Miranda* gave every suspect the right to counsel prior to interrogation, Justice John M. Harlan, in dissent, bitterly tolled the confession's knell: "This doctrine . . . has no sanction, no sanction. . . . It's obviously going to mean a gradual disappearance of confessions as a legitimate tool of law enforcement."

The knell was sounded far too prematurely. As the police well know, many suspects talk without regard for the consequences. An excellent example of this phenomenon is found in the lie-detector interrogation of Jack Ruby, the admitted slayer of Lee Harvey Oswald, who faced the death penalty should the state be able to prove premeditation. At one point in the interrogation, Ruby was asked a key question by the FBI polygraph operator, Bell Herndon: "Did you tell anybody that you intended to shoot Oswald at any time before you did it?" There ensued this exchange between Ruby and his attorney, Clayton Fowler:

> FOWLER: Again, I don't believe certainly he understands the full complicity of this thing. If there are any questions that are asked that show premeditation on his part, I would respectfully ask that he decline to answer and that you decline to ask it.
>
> RUBY: But it's already in there. I've already told it to the Warren Commission.
>
> FOWLER: Now, if there is an area that has been covered already and you still wish to go into it—I don't want this man—
>
> RUBY: So, would you mind calling Alexander in? [William Alexander, assistant district attorney of Dallas County]
>
> FOWLER: Listen, Jack, will you please listen to me? This man

got up down there and asked the jury to send you to the electric chair.

RUBY: I know it.

FOWLER: He has not changed his opinion yet, and he will again ask it at some later date. Now, is this the kind of man you want to pussyfoot around in here with and let listen to these questions? Just "Yes" or "No." If it is, we'll bring him back in.

RUBY: Yes; I want him in here, and I want you to ask him to come in, please.

FOWLER: . . . I would like this record to reflect that this is against the advice of his attorneys present, and that it will be very detrimental to, No. 1, his appeal, and No. 2, perhaps any clemency that might be asked for in the future, and No. 3, for the actual trial of the case on its merits, if such ever occurs.

In the relatively brief interval since the decisions, all indicators suggest that the results will not be as disastrous as the pessimists predicted. According to a *Saturday Evening Post* editorial of July 30, 1966, a New York *Times* reporter who sat in on a number of interrogations found that the new rules produced no dramatic lessening of the will to confess. "By and large," remarked a detective, "they readily admit what they've been doing even after they've been told of their rights." In July 1966, just after *Miranda*, District Attorney Evelle Younger of Los Angeles County, which has the largest criminal caseload in the nation, ordered a survey on the effect of the new rules. Of 790 defendants who were duly informed of their rights, 433 (nearly 55 percent) went ahead and confessed anyway, a percentage that "amazed" Younger. Evidently, he said, "conscience usually, or at least often, drives a guilty person to confess."

Even more revealing was the survey's finding, based on 2,780 felony cases studied, that confessions were essential to successful prosecution "in only a small percentage of criminal cases." The apparent explanation was that in most crimes the defendants were either caught *flagrante delicto* or observed by witnesses.

One overlooked aspect of the confession controversy is that the suspect who clams up and refuses to say anything at all is in a way furnishing evidence against himself. Under some laws, it is a rebuttable presumption that failure to deny a serious accusation is unnatural and in itself a sign of guilt known as an "adoptive admission." Even where this is not the law, juries are inherently suspicious of defendants who remain silent. Knowing this, most experienced criminals try to set up an alibi or at least supply a plausible explanation for the set of circumstances that has trapped them. Hence the astute investigator remains in the driver's seat despite the courts' diligence on civil liberties. In an article in the American Jurisprudence *Trials* series, "Investigating the Criminal Case," I encouraged the investigator to "persist in asking the suspect about details and fine points of the story. In this way the suspect will entrap himself in inconsistencies and absurdities which, if he remains adamant in spite of them, can be used in court to discredit his tale."

Most experienced lawmen privately acknowledge that the confession alone is a singularly unreliable instrument of justice. There are many persons caught in the police net who are pathological liars or otherwise untrustworthy, who cannot be believed even when they are incriminating themselves. Any student of psychology who has read Theodor Reik's *The Compulsion to Confess* would look skeptically on the uncorroborated confession. False confessions given voluntarily fill the chronicles of criminal justice. In the decade-old "Black Dahlia" case in Los Angeles, the sensational Elizabeth Short murder investigation, there have been approximately 200 "confessions." The frequency of spurious confessions is such that some states now require that in major cases an admission on the part of the accused must be corroborated by independent evidence.

Yet in the face of the confession's proved unreliability, uninformed and intractable segments of the police community continue to impugn the wisdom of the courts. In his memorable outburst in November 1964, only months after the *Escobedo* decision, J. Edgar Hoover took a swipe at the "bleeding heart" judges of the Supreme Court for what he conceived as oversolicitude for the rights of the accused. On May 27, 1967, the G-man chief's hard-line ally, Thomas Cahill of San Francisco, ripped recent court decisions that put "a wall of protection" around the criminal before an audience of Scottish Rite Masons. The pair was merely articulating the sentiments of the majority of police chiefs.

This charged rhetoric obscures a central fact: the de-emphasis of the confession will give law enforcement a tremendous boost toward professional status. For one thing it will ventilate the lingering malodor of the squeal room, a contributing factor to the low esteem in which the police are held. And it will upgrade the investigative process. As former Supreme Court Justice Arthur Goldberg pointed out in concurring with *Escobedo*: "A system of law enforcement which comes to depend on the confession will, in the long run, be less reliable than a system which depends on extrinsic evidence independently secured through skillful investigation. If the exercise of constitutional rights will thwart the effectiveness of a system of law enforcement, then there is something very wrong with that system."

The Detroit department, under Commissioner Ray Girardin, a former police reporter, took Mr. Goldberg's words to heart. It began to give first priority to digging for facts rather than bringing in suspects for the interrogation ritual. The results were eye-opening. Detective Chief Vincent Piersante reported that in 1961, before *Escobedo*, confessions had been deemed "essential" to 20.9 percent of homicide cases; in 1965, the first full year that suspects were advised of their rights, the percentage plunged to 9.3 percent as sharper sleuthing took effect. And surprisingly, the police still got their confessions—more than before.

The overreliance on confessions has dissuaded a large segment of the police from acquiring and burnishing investigative skills. "Once [some police] get a confession," I stated on the *Playboy* "Crisis in Law Enforcement" panel, "they think they have a case all locked up, and this leads to sloppy corroborative detective work. Then, when they go to court and have their case shot full of holes, they wail that the court is coddling the criminal."

With the handwriting on the wall, today's police investigator will have to develop a proficiency—or go on blaming the courts for his own inadequacies. The drafters of the 1872 India Evidence Act, which installed safeguards in India similar to those the Supreme Court has enunciated, foresaw the tendency toward shortcuts: "It is far pleasanter to sit comfortably in the shade rubbing pepper into a poor devil's eyes than to go about in the sun hunting up evidence." Almost a century later a Florida police official colorfully remarked that the Supreme Court's rulings will be "getting the guys who depend on confessions off their duffs" and out searching for reliable evidence.

What the times demand are police officers well grounded in the fundamentals of their profession and familiar with some of the new, sophisticated techniques. Modern investigation calls for the ingenuity and imagination to add new wrinkles to the standard techniques—plying informers for tips (in April 1967, the Supreme Court upheld the constitutionality of the informant system), skillfully questioning witnesses, poring over records, and employing deductive reasoning.

More and more, the immutable, dispassionate scientific aids

are assisting in crime solution. As a result of the court decisions, state and local police agencies in New York have formed the National Association of Police Laboratories to improve the efficiency of police laboratories. "With the confession rulings and the increasing presence of science in everyday life, there's never been a greater reliance by the prosecutor on physical evidence tested under the highest possible standards," stated the group's president, Dr. Bernard Newman, in the New York *Times* of January 22, 1967.

Augmenting conventional scientific examinations such as microscopy and chemical analysis are the recent techniques of nuclear activation analysis, a process so sensitive it can detect a thimbleful of acid in a tank car of water, and Voiceprinting, an electronic method of positively identifying the human voice.* Experimentation is under way on "air prints," the testing of air samples from a crime scene to identify body odors emitted by the criminal. In a California case recently the mathematical law of probability was used to match fragmentary descriptions of a man-and-woman mugging pair to a husband and wife so convincingly that a jury brought in a guilty verdict.

Yet the battle of the police versus the courts promises to go on indefinitely. Mention the Painten case to Boston police, for example, and they shake their heads in bewilderment and disgust. Donald M. Painten had been convicted of the 1958

---

* Voiceprints have already been instrumental in solving several criminal cases, the first being bomb-threat calls to a Connecticut industrial plant. The most dramatic use to date was in the burglary and arson trial of Edward Lee King of Los Angeles. Following the Watts riots of 1965, CBS-TV newsman Bill Stout offered $100 to any person who would tell what he did during the riots, on the condition his identity would not be revealed and his face would not be shown. One man told of participating in looting and burnings of a drugstore, a liquor-store and a furniture store. When King was subsequently arrested on a narcotics charge and Stout's business card was found in his wallet, he was suspected of being the "mystery voice" on the CBS taped interview. He was indicted for burglary and arson and, largely on the testimony of a Voiceprint expert, was convicted. The case is presently under appeal.

robbery of the People's National Bank of Marlboro in which $10,500 was taken. He appealed on the grounds that a police search which uncovered evidence used against him was illegal. The circumstances of the search are set forth in the opinion of the U.S. Court of Appeals:

> Very briefly, two policemen, knowing of a holdup but having no substantial clues, came across petitioner and one Ash, and followed them to petitioner's apartment. Their grounds for suspicion did not, even remotely, amount to probable cause for arresting either Ash or petitioner, either for the holdup or for any other crime. After arranging for plainclothesmen to station themselves at the back of the building, one of the uniformed officers then knocked on the door. He testified as follows:
>
> "I rapped on the door, and a voice said, 'Who is it?' I said, 'Police officers.' The door opened about three inches, and Mr. Painten looked out at me. He saw us. I had my badge in my hand. He said, 'Will you wait a minute?' I said, 'Sure.' He closed the door. As he closed the door, maybe ten seconds later I heard what to me sounded like a window opening and closing. Then, a few seconds after, the door was opened, and we were allowed to enter. . . . I asked who lived there. Painten volunteered it was his apartment."
>
> After entering the apartment, the police noticed a bulge in Ash's pocket, and removed some $200 in crumpled bills. They then called to the plainclothesmen to come up, and received the response that "someone" had thrown "something" out the window. This information led to the discovery on the fire escape on a floor below of a paper bag containing two pistols and some cartridges. Petitioner was thereupon arrested; the apartment was searched, and a large amount of currency was found under a mattress. At petitioner's trial the guns and bullets were introduced as evidence.

The appeals court, which delivered its opinion in 1966, reversed the conviction of Painten on the doctrine established in *Mapp v. Ohio* in 1961, a landmark case. Cleveland police, acting on a tip that gambling paraphernalia would be found in a rooming house run by Mrs. Dollree Mapp, entered the building by waving a piece of paper they said was a search warrant. They ransacked the premises and found no gambling paraphernalia, but took with them some pictures and literature they claimed were obscene. Mrs. Mapp was convicted of possession of obscene material, although no search warrant was produced in court. The Supreme Court held that the police had breached the Fourth Amendment, which "forever secure[d] the people, their persons, houses, papers and effects, against all unreasonable searches and seizures under the guise of law. . . ." The decision set up the so-called exclusionary rule, which dictates that evidence obtained illegally is inadmissible in court. While the rule bars evidence secured in promiscuous, indiscriminate "fishing expeditions," it does not prevent police from conducting a search for specific evidence they have probable cause to believe is present.

In the Painten decision, Chief Judge Bailey Aldrich concluded: "It is apparent that the police, knowing of a crime and knowing that Ash and petitioner were suspicious characters, but having no reason to connect them with the crime they were investigating, set out to arrest and search the men in the hope that evidence would develop. It is precisely such tactics that the Fourth Amendment makes unlawful." Boston detectives told me they had "checked out" Painten because of a prior criminal record, and since they had not conducted themselves in a blatantly lawless manner, they were quite put out over the "technicality" that ruined their conviction. They were also irritated at the reckless conduct of the Cleveland police, which provoked the exclusionary rule. "I used to have a district where there was a lot of action," said one detective, "and I used my instincts to stop a likely person. I found all kinds of violations." With the exclusionary rule, the detective must have probable cause, not mere instinct, and he is rather disgruntled over this curb on his powers.

Hindsight, which is always much easier than foresight, suggests that in the light of the *Mapp* decision, the police jumped the gun in barging in on Painten only because he had a prior record. If he was a suspect for this reason, a more painstaking investigation of his activities and his links with the crime would probably have produced sufficient cause to obtain an arrest warrant, and his premises could have been lawfully searched incident to arrest.

While the police frustrations in trying to do their job under stricter guidelines can be appreciated, it must also be pointed out that only a miniscule fraction of the total police transgressions, ranging from rank misconduct to impropriety, ever reach the courts. Negro guitarist Jackie Washington, for instance, was allegedly beaten without provocation by two Boston patrolmen, yet the internal affairs section of the department supposedly whitewashed the epidode. One young Negro complained to me, "Man, they don't ask you a question without giving you a chop with the forearms." A Negro taxicab driver told me he had picked up a fare the night before, a distraught Negro girl who had just gotten out of a police patrol car. The two white cops, she said, had pulled her off the street and driven around taking turns having intercourse with her; she had consented because she was carrying a bottle of whiskey and they had threatened to "bust" her for intoxication.

A Boston law school student who served as a researcher for the President's National Crime Commission by riding with police in patrol cars during their rounds was appalled at what he saw. "There was sleeping on the job, confiscating of beer from stores and bars, bigoted talk, constant criticism of superiors, verbal abuse of persons questioned, and some physical abuse," the law student told me in a private discussion. "We estimated that 30 to 50 percent of police time in Boston is wasted." He concluded that about 10 percent of the officers were members of the Birch Society, and that an overwhelming percentage of the rest held Birch beliefs. He felt that the commission's report on this phase of the research only hinted at the actual state of affairs; that it has been toned down in order not to undermine proposed legislation to increase police powers.

The commission report, incorporating similar research in Chicago and Washington, was indicting enough in its own right. Based on observations of 5,339 encounters between police officers and citizens on 850 eight-hour patrol shifts, it concluded that 15 percent of the street interviews between policemen and Negroes contained some form of overt hostility or prejudice by the officer against the Negro; that of twenty incidents of brutality or excessive force, the overwhelming number were directed against poor and indigent citizens both white and Negro; and that many incidents of corruption and payoffs seemed to be "highly organized." That this may be only the tip of the iceberg is indicated by the fact the police were aware they were being monitored. Executive Director James Vorenberg of the commission commented that he hoped the survey did not reflect a national pattern, but if it did, it "should be a red flag for police administrators."

One of the most redundant police charges is that the courts are not merely interpreting laws but are in effect creating new laws hindering the police—the last bulwark between society and the criminal. By the same token, it can be said that the courts are the last bulwark between society and the police.

14

Birchers in Blue and the Red Hang-up

From New York to California, a prairie fire of right-wing activity has swept through the nation's police system. Imbued with the John Birch Society's radical brand of anti-Communism, police are using their powers in almost vigilante fashion to harass, intimidate, Red-bait and blacklist not only avowed Communists but liberals and others whose views are politically left of center.

Mostly submerged, sometimes surfacing, the tactics are disturbingly reminiscent of one of the greatest anti-Communists of all time, Adolf Hitler. The American police are still far short of a Gestapo—most would indignantly reject the comparison—but their proclivities have been too obvious to ignore. Take, for example, the fact that one of the most capable and politically moderate police chiefs in the United States has been one of the victims.

Edward J. Allen has impressive credentials. He comes from a police family; his father, uncle and older brother were policemen. In 1936 he joined the Erie, Pennsylvania, department and quickly earned a reputation as a hard-nosed, incorruptible cop. In 1948, on the recommendation of the FBI, he was named chief of police in Youngstown, Ohio, by a reform mayor determined to rid the city of racket rule. Allen fearlessly took on such crime-syndicate bigwigs as Pete Licavoli, head of the notorious Purple Gang; Vito Genovese, reputedly the nation's number-one crime czar, and Charles "Lucky" Luciano. His achievements were of such an order that his colleagues named him chairman of the Organized Crime Committee of the International Association of Chiefs of Police.

In 1955, with the endorsement of Ohio's Governor Frank Lausche, the hard-driving troubleshooter moved to Santa Ana, California, to clean up a force ridden with internal dissention and graft scandals. His sure hand transformed the force into a model of efficiency: it earned a wide reputation for its traffic safety record and its ability to solve cases at a rate 50 percent above the national average. But to a clique of officers who were members of the John Birch Society, Allen's talents were secondary to the fact that he was a political moderate, and he became a marked man.

In 1964, Allen was the target of a subversive plot that wracked the department and inflicted wounds that still have not healed. Its object was to roust Allen from office and replace him with a chief who would be in effect a puppet of the Birchers. The power grab took the alternating forms of harassment and attempts to discredit Allen. His home telephone rang late at night and before dawn, unordered flowers and other merchandise arrived C.O.D., fire trucks raced to his home on false alarms, advertisements appeared that he had automobiles or dogs for sale, and unsummoned taxis came to pick him up.

In trying to impugn the integrity of their chief, the Birchers circulated what City Manager Carl J. Thornton termed "anonymous and libelous" pamphlets questioning his honesty and morality. Once, for instance, when Allen accepted an honorarium for a television appearance, he was accused of bribetaking. Some of the pamphleteering was done through the

Police Benefit Association, which was under the control of the Birchers; the association put out news bulletins with coded messages condemning the chief. Some was done by mail—members of the City Council received copies—and by handouts from police cars parked around headquarters.

When the situation became unbearable, City Manager Thornton ordered a full investigation under the direction of an independent local attorney. "The situation has, in my opinion, become intolerable and potentially a danger to the welfare and safety of the people of the community," he said. Almost simultaneously, Chief Allen fired two alleged ringleaders, a captain and a lieutenant, for refusal to answer questions about police matters and about the Police Benefit Association. The officers were not being dismissed, Allen said in the Los Angeles *Times* November 7, 1964, for any possible membership per se in the Birch Society. "It was a question of insubordination and failure to cooperate."

The investigation determined that the clique consisted of some dozen Birchers and sympathizers who, it was confirmed, had attempted to seize control of the department. After almost eight months of personnel board hearings, the two dismissals were modified to seven months' suspension without pay.

Where the Bircher police had failed, the City Council almost succeeded. Santa Ana is the hub of Orange County, a sprawling metropolitan area of more than one million people between Los Angeles and San Diego; its political climate is as reactionary as the weather is balmy. In 1964 the county bucked the national trend by going 56 percent for Barry Goldwater, and it boasts the only avowed Birch member in the California legislature. The *Freedom* newspaper chain, which blankets the county, is published by a man who denounces public schools and libraries as socialistic and advocates private police in lieu of a public force.

Thus in Santa Ana it was not at all unusual that the Birch

Society, through its aggressive tactics, should have placed several members on the City Council, and not at all unpredictable that the council should be split on the Allen versus the Bircher cops issue. At one point the council was on the verge of asking for the chief's resignation, but it finally settled for the reduced penalites against the two fired officers.

In July 1965, I talked to Chief Allen at police headquarters in the opulent new Public Safety Building. His office is unusual for a police chief: there is piped-in classical music, a statue of St. Francis of Assisi and a copy of Gainsborough's *The Blue Boy* (ironically, the original painting hangs in the Huntington Art Gallery in nearby San Marino, Western regional headquarters of the John Birch Society). The lone symbol of his metier is a nightstick hanging on the wall, a relic of his rookie days on the beat in Erie.

Nor is Allen cast wholly in the police chief mold. Certainly he is in character in decrying the "overdose of sex being shoved down the throats of young and old Americans by the hucksters of Madison Avenue and Hollywood," in lamenting the court decisions he feels have hampered law enforcement, and in regretting the lack of respect generally accorded the police. And as a disciplinarian who does not drink or smoke, he is considered by some to be "unreasonable, dictatorial and too strict."

Yet the stern-faced man with the piercing blue eyes is not insensitive to the world outside the police sphere. His mood lightens when he talks of art, music and man's nobler instincts. He is, of all things, a passable poet, turning out verse on myriad subjects. More in keeping with his background, he also authored *Merchants of Menace: The Mafia*, an authoritative book drawing on his boundless knowledge of the underworld.

Not all who attempted to undermine him were Birchers, Allen told me. "But the John Birch Society was the cement that bound them together. If they got into difficulties, they felt the Society would support them." Some citizens who were Birchers gave the dissidents help, he said, but others flatly stated they did not approve.

At the time I talked to Allen, the hubbub over Birchism had subsided and a state of uneasy truce prevailed. The two suspended officers had returned, and all concerned had professed a desire to return to the normal order. But judging from the chief's conversation, he retained a visceral feeling that a loaded gun was still pointed at his head. "I know they got to read all my mail," he said. "They accused me of using official stationery to correspond with my police friends in the East. And I suspect they still read it."

The Santa Ana experience has been duplicated, to one degree or another, in many departments across the country. In 1963 in Philadelphia, when it was discovered that some fifteen officers were Birch members, Mayor James H. J. Tate acted with dispatch in withdrawing them from general duty, initiating disciplinary proceedings and probing the extent of Birch entrenchment in the force. Following the doctrines of the society, Tate contended, would detract from the officers' effectiveness. "This is a situation where they are not attuned with law-enforcement problems," he told the press. "They are against certain groups in the big cities. The police department . . . should be above reproach." Tate compared certain Birch Society traits with those manifested in the early days of Nazism and Communism and took the position that police officers who espoused them could not impartially perform their duties.

In Independence, Missouri, a large suburb of Kansas City, Chief Orson F. Myers suspected that a number of policemen were members of the Minutemen, an ultraright paramilitary group headquartered nearby. Like the Birch Society, the Minutemen have made a special effort to proselytize law-enforce-

ment officers. Myers, a retired FBI agent, demanded that Minutemen resign forthwith or face being fired. In October 1966,
when a Minutemen band was intercepted by New York City
police on their way, police said, to fire-bomb leftist summer
camps in upstate New York, with a possible high toll of human life, it was revealed that two New York state policemen
were members of the organization and had tipped off the
Minutemen on the camps' layouts and police emergency plans.
In December 1967, Chicago Superintendent Conlisk professed
"shock" when a nucleus of six Ku Klux Klan patrolmen was
discovered; three resigned, and three were suspended.

In Trenton, New Jersey, Chief Louis Neese incorporated
sections of a Birch "Support Your Local Police" circular into
a declaration of departmental policy. The circular tags criticism of the police as Communistic, blasts the CBS television
documentary "Biography of a Bookie Joint" as "designed to
make all working 'cops' look like grafting bums," charges that
the federal marshals overseeing integration at the University
of Mississippi "actually created most of the rioting," and describes the civilian review-board concept as the product of
"gullible do-gooders and bleeding hearts."

Paradoxically, the sophisticated city of New York supports
a police department in which Birch-style activity is brisk if not
rampant. During the 1964 Goldwater-Johnson campaign,
Bircher policemen peddled copies of *None Dare Call It Treason* in precinct stations; the ranting tract accuses successive
Presidents beginning with Franklin D. Roosevelt of selling
out to the Soviets and exhorts readers to join the John Birch
Society. "Support Your Local Police" circulars blossomed on
bulletin boards, and on election eve the radios in 700 police
cars burst forth with Goldwater campaign slogans.

The police brass reacted to these breaches of regulations
with a boys-will-be-boys attitude. The radio incident was
brushed off as "just kidding around over the air," despite the

fact that extraofficial transmissions are in violation of both departmental and Federal Communications Commission regulations. The Birch propaganda on the bulletin boards was also overlooked. In an extraordinarily disingenuous statement, Deputy Commissioner Walter Arm said he knew of no Birchers on the force and did not plan to look for any; shortly thereafter the regional director of the Birch Society, Thomas J. Davis, boasted there were at least 100 Birchers on the force. Commissioner Michael Murphy gingerly sidestepped the issue by putting it on a strictly legal plane, and in 1966 departmental and city attorneys ruled that the society was not a political organization within the meaning of the state penal code and city charter, thus making police membership not illegal.

The Los Angeles department is probably the most "yahoo" police group in the United States. Early in 1965, John Rousselot, then national public relations director of the John Birch Society, claimed 2,000 members among Los Angeles County law officers. When I talked to him in September 1965, he qualified this somewhat by saying that the figure included all levels of law enforcement—prosecutors and their staffs, judges and court staffs, and federal agents.

If accurate, the 2,000 figure is a staggering concentration of militant ultrarightists in law enforcement. Yet the profusion of Birch activity on the Los Angeles department suggests that the estimate is not grossly exaggerated. During the 1964 Presidential campaign, police patrol cars could be seen pulling up at the pet-food plant of the late Dr. D. B. Lewis, radio sponsor of Robert Welch and Billy James Hargis, who willed $1,000,-000 to the society, to obtain supplies of right-wing literature, including *None Dare Call It Treason*. The propaganda was openly distributed from the patrol cars.

The pro-Goldwater partisanship became so blatant that Chief Parker, noting that "members of the department are thoughtlessly wearing campaign slogans and insignia on visible portions of their clothing while on duty," issued Memorandum No. 32 dated September 14, 1964, which ordered that officers "refrain from becoming identified with any political controversy while engaged in the official performance of duty." An officer who flaunted the order by selling right-wing political tracts in the jail was handed a fifteen-day suspension.

Judging from the bulletin boards in the precinct stations, the extremist infection is highly virulent. One notice posted by authority of the watch commanders announced the appearance of Karl Prussion, an ex-Communist who now prowls the right-wing lecture circuit giving dire warnings of the Red menace, at the Police Academy on March 19, 1962. "You will hear a man who knows what the Communist Party has done, and is doing," puffed the notice. "How they planned the San Francisco riots, and the subsequent charges of police brutality!" Another notice advised that *Human Events* would be received at every precinct station, the cost to be borne by "interested people [who] have gone to great expense to bring you this important news publication." The notice instructed that each issue was to be filed "for immediate and future reference," and that each precinct custodian "arrange with members of the other shifts or watch to assist you in the maintenance of *Human Events* during the periods you may not be on duty." *Human Events* is an ultraright tabloid started in 1944 under the patronage of Gen. Robert Wood and several other members of the old America First Committee. At one time or another it has labeled Walter Reuther "a ruthless labor dictator and one of the most mischievous Socialist leaders in the country"; lumped together "the leftists, the one-worlders, the modern educationists"; and alluded to the ugly activity of the bus-riding integrationist agitators."

The appearance of Prussion and the distribution of *Human Events* were but two of the many activities sponsored by the Fire and Police Research Association of Los Angeles (Fi-Po), a shrill propaganda apparatus that is unprecedented in the nation's major public protection services. Fi-Po describes itself as "composed of active, sworn members of the Fire and Police Departments of the City of Los Angeles. Our objective is to inform the membership and the general public of the subversive activities which threaten our American way of life. The organization researches and disseminates only documented and factual material."

One "factual" scoop, published in a 1963 issue of *Fi-Po News,* was the disclosure that folk music was a Communist plot. "L.A. ARRESTS EXPOSE COMMIES!" screamed the headlines in the March 1964 issue. "Folk Music Center Seen as Recruitment Base—Interlocking Front Activities Unmasked." The lead sentence of the article read, "FBI Chief J. Edgar Hoover's warnings that this nation's youth is the number one target of the Communist Party have been confirmed by accelerated Party activity, coupled with recent arrests in Hollywood." The article strained mightily to implicate folk singing and folk music as an integral part of the Communist conspiracy, and was so ludicrous that the wire services impishly picked it up and made Fi-Po something of a nationwide laughingstock.

Fi-Po also arranges for the appearances of prominent right-wing speakers before police audiences. The August 1961 edition of *Fi-Po News,* for example, announced a program at the Police Building Auditorium featuring Dr. Fred Schwarz of the Christian Anti-Communism Crusade, who "gave up a flourishing medical practice to devote full-time to fighting this atheistic menace." It was also advertised that Fi-Po had concluded arrangements with Dr. Schwarz for police officers to attend his Southern California School of Anti-Communism at the special fee of $10, "half the regular price." The "very serious problem of Communism" would be taught by such instructors as Herbert Philbrick, author of *I Led Three Lives,* and W. Cleon

Skousen, who wrote *The Naked Communist*. Philbrick, a one-time infiltrator of the Communist party in Boston for the FBI, is now a professional lecturer on the anti-Communism circuit. Skousen is an ex-FBI agent, former chief of police in Salt Lake City and editorial director of the police periodical *Law and Order*, and national functionary of the John Birch Society; his 1966 paperback book, *The Communist Attack on U.S. Police*, has been widely disseminated among the nation's departments.

Fi-Po's prime mover is Sgt. Norman H. Moore of the Los Angeles force. Moore is chairman of the State American Legion Subversive Committee and an informal lobbyist in Sacramento for Fi-Po-sought legislation; during the 1964 campaign he took a leave of absence to serve as a Goldwater bodyguard. It was Moore who wrote the folk-music canard, and the right-wing Town Meetings for Freedom was sufficiently impressed to select him for its annual Special Services Award.

Another Fi-Po stalwart is Gordon M. Browning, a veteran of nineteen years on the Los Angeles department. Browning averages three speeches a week on the subject of "internal and external subversion" and appears frequently at Birch-sponsored events. On March 5, 1965, for instance, he gave a talk called "A Police Officer Looks at the Current Problem" before the North Hollywood Chapter of the Birch Society that was billed as an exposé of "the subtle, well planned attacks on our police organizations by the Communists, the Fabian Socialists, and their fellow travelers on the Extreme Liberal Left."

Fi-Po provides a "service" for industry and commerce in the form of "loyalty checks." For a fee of $10, the client submits the name of a prospective employee, which is reportedly checked against the files of the police "Red Squad" and the main criminal files. John Rousselot of the Birch Society mentioned to me that his organization occasionally utilizes the Fi-Po service. Given Fi-Po's basic political orientation, one can easily imagine the criteria by which individuals are adjudged security risks.*

A damning commentary on Fi-Po's overzealousness is the bizarre attempt to smear Senator Thomas Kuchel of California, who has been tagged a "liberal Republican" by right-wing extremists. Actually a moderate, Kuchel has spoken out against extremists of either pole, an act which prompted the right-wingers to mark him for political extinction. The Senator first became aware of what was afoot when he discovered an affidavit circulating among Congressmen, Senators and newsmen that accused him of a homosexual act.

The affidavit had been signed by tavern owner Norman H. Krause, a former Los Angeles policeman. It alleged that Kuchel had been arrested in 1950 on a drunk-driving charge, at which time he was observed participating in an immoral act. The affidavit was absolutely untrue; the Senator had not been in any way involved in the incident. The two men who had been arrested worked in his office at the time, when he was state controller. Moreover, they were not participating in an immoral act; it was a simple case of driving while intoxicated, for which they were duly convicted.

On February 18, 1965, a Los Angeles grand jury returned an indictment charging four men with conspiracy to commit criminal libel against Kuchel. One was ex-policeman Krause. Another was John F. Fergus, a public relations man for Eversharp-Schick, Inc. A third was Francis A. Capell, whose

---

* Fi-Po's service is unique in the American police system only in that it exacts a fee; many individual departments and officers leak confidential information to persons and firms with whom they have cordial relations. In his 1967 book *Inside the F.B.I.*, former special agent Norman Ollestad quotes an assistant to the director of the FBI as saying during a training class lecture that "one of the Bureau's *unofficial* services to the community is our practice of providing businessmen with inside information about job applicants and about their current employees as well, if they request it. Which is a great help in keeping those bad apples out of their organizations. Employees whose questionable loyalties have been known to stand in the way of their respective companies receiving important military contracts. . . ."

anti-Semitic *Herald of Freedom* reportedly was about to pub-
lish the libel. The fourth, who served as a go-between, was Jack
Clemmons, a Los Angeles police sergeant who resigned prior
to the grand jury proceedings. Clemmons was a past director
of Fi-Po.

The grand jury investigation disclosed that thousands of
copies of the bogus affidavit had been sent through the mails
and distributed by right-wing bookstores. One copy had even
been deposited, without Kuchel's knowledge, in the files of
the Senate Internal Security Subcommittee headed by James
O. Eastland of Mississippi. "This case drips with malice," commented Kuchel, who had made the courageous decision to
bring the matter out in the open despite the leperous effect of
the homosexual label, false as it was.

The ultra-right-wing activity that has broken out in the nation's police system is the outcropping of its solidly reactionary
structure. As Chief Parker blithely put it in explaining the
Birch hassle down the line in Santa Ana, most of the nation's
police are "conservative, ultraconservative, and very right
wing." The bias is nowhere more visible than in the Los Angeles department, clearcut, for example, in Parker's prosecution
of Michael Hannon for "contentious conduct per se" in participating in civil rights activity, while winking at rampant Birchism in the ranks.

The inherent conservatism of the police is hardened by their
feeling of being unjustly maligned and deprecated. "Why must
we be exposed to sneers, insults and abuse when we're merely
doing our duty?" moaned former New York Commissioner
Michael Murphy. Since their severest critics seem to be partisans of the left, the police reflexively polarize to the right. "It
is a human reaction to the treatment police are afforded by
liberal groups," Parker was quoted as saying in the Los Angeles *Times* on November 7, 1964. "They are driven together
as fellow-sufferers."

In this self-pitying frame of mind, the police are susceptible to the blandishments of the right-wing groups that consider them, as part of the nation's security force, prime targets for recruitment. The Birch Society and like-minded groups pander to the police need for sympathy and recognition through such devices as the overweening "Support Your Local Police" program.

The problem of Birchers in blue is not readily soluble. Like anyone else, a policeman is entitled to his private viewpoints, provided he does not engage in open political activity. Philadelphia's home charter bans "partisan political activity," while New York departmental regulations forbid membership in "any organization that is politically motivated, whether right wing or left wing," and most major departments are bound by similar rules. Birch spokesmen contend that the society is no more political than, say, the American Legion, and that policemen have an absolute right to join. During the Santa Ana hassle, newspaper ads in defense of the Bircher cops proclaimed that the society was "educational not political," and this fine point has invariably been recognized by police authorities. But the New York *Times* in an editorial November 19, 1964 was not so sure. "Is an organization that carries out political action a political organization?" the *Times* asked. "This is the question to be asked about policemen joining the John Birch Society."

Some critics of police Birchers take the position that membership in a secret, monolithic organization such as the Birch Society is by itself incompatible with being a public servant. This was the stand of Mayor Tate of Philadelphia, who said that police who joined "had limited their capability and usefulness." Some right-wing secret groups such as the Minutemen demand that members take an oath giving their first loyalty to the organization, which, of course, is irreconcilable with being a policeman. Possibly the most generally reasonable position is that of the ACLU, a zealous watchdog of individual freedom, which has said it can "see no reason for a policeman being forbidden to belong unless membership adversely affected his work."

In many instances, however, the extremist policeman, whether he is a member of the Birch Society or unaffiliated, is influenced by his ideological beliefs to the point where they adversely affect his work. The police possess wide discretionary latitude; they cannot enforce all the law all the time but must give priority to those offenses they believe most gravely affect the community and involve the most troublesome offenders. In this context, the most grave offenses and the most troublesome offenders well might be, in the eyes of a Birch-sympathizing policeman, those frowned upon by the social and political creed of the John Birch Society.

These right-wing prejudices on the part of the police show up most pointedly in the hounding of leftists, liberals, review-board proponents, civil rights demonstrators, anti-Vietnam war protesters, campus radicals, and just about anyone who is not a brass-band patriot. Every department of any size has what is variously called a Subversive Squad, an Intelligence Unit, or a Red Squad. With their jurisdiction tenuously hinged on archaic state antiradical syndicalist or antianarchy laws, or no law at all, they constantly pry into the public and private activities of Communists and Socialists, liberals and intellectuals, beatniks and peaceniks, et al., while ignoring the subversive menace from the right. The Red Squads, few of whose members are politically sophisticated, operate on the blind assumptions that the tides of social reform are inevitably tinged Red and that criticism of the police is invariably Communist-engineered (a wishful notion first advanced by J. Edgar Hoover apropos of the FBI). Their purported mission duplicates that of the Domestic Intelligence Division of the FBI, which has primary responsibility for internal security, but their sorry record of un-American activity indicates they are more interested in branding and baiting than in bona fide countersubversion.

In an article in *The Nation* of August 30, 1965, Chicago *Daily News* reporter Lois Wiley outlined the method by which "you get identified by the 'red squad' ":

> Police photographers take pictures of civil rights demonstrators, peace marchers, pickets at House Un-American Activities Committee hearings, and the audiences at meetings sponsored by groups suspected of being very left wing. Recently the police photographers have also been snapping pictures of spectators at Board of Education meetings [Chicago integrationists were clamoring for the removal of School Superintendent Benjamin Willis]. "I walked into the room one afternoon and suddenly this camera was pointed at me," says one bemused University of Chicago economics professor who happened to be interested in a high school addition the board was considering. "Is that constitutional?" If your picture pops up often enough, you get in the "red squad" file of left wingers.

As former Chicago sheriff Joseph Lohman observes, the photographs are not "sanitized," and anyone who habitually attends events that are suspect in police eyes becomes an *"ex officio subversive."* *

Although the targets of Red Squad attentions are almost never prosecuted—and thereby afforded due process—the squads are used in a number of extralegal ways. On occasion, a demagogic politician uses their supposed inside knowledge to drag a red herring across the path of an opposition candidate or cause. In his battle with the anti-Willis demonstrators,

---

* On December 7, 1967, the New York police arrested 100 antiwar demonstrators in a group that had been given permission to parade peaceably. Herded to the Seventh Precinct Station, they were photographed with Polaroid cameras, and arrest cards containing personal data were filled out. The police acknowledged they had made a mistake in arresting them in the first place—"some wires got crossed," explained a police spokesman—but would not return the photographs and arrest cards to some of those arrested who insisted on having them.

Mayor Daley branded "many of the people" opposing Willis as "Communists" on the basis that "police department files show this is true." In his battle against the New York review board, PBA President Cassese defamed board proponents by stating that many of their names were in a "black book" at police headquarters.

Red Squads are also an effective means of intimidation. In 1964, for example, middle-of-the-road Democrat Raymond Johnson ran for the state assembly in Orange County, California, on a "Beat the Birchers" platform. When he and a group of supporters picketed a Birch rally featuring council member Dr. Revilo Oliver (who had advanced the idea that President Kennedy was assassinated because he had not gone along fast enough with the Communists), members of the Santa Ana police Red Squad, overlooking the many radical rightists in the crowd, photographed the pickets and told each, "It's for the file." Perhaps encouraged by this display of police partisanship, a secret council of Young Americans for Freedom reportedly discussed bombing Johnson's campaign headquarters, relenting only when someone argued it would make him a martyr.

Perhaps the most craven activity is in blackballing suspected "subversives" in the employment market and preventing them from earning a livelihood. In a way reminiscent of the "faceless informers" in vogue during the McCarthy era, the police let employers or prospective employers "take a look" at the suspect's Red Squad file, with its raw and unevaluated charges, or display to them police photographs which are in themselves intimidating. As a harassment technique, I recall, this was in great favor with FBI agents as well.

When Communist party rolls dipped below the 10,000 mark in the early sixties, the Red Squads, taking their cue from such lurid remarks of the FBI director as "the W. E. B. DuBois Clubs are new blood for the vampire of international Communism," found greener pastures Red-hunting on the nation's college campuses. In its March 27, 1967, issue, *Newsweek* reported: "Few demonstrations on campus fail to attract a host of camera-laden FBI agents, campus or local police and free-lance spies, and on some campuses political spying is well-organized. . . . At the University of Texas, where a recent meeting to hear a left-wing speaker drew an audience of thirty-five, a third of them investigators eyeing the crowd, spying is a popular pastime. The deans, the local police, the Texas Department of Public Safety and the FBI all keep files on leftists. . . ."

For years, one of the most familiar anomalies on the Berkeley campus scene was the balding figure of Inspector Charles O'Meara of the Berkeley police Red Squad. Until his recent retirement, O'Meara spent a virtual career building up exhaustive files on suspect students and nonstudents. His successor, Inspector Edwin Skeels, explained, in answer to student complaints of Red Squad harassment, in a San Francisco *Chronicle* interview February 18, 1967, "We like to keep tabs on large groups of people that present possible problems." On this vague presumption, a police officer using the pseudonym "Jim Majors" infiltrated the Vietnam Day Committee, and another ostentatiously photographed participants in a march to Sacramento to protest the tuition proposals of incoming Governor Ronald Reagan.

The stepped-up activities of the Red Squads have fostered an environment of suspicion and intimidation on the campuses and off. When the State University of New York at Buffalo recently announced plans to move its campus to suburban Amherst, alarmed citizens voted to authorize funds for the creation of an Amherst police Red Squad. The proliferation of Red Squads, with their indelible blacklists, has just about destroyed the old adage that campus political firebrands wind up as captains of industry and leaders of government.

There is a drive under way by the police establishment to cloak this official vigilantism in legality. In testimony before the Senate Internal Security Subcommittee on June 24, 1966, Executive Director Quinn Tamm of the influential International Association of Chiefs of Police welcomed the opportunity to "present our views on one of the most serious law-enforcement problems of our time—how to deal with subversion." In the IACP's view, countersubversive investigations belonged primarily in the hands of local, not federal, authorities. "We are particularly concerned with the need to restore the efficacy of state laws against subversion and the right of each state to investigate subversive activities within its borders," pleaded Tamm. What he was advocating in effect is that the local police should be watchdogs of our loyalty to the United States.

Tamm's dialectics were chilling. "For the past few years," he said, "concern about Communistic subversion has generally been dormant except for the continuing vigilance of such groups as this subcommittee, national patriotic organizations, and our law-enforcement and military-intelligence agencies. Certainly the concern that culminated in the Smith Act of 1940, the Internal Security Act of 1950, and the Communist Control Act of 1954 has substantially abated. We of the police believe that such vigilance must continue and must be increased."

One senses the ominous ring of a neo-McCarthyism implemented with vastly expanded local Red Squads. Lest there be any doubt who the victims would be, Tamm explained that the Communist apparatus continues to function "with the help of misguided do-gooders and calculating leaders of so-called social reform groups. . . ." Voicing the police frustration at having to maintain law and order on both sides of the political fence, he regretted that the police have to be " 'observers,' manning barricades against Young Americans for Freedom, who are picketing the [Communist] meeting—in effect providing protection to the meeting." The police, he said, are "impotent to take the action they should properly be taking to protect us against subversion and sedition—rooting out and bringing to justice those who are blatantly advocating sedition and subversion of our government. . . . While the Communists have been given increasingly greater latitude by judicial decisions, at the same time the police have been increasingly restricted."

What Tamm seems to be promoting on behalf of the nation's police executives is a nationwide inquisitorial network of Red Squads acting under uniform and stringent state antisubversion laws. Inferentially, the zeal of the FBI in internal security investigations has not been sufficient to suit the police, and one shudders to think what forms their Red-hunting might take.

15

The Police Lobby

"We are not a lobby," asserts Charles E. Moore, Jr., publicity director of the International Association of Chiefs of Police. "We are a nonprofit educational organization—we respond to Congress when asked." In the conventional lobbying sense, Moore's disclaimer is true. The IACP does not retain a paid, registered lobbyist on Capitol Hill, else it would lose its tax-exempt status. But despite this distinction, the voice of the IACP is a powerful one. It is heard not only in the halls of Congress but, through a well-financed publicity program, across the nation. It walks like a lobby, it talks like a lobby—and it gets the police message across.

The glib, personable Moore is well qualified as a police spokesman. He was born in Mobile, Alabama, forty-two years ago, and following naval service in World War II graduated from the University of Alabama with a Master of Arts degree in journalism. After a stint with the Mobile *Press-Register*, he entered the FBI in 1951, serving in Phoenix and Peoria before being assigned to the bureau's publicity department (the Crime Records Division) in Washington. He quit the FBI in 1961 to join a Washington public-relations firm. In 1962 he moved over to the IACP.

Moore works out of IACP headquarters, an ancient elegant graystone mansion with curving balustrades and marble floors, located near DuPont Circle at 1319 18th Street N.W. On the day I talked to him he was about to start a search for larger quarters; the IACP is growing fast.

"We have some 6,200 members," Moore informed me. "Eligibility starts with captains if they are in charge of a division. Industrial security officers are also eligible." The IACP is represented in 63 countries of the free world, although the overwhelming majority of the membership is in the United States. In addition to the active and life members, says Moore, there are 893 associate members, as well as 100 sustaining members who pay a $100 initiation fee. These latter two categories are made up of police buffs, although, Moore claims, their membership cards do not provide immunity from arrest.

The IACP is financed largely by membership dues, grants, and contributions from large corporations whose interests parallel those of law enforcement. Recent contributors have included the American District Telegraph Company (the ADT burglar alarm system); the Mosler Foundation, whose contribution was initiated by the government sales division of the Mosler Safe Company; the General Telephone and Electronics Corporation (through the director of security); and the Wackenhut Corporation, the nationwide personnel screening group once retained by the governor of Florida as a private spying agency. In 1964 the Ford Foundation awarded the IACP a $100,000 grant over four years to assist in its studies.

Although the IACP was founded in 1893, it remained of modest size until the rapid expansion of the sixties. Now it boasts a full-time staff of more than fifty. The executive director, Quinn Tamm, is a former FBI assistant director who had a falling out with J. Edgar Hoover in 1961 and retired from the bureau; his brother, Edward A. Tamm, also at one time an FBI assistant director, is a federal district judge in Washington. The administrative assistant to Tamm, Jeptha S. Rogers, was for many years an inspector in the FBI's Training and

Inspection Division maintaining liaison with police agencies; he retired from the bureau in 1962. There is a sizable contingent from the Oakland, California, Police Department, including George W. O'Connor, director of the Professional Standards Division.

The IACP staff is concerned with a broad spectrum of police problem-solving. It operates a managerial self-appraisal service that has been utilized by more than 100 law-enforcement agencies, including police in Chicago, Washington, Dallas and, presently, New York, where an analysis of crime records is under way. The results are not always pleasing to the agencies. In Boston, for example, the IACP recommended that the ratio of 4.1 policemen to every 1,000 citizens—well above the national average—be cut back. "The ratio is misleading," contends Deputy Superintendent William A. Bradley. "Boston is the only city that more than doubles its population in the daytime." Among other IACP projects are a Highway Safety Division, which is trying to devise ways and means of alleviating the carnage on the nation's highways, and the Center for Law Enforcement Research Information, which currently is concentrating on guidelines for dealing with the "explosive social problem."

A major area of IACP interest is in the upgrading of police standards, which admittedly fall far short of professionalism. "We are trying to induce legislatures to pass uniform minimum training laws," relates Moore. "You can't become a barber or mortician in many states without a license. The same should hold true for police." In some states, he advised, a surcharge is added to court fines which helps pay for police education. In IACP's viewpoint, the current lack of education is a stumbling block to professionalization. "Most police have only a high-school education or less," says Moore. "They join for security and retirement."

In its push for professionalization, however, the IACP has

avoided the problem of police corruption like the plague. With respect to IACP surveys of police agencies, Moore remarked: "We're not investigators—we don't look for corruption." The IACP is in fact hypersensitive about the police image. In 1966, when the National Broadcasting Company televised a lengthy, in-depth documentary on organized crime which showed several examples of police taking payoffs from racketeers, Executive Director Quinn Tamm fired off an angry letter to NBC President Julian Goodman. Charging that the documentary's producer, Fred Freed, had sought sensationalism rather than objectivity, Tamm asserted: "I called Mr. Freed, he visited our headquarters here in Washington, and I offered him any assistance we could provide with regard to producing an accurate picture of crime and the police role. His attitude did not indicate that he desired any data of a constructive nature. You have done the police, the public and your network a great disservice."

Goodman replied evenly that the documentary "pointed out that there are some corrupt police officers and public officials whose venality nourishes crime. . . . Mr. Freed and the men who worked with him on this program are experienced, skilled reporters, whose only commitment is to the truth, and they reported the facts as they found them, accurately and fairly."

The IACP also assists local agencies in their public-relations programs. Available from headquarters is a series of IACP movies. One, *The Door Was Locked,* is billed as "a 'key' movie every law-enforcement agency can use to show the homeowner and apartment dweller how premises can be best secured against intrusion by criminals." Produced with the cooperation of the Schlage Lock Company, it sells for $200. Another, *Attack!,* is boosted as "ideal for showing before all types of audiences—and it is particularly effective for screening before women's groups." Noting that forcible rape was up 9 percent in 1965, the blurb claims the film "shows women how they

can protect themselves against . . . ATTACK!" The advertis-
ing virtually guarantees that women viewing the films will embrace their local police as indispensable guardians of their
chastity.

Tamm, a stern-faced man with close-cropped white hair,
spends considerable time on the lecture circuit promulgating
the police viewpoint. In a talk before the Beaumont, Texas,
Lions Club September 1, 1966, he said: "Today, we too often
see and read of the young people on campuses and in our
streets flaunting the law because they say they had no part in
making the law. We see them, as evidenced on the Berkeley
campus, in a state of open rebellion, cleverly egged on by
known subversives, and cheered on by some of the maudlin,
oversentimental, self-claimed idealists from the faculty. We
read of some of them performing near-treason by burning
their draft cards and joining with the Communist sympathizers in tirades of denunciation against our nation's effort in
Vietnam to contain Communism."

At a testimonial dinner for Sheriff J. Howell Flournoy of
Caddo Parish, Louisiana, on April 20, 1966, Tamm spoke in
equally lurid tones: "Mobs stage insurrections in our streets,
on our campuses, even in our nation's Capitol, the citadel of
the world's hopes for freedom. And when those who are sworn
to maintain law and order perform their duty with a calmness
and fortitude that never ceases to fill me with pride, they are
reviled by cries of 'police brutality.' " Before an industrial
security conference in Dallas May 17, 1966, he proffered that
strict surveillance, surprise checkups and other antitheft techniques used on employees by management were "a sad commentary on the morality of the American worker."

In a speech before the New England Institute on Police and
Community Relations April 24, 1966, Tamm termed the Chicago department's Operation Crime-Stop, in which citizens
are urged to report suspicious persons or actions, a "police-com-

munity relations program." And in an address to the Citadel of Faith and Freedom Victory Rally in Orlando, Florida, March 22, 1966, he mixed biblical intonations with another slam at civil disobedience. "As man applies the abrasive flint of civil disobedience to the steel of our laws," he warned, "dangerous sparks are set flying which threaten the very foundations of our form of government."

In painting these morbid pictures of widespread chaos, corruption and near anarchy, Tamm is striking the kind of propaganda upon which the policy lobby has based its plea for more authority and tougher laws. Writing in IACP's monthly magazine *Police Chief* in March 1967, he summed up the fearmongers' case: "The crime rate is spiraling upward in alarming proportions; crime is increasingly more vicious and of shocking notoriety; civil rightists and protesters against all manner of real and imagined wrongs have been guilty of appalling excesses; more and more crime is being committed by the young and the very young generations; the police have been made less and less effective because of severely restrictive court decisions and a growing vociferousness among the liberal community which calls for stripping police of traditional devices of detection; and, as President Johnson has pointed out, there is a fear beginning to pervade the law-abiding elements of our society."

To get desired legislation, the IACP has now appointed a full-time nonlobbyist. In the February 1967 *Police Chief* Tamm disclosed: "A number of conscientious federal lawmakers have contacted IACP headquarters seeking guidance concerning legislation which they would like to introduce, and we have responded. The tempo of this interest has increased to the point where we have designated a staff member to make himself available at all times to answer Congressional inquiries for advice and assistance."

Many of the lawmakers beating a path to the door on 18th

Street bear impeccable credentials as ultraconservatives. One IACP-sought piece of legislation would make it a federal crime to travel or use any facility in interstate commerce with intent to incite a riot or other violent civil disturbance, and for other purposes. Bills to provide this amorphous law, which could become a dangerous tool of political zealots, have been introduced by Congressmen Paul A. Fino of New York, Dante B. Fascell and William C. Cramer of Florida, Craig Hosmer of California, and J. Irving Whalley of Pennsylvania. Whalley has also sponsored HR 2548, which would provide compensation to survivors of local police killed while apprehending persons for federal crimes.

The IACP can also count on the solid support of the American Legion, which has had considerable experience in influencing legislators on veterans' matters. The Legion and IACP are ironing out an agreement for the exchange of speakers to explain the American Legion's program "in support of law and order" and "how Legionnaires can support the efforts of police."

In the American Legion magazine of April 1967, an article entitled "Our Downgraded Police: A National Peril" proclaimed that "as mobs, courts and propagandists make police work tougher, more thankless and riskier, it is harder to find and keep good cops." No slouch at propaganda, the magazine juxtaposed a photograph of a bloodied policeman with a milling scene at a "Stop Police Brutality" demonstration of the W. E. B. DuBois Clubs. "Even the Communists' wild and vague charges against police get straightfaced nationwide publicity," complained the caption.

Ironically, one bill IACP wants badly would in effect prevent police officers from becoming eligible for Legion membership. "The police are prime targets for draft boards," says Charles Moore. "We object to the raiding. Departments are rarely up to authorized strength as it is." The bill would give sworn police officers blanket immunity from the draft. Another item on the IACP's most wanted list is legalized wiretapping by police in the investigation of "organized crime." Although the President's National Crime Commission recommended against giving the police such vaguely founded prying powers, Chief Thomas Cahill of San Francisco, the only police member of the commission and an IACP official, signed a minority report advocating the use of wiretapping.

The reluctant lobbyists of the IACP manage to wangle invitations that give their viewpoints maximum exposure. Early in 1967 the Senate Judiciary Committee's Subcommittee on Criminal Laws and Procedures began hearings that its dour chairman, Senator John L. McClellan of Arkansas, said he hoped would be "the turning point of the struggle against lawlessness in this nation." The roster of witnesses was palpably loaded with proponents of law enforcement's hard line. Federal Judge J. Edward Lumbard of New York saw the crisis in law enforcement as of such magnitude that "the old arguments against wiretapping are no longer weighty." District Attorney Aaron E. Koota of Kings County (Brooklyn), New York, decried Supreme Court rulings on confessions which, he said, enable criminals to walk the streets "secure in the knowledge that they cannot be punished for their crimes. . . ."

The IACP's Quinn Tamm also used the subcommittee as a forum to deliver a searing diatribe at the courts. "I am certain that the framers of the Constitution never intended it to be distorted into a technical instrument for the benefit of depraved criminals," he was quoted in *U.S. News & World Report* of March 27, 1967. "I am of the firm opinion that the majority of the decent people in this country have had about enough of a judicial system which allows criminals to roam the streets and commit vicious, depraved acts, time after time. . . ."

The 1964 turmoil on the campus of the University of California at Berkeley provides an insight into how the nonlobby works. In its April 1965 issue *The Police Chief* carried a feature article, "Anarchy On the Campus: The Rebels and the Law." The author, Charles Moore, was "invited" to Berkeley by Police Chief Addison H. Fording, an introductory note explains. Fording believed, it is stated, that "the experiences of the police agencies involved [in the civil disobedience disorders] may be of assistance to other agencies should they encounter similar problems." The cost of researching the article was borne by the IACP's Institute for Police Management.

The article quickly digressed from pure management analysis, however. "One of the more alarming aspects of these student demonstrations," wrote Moore on the first page, "is the ever-present evidence that the guiding hand of Communists and extreme leftists was involved. As Berkeley Chief . . . Fording pointed out, 'According to those experts who are best informed regarding Communist plans for world domination, a basic objective is to capture the minds of students and whenever possible to take over institutions of higher learning.' "

Moore tried hard to capture the spirit of Fording's Machiavellian theory. He quoted a graduate student's letter to the editor of the now-defunct San Francisco *News Call Bulletin:* "The handiwork of professionals is everywhere in evidence— information booths, buttons, machine-printed signs, bull horns, walkie-talkies. . . . Can this be the spontaneous rebellion of downtrodden students?" His news sources hardly bear a reputation for dispassionate reporting. The Oakland *Tribune,* owned by the family of former Senator William Knowland, has consistently pictured Berkeley campus activity through Red-tinted filters. The San Francisco *Examiner,* bellweather of the Hearst chain, ran a photograph of a throng at the campus' Sather Gate with a circle around Albert "Mickey" Lima, an avowed Communist functionary—as "proof" of Communist penetration of the Free Speech Movement. Veteran crime reporter Ed Montgomery of the *Examiner*, a police dogmatist, was unskeptically cited for "detecting" activists with "Communist connections," among them "a teaching assistant who is a close associate of the chairman for the Communist Party for northern California" and "the sister of one of the suspended students who has been associated with the Communist-infiltrated Women for Peace. . . ."

Moore's other finger-pointer was even less objective. The *Washington Report* of the American Security Council, an ultraright organization that combines a "loyalty-security blacklist" service to industry with bristling advocacy of the cold war "hard line," was credited with five identifications, including "the son of a former *Daily Worker* editor." And *Tocsin*, a militant weekly of the radical right (Moore calls it a "West Coast anti-Communist weekly"), was liberally quoted as if it were a reliable source.

Moore's perception of the "guiding hand of Communists" behind the Berkeley struggle surpassed the conclusion of J. Edgar Hoover, who told a House appropriations subcommittee on March 4, 1965, that the demonstration, "while not Communist originated or controlled, has been exploited by a few Communists for their own end." Nevertheless Moore's performance earned him another invitation, this time to testify before the Senate Internal Security Subcommittee "with respect to student demonstrations and the influence of subversive elements." Moore's testimony, carried by the wire services, received, according to the *Police Chief* of April 1966, "wide publicity in the nation's news media." The article had received "wide acclaim," it was noted, and a reprinting of 3,000 copies had been distributed.

When he was later invited before the same subcommittee, as recounted in the previous chapter, Quinn Tamm referred to Moore's article and testimony and refreshed the Senators' memories that Moore had "listed several individuals as either members of, or connected with, the Communist party or its affiliates." With this sequence of lobby by invitation, the IACP launched its offensive to secure local police jurisdiction over political beliefs. "We need tighter state laws on extremism," Moore told me. "As it is, the federals have the widest authority." It is a frightening prospect: that our local police, many of them rabid right-wingers, will be handed police powers over thought.

At the line level, the policemen's lustiest voice is the Fraternal Order of Police, whose national headquarters is in Cincinnati, Ohio. The FOP, which elected John Harrington its national president in order to focus on the Philadelphia review board, lobbies unabashedly. The national lodge in Washington maintains a legislative committee which duns Congress on legislation affecting police; among current bills being promoted are HB 15594, which exempts police pensions from federal income tax, and SB 3165, which provides a $25,000 indemnity for the dependents of police officers killed while engaged in a federal case. State lodges of the FOP also have legislative committees which lobby for increased police benefits, better working conditions and the abolishment of review boards.

We have already seen the political potency of the Patrolmen's Benevolent Association's New York chapter in its successful fight against the New York review board. It spent half a million dollars, with a million and a half more in reserve, on a well-managed campaign that would do credit to the central committees of the major parties.

There is also a proliferation of police groups organized on a state and local basis that exerts pressures on legislators and politicians. The largest of these are the various state peace officers associations, which have been uniformly vocal in denouncing court decisions, attacking review boards, and perceiving Communists as the instigators of criticism of the police. For example, on October 29, 1966, Lt. Bill Kolender of the San Diego force told a San Francisco convention of the 24,000-strong Peace Officers Association of California that Communists are secretly behind the plot to establish review boards. "It's a move to discredit the police," he revealed.

The Peace Officers Association of California is one of many state-level police organizations that support a paid, full-time lobbyist in the state capitols. Its man in Sacramento is Herbert Ellingwood, who is euphemistically titled Legislative Advocate; he also represents the District Attorney's Association of California, whose legislative interests largely parallel those of the police. A paper delivered to the Police Research and Development Institute at Oakland on April 21, 1965, by Ellingwood is rather illuminating on the subject of police lobbying. "Legislators have voiced their opinion often in the form of a plea that they must rely on special interest groups to call a legislator's attention to problems and to advise him as to the best and most acceptable solution," said Ellingwood in justifying lobbying activity.

"And who knows more about criminal law problems than law enforcement?" Ellingwood rhetorically asked. "No professor, judge, defense attorney, or *so-called civil liberties representative* [italics added] knows as much about our problems as we do. Each of these groups might have something important to say. But the law enforcement officer, who is trained and educated, who walks the beat every day and relieves it every night, who meets the crook by looking down the barrel of a sawed-off shotgun, who chases speeders at dangerously high speeds, who knows and understands juvenile delinquency as no one else can, who converses one minute with the prostitute and con artist and in the next minute enters the legal jungle of the judiciary, must be in the best position to inform the legislature about law enforcement problems."

There are, of course, many legislators who are fascinated

with the police mystique—and the theory that the police know best. The efficacy of police lobbying in California was synopsized by Ellingwood: "It is not possible to list the many notable achievements of law enforcement legislative activity. We can look with pride to such things as the Commission on Peace Officer Standards and Training, the state teletype system, the State Department of Justice, the laws on conspiracy, the narcotic penalty and rehabilitation program, and many others as our work product. In addition, we have been able to retain the death penalty, stop unworkable changes in criminal responsibility, and indicate to the legislature many proposals which would have a detrimental effect on the citizenry . . . law enforcement's role in legislative matters must be one of aggressive leadership. . . ."

Many of the indigenous police groups are represented nationally by the International Conference of Police Associations, incorporated in 1954 as a nonprofit organization with headquarters in Washington. ICPA's executive director, Royce L. Givens, maintains regular liaison with Capitol Hill. "We do not engage in lobbying as such," declares Givens. "However, I do make contact with members of Congress when requested to do so by officers of our member associations for information and so forth."

Some idea of ICPA's interests can be gained from the remarks of speakers at its annual convention on July 16, 1966, in San Francisco. Father Marcolinus Nouza, an author and a graduate of the Oakland Police Academy, attributed much of the clamor about review boards to "concerted efforts by Communists" bent on hampering law enforcement as a means of "breaking down the moral fiber of the country." And, he added in a blast at the courts, "Crime is becoming the law of the land and the law of the land is becoming a crime." Another speaker, Officer Ted Coombs of the Los Angeles Fi-Po Research Association, alleged that war-on-poverty funds were being diverted to political purposes by persons with "known subversive backgrounds" and called for the background exposé of those persons.

The ICPA operates a Committee on Subversive Intervention into Law Enforcement, which acts as a sort of clearinghouse for the exchange of Red Squad information between cities. Its chairman is Inspector Henry W. Kerr of the Los Angeles department, who is also on the board of directors of the Fi-Po Research Association. In a presentation before the 1964 annual convention of the ICPA (published in the September 1964 issue of *The California Highway Patrolman*), Kerr took off on review boards in general and one of their proponents, Roger M. Baldwin, in particular. "It is interesting to note," said Kerr of the ACLU stalwart, "that Baldwin has been reported as having more than 100 Communist-front affiliations." Kerr damned Baldwin for being on a committee working for the repeal of the Smith Act of 1940, the McCarran Internal Security Act of 1950 and the Communist Control Act of 1954. What the inspector failed to point out was that most of the opposition to these acts stems from non-Communists who view them as repressive police-state measures.

Probably the least sophisticated and most strident of the nonlobbies is the Florida-based National Police Officers Association of America, Inc. Although NPOAA has only 10,000 full-time officers in its membership, it professes to be "serving the interests of over 480,000 professional law enforcement officers." To this end it operates a "Congressional Liaison Office" in Washington. A "Legislative Bulletin" to members outlines the function of the office: "Law enforcement officers, professionally, have been the 'Fall Guy' for every minority complaint in the nation. . . . NPOAA *is not standing idly by*. About $.15 from your membership dollar [the dues are $8 per year] is being used to offset distortion, falsehoods and lies. NPOAA however is not a lobby. We present legislative information to you."

The founder of NPOAA is Frank J. Schira, a former Chicago police officer who serves as executive director; Matthew A. Landers, also an ex-policeman, is national president. "Our national officers are straight from the front line of law enforcement," Schira assures members, "and not political hacks or paper shufflers." Schira's editorials in *Valor*, "The Official Police Review," are equally blunt, and members are hardly at a loss as to where NPOAA stands.

In the October-December 1966 issue, Schira proclaims what amounts to a brief manifesto. "The hue and cry of 'police brutality,'" writes the burly, tough-talking Schira, "is the most successful propaganda effort ever devised by the combined efforts of the criminal, the Communist, and the ultraliberal wing of this nation." As he sees it, accusations of brutality have been "a smokescreen, a cover, to turn the public eye from the real purpose—which is to destroy law and order in every community and to openly allow rape, murder, riot and theft at will."

The civil rights movement, too, is a diabolical conspiracy. "Law enforcement officers have known for years of the Red (Communist) influence in matters of civil rights and their leaders. Professional paid agitators have given rise to a national movement of rebellion of authority. Combined with the criminal element within their ranks, this makes an evil alliance." The NPOAA is also against social security to replace pensions, the currently proposed firearms legislation, and abolition of capital punishment. "We see no justification in letting animals who kill live," reasons Schira.

Schira flatters himself that this kind of "calling a spade a spade" will draw enemy fire, and he is prepared for it. "You can expect attacks on the organization to begin with from the extreme left and the 'do-gooders' who preach love and kisses for criminals," he counsels members. "Know your enemy."

The NPOAA also boasts a women's auxiliary composed of wives, daughters, mothers and sisters. An advertisement in *Valor* soliciting the ladies to join promises a handsome car emblem: a policeman with women and children in the background and the slogan "OUR POLICE—STRENGTH OF INTERNAL PEACE."

Another member of the NPOAA family is the Order of Michael the Archangel Police Legion, described as an "association of police chaplains." The national chaplain is the Right Rev. Bartholomew R. Fox, an Eastern Rite priest, who has inaugurated a "Pray for Police" project he hopes will "offset the deception by 'leftist' elements who are using religious organizations to abuse police and preach civil disobedience." A notice in *Valor* advises: "Donations are needed by the OMA to carry on its work." The donor receives an "honorary" membership card and a "beautiful silver emblem" inscribed with the motto: "PRAY FOR POLICE."

NPOAA members are provided not only spiritual inspiration but physical comforts. At its Venice, Florida, headquarters, NPOAA makes available "Florida vacation homes"— three-bedroom houses with television sets and swimming pools —at $75 per week. And to help its members identify with the organization, there is an assortment of sundry items bearing the NPOAA insignia—blazer emblems, lapel pins, pens, cigarette lighters, T-shirts and bumper emblems—that can be purchased by mail-order.

On Route 41 near Port Charlotte, Florida, the NPOAA runs a unique enterprise called the National Police Museum and Hall of Fame, created in 1955 to honor police officers killed in the line of duty and "to be certain that their heroism and great sacrifice is not in vain. . . ." The Hall of Fame provides the families of the deceased "a special posthumous citation, a

Medal of Valor, and places the name, department and rank of the officer in a memorial section of the Police Hall of Fame." The spacious building was "officially opened on October 15, 1960, with a message from Presidential candidate John F. Kennedy. Four years later his name, along with that of Officer J. D. Tippitt, was placed among those honored."

The museum section of the building boasts police equipment and crime weapons valued at over $100,000. "Hundreds of thousands of Americans have toured the building since it was opened," says the NPOAA, "and all have praised highly the story told here." One aspect of the story portrays "the horrors that face those who break the law." On the floor are police motorcycles and in showcases a gruesome array of confiscated weapons. The FBI's "Wanted" posters of Top Ten Fugitives are displayed, just as they are in post offices. "It is surprising how often the many visitors to the Hall of Fame recall knowing some of these arch-criminals in their home town," a *Valor* article on the museum straightfacedly notes.

In January of 1966, the NPOAA opened its National Police Academy for the training of police officers. The first class graduated, *Valor* reported, "from a day-long seminar on Subversion, Espionage, Sabotage and Explosives." Correspondence courses in police crafts also are offered.

The NPOAA bestows a variety of awards on worthy recipients. One is the Crime Analysis Award for "reduction in crime" in the "war on crime." The 1966 version went to Superintendent O. W. Wilson of Chicago and was bestowed by Chairman "Z" Frank in ceremonies at police headquarters. Another is the Honor Legion "similar to the Military Purple Heart;" it automatically goes to any police officer injured in the line of duty.

In turn, NPOAA is proud of the recognition it has received. Schira has been appointed to the American Legion Law and Order Committee by National Commander Eldon James. In

1966, the right-wing Freedoms Foundation at Valley Forge gave NPOAA its George Washington Honor Medal Award for "an outstanding accomplishment in helping to achieve a better understanding of the American Way of Life." NPOAA puffs that it has received laudatory letters from President Johnson and J. Edgar Hoover. But all is not accolades. One prominent police executive confides that he turned down a request to be listed on NPOAA's board because he considers the outfit "too commercial." And the Florida Chiefs of Police Organization, which has the closest perspective, has disowned NPOAA.

Yet the nonprofit business of police promotion must be brisk, for in 1966 Gerald S. Arenberg, NPOAA's assistant executive director, and two other associates broke away to found the rival American Federation of Police, Inc. Located across town in Venice, AFP has already formulated plans for an International Police Hall of Fame and Museum. It also intends to broaden its base by attracting watchmen, private investigators and police buffs, and to this end has organized an International Association of Auxilary Police.

Arenberg's cant will probably be as shrill and truculent as Schira's. Just before he left NPOAA, he wrote in *Valor*: "We are at war with an enemy just as dangerous as the Viet Cong in Southeast Asia. These protesters and rioters are criminals. . . . What should a police officer do when called an 'S.O.B.' or other degrading terms when dealing with criminals? Simply smile and say 'Sir, tsk, tsk'? . . . A police officer is human and will react to violent words or violent acts . . . if the public turns away from these dedicated and loyal policemen dying on our streets, it is just one final step further toward the Communist take-over when law and order no longer prevail in the land of the free and the home of the brave." Such ringing rhetoric has not stirred NPOAA's patriotic soul, however: it passed a resolution forbidding any NPOAA officer from joining AFP.

No discussion of the police lobby is complete without in-

cluding the role of the FBI and its director whose influence
with the Congress, the public, and the police community itself
cannot be underestimated. By virtue of its spectacular successes
against the flamboyant public enemies of the thirties coupled
with an absence of any corruption scandal, the FBI under
Hoover has achieved a reputation as the *sine qua non* of police
efficacy. Hoover himself has become the titular head of American law enforcement.

As far as the public is concerned, Hoover holds a virtual sole
proprietorship as the voice of law enforcement. He has never
been reticent about exercising it, and his turgid, doomsday
rhetoric has set the lawman's tone for some forty-odd years
now. Criminals, he once said, are "a horde larger than any of
the barbarian hosts that overran Europe and Asia in ancient
times." They were "craven beasts," "public rats" and "scum
from the boiling pot of the underworld." "I'm going to tell
the truth about the rats," he vowed in his 1938 book *Persons in
Hiding*. "I'm going to tell the truth about the miserable politicians who protect them and the slimy, silly or sob-sister convict lovers who let them out on sentimental or ill-advised
paroles." In 1963, as his fortieth anniversary as director approached, not much had changed. The surge in crime, he
warned, "foretells a tragic breakdown of law and order which
will require drastic action to avert chaos."

Hoover's opinions are widely propagated in the daily press
and, to his law-enforcement audience, in the monthly *Law
Enforcement Bulletin* and the regular *Uniform Crime Reports*
published by the FBI. In a 1959 edition of the *Reports*, for
example, a "Crime Capsules" column declared: "Proponents
of capital punishment cannot find support for their cause in
the study of state murder rates, since the results are inconclu-
sive." By the same token, neither can the proponents, of
whom Hoover is the leading spokesman, support their contention that capital punishment is a deterrent to crime. Unfortu-

nately, the outdated concepts of the prestigious FBI director
have gained wide popular acceptance because of their *ex officio* authority and in the process have impeded crimino-penal
progress, bound up as it is in the climate of public opinion.
"Irrespective of all the tested knowledge by students in the
field," notes Howard B. Gill, director of the Institute of Cor-
rectional Administration at the American University, "a tenta-
tive and at times raw statement by J. Edgar Hoover in the
Reader's Digest carries more weight than one hundred research articles in the *Journal of Criminal Law, Criminology
and Police Science.*"

To the police and a large segment of the public, Hoover is
the father figure of theological anti-Communism. He admired
Senator McCarthy as "a man who is not going to be pushed
around," and his own pronouncements during that oppressive
era helped condition public opinion for the "antisubversion"
laws that were enacted. One way or another, he has kept the
pot boiling. When the Communist party, U.S.A., became so
enfeebled in the early sixties it could barely muster 6,000
members, Hoover discovered new threats to internal security
on the nation's campuses.

W. H. "Ping" Ferry, a former reporter now with the Fund
for the Republic, termed Hoover "the indubitable mandarin
of anti-Communism in the U.S." and his claims "sententious
poppycock" in a speech on August 6, 1962, before Western
Democrats in Seattle. But the scare-mongering has, as Walter
Reuther put it, conditioned "the public's frame of mind upon
which the radical right feeds." Hoover is probably the one
individual most quoted by the extreme right. In the tract
None Dare Call It Treason, for example, author John Stormer
quotes the FBI chief on Communism no fewer than seventeen
times. At the same time, the right wing has showered
Hoover with "patriotic" honors. In 1961 he received the Freedoms Foundation award for his "anti-Communist writings,"

and in 1965 the American of the Year trophy of the ultraright Americanism Educational League. There is hardly an issue of *American Opinion, Human Events* and the other right-wing periodicals which does not contain at least one Hoover saying.

Few in Congress dare deny the FBI director his wishes. The waspish chairman of the House Appropriations Subcommittee, John Rooney of Brooklyn, boasts he has never denied the FBI "a penny" of its requested budget. FBI liaison men pave the way with various friendly committees on Capitol Hill to assure that Hoover's appearances are without hitch. At one time the FBI had to wait a week before entering kidnap cases, after which time it could be presumed the victim had been taken interstate, but the chief G-man's powers of suasion have whittled the waiting period away. When the FBI failed to crack the million-dollar Brinks robbery within the five-year statute of limitations, Hoover prevailed upon Congress to lengthen the statute to seven years.

On the other hand, Hoover's frown can make the passage of legislation a difficult if not impossible task. He was instrumental in staving off for three years the 1967 consular treaty with the Soviet Union by aligning himself with the conservative bloc in Congress that opposed it. As this is written, Hoover appears to have successfully eliminated from the The National Crime Act (the "Safe Streets" act) a research provision that would explore the causes and possible cures for crime and is trying to block a bill, favored by the Attorney General, that would provide for an assistant attorney general to oversee such research; over the years he has opposed studies that might produce viewpoints differing from his own. In 1949 he had his way in pulling the United States, a charter member, out of Interpol, the international cooperative group that serves as a nerve center tracing border-skipping criminals, because he felt the return of a criminal to an Eastern European country was politically motivated.

The heavy shadow of the FBI director even fell over the President's National Crime Commission in its deliberations on the abolishment of capital punishment, the legalization of marijuana, and the banning of wiretapping and bugging. In a wrap-up article on the commission's work on February 24, 1967, *Life*'s Richard B. Stolley disclosed that there was fear on the part of some commission staff members over the reaction of the FBI and Hoover, long a harsh traditionalist on the causes and cures of crime, to such "liberal" proposals. Moreover, he notes, the commission report was obliquely critical of the FBI's enterprise in gathering statistics and fighting organized crime. "If Hoover is annoyed enough," he concluded, "his powerful friends in Congress may not be eager to pass proposed regulations or to appropriate money for recommended research and training programs."

A major recommendation of the commission was increased emphasis on crime prevention through antipoverty and rehabilitation programs rather than punitive measures. In a public statement, Hoover denounced the recommendation, calling it "a tendency to ignore punishment as a deterrent to crime. . . . Coddling of criminals and soft justice increase crime," he declared. "Denials to the contrary have no validity." But the fact remains that during Hoover's forty-four-year tenure as director, during which his views have prevailed, the crime rate has spiraled steadily upward.

The relationship of the police establishment to Hoover and the FBI is an ambivalent one. Since Hoover is the star salesman of the police viewpoint, he is openly espoused by the police. "We have our squabbles with the FBI," a Los Angeles police official told me, "but we keep them to ourselves because the FBI's reputation rubs off on all of us."

Indeed, the IACP, whose staff is topheavy with former FBI agents, is obedient to Hoover's desires. One example occurred at the 1960 annual convention of the IACP in Washington.

Chief Edward J. Allen of Santa Ana, who had been appointed chairman of the Organized Crime Committee by dint of his outstanding success against the syndicate hoodlums in Youngstown, Ohio, introduced a recommendation that a national clearinghouse on crime syndicate intelligence be established. The late Capt. James E. Hamilton of Los Angeles, who had set up that department's effective intelligence operation, was in agreement, asserting that "the definite lack has been on a federal level in furnishing local departments information as to the movement of national figures." There had been repeated calls for such a clearinghouse since the Kefauver hearings exposed the organized crime menace.

To Hoover the idea of an agency that might rival his own was insufferable. In an address to the assembled chiefs, he termed the proposal a "grandiose scheme" which might establish "an all-powerful police agency on the federal scene." It was a spurious polemic, for the proposed clearinghouse would possess no police powers at all. But the chiefs got the message. At a board meeting shortly thereafter they suspended the Organized Crime Committee; after a suitable hiatus it was reinstated with a new chairman, Thomas Cahill of San Francisco, who is more amenable to Hoover's point of view.

"Hoover controls the IACP and used his influence to abolish the committee," Allen contends. "I respect Hoover, but on this score he was dead wrong. I admire a man who could admit he is wrong, but Hoover wouldn't do it." Allen is philosophical about the FBI's hegemony over the IACP, but he does resent the ridicule heaped on him by a high FBI official in front of his police colleagues for believing in the existence of the Mafia.

Of late the FBI's influence has far outweighed its contributions to law enforcement. As a ranking Boston official put it, "Hoover should have quit when he was on top years ago. Now he's a step behind." In their day, the FBI police training schools and the prestigious FBI National Academy were model programs, but their continued accent on the mechanics of the trade without attention to the noncriminal aspects of modern law enforcement has made them quasi-obsolete. And there is growing resentment over the *quid pro quo* attached to FBI training services. National Academy graduates, for instance, are regularly contacted by G-men; the FBI uses them as antennaes within their departments. "The FBI doesn't realize that National Academy graduates aren't FBI agents," commented one chief, "but that their first loyalty is to the municipality."

The pervasiveness of FBI influence in the law-enforcement establishment contributes immeasurably to the stagnation. The majority of FBI agents who resign or retire join other law-enforcement agencies, and they often bring bureau policies and procedures with them. A clear-cut example is the New York state police. In 1959 Arthur Cornelius, Jr., the agent in charge of the Albany FBI office, retired to become superintendent of the state police. Since that time there has been a steady influx of retiring FBI agents, including an assistant director, into the ranking positions; the career incumbents were either shunted aside or forced into early retirement. Not long ago I talked in private to two veteran police troopers, and they described what has happened.

The nepotism, they said, has deteriorated morale, and there is an exodus of the more promising men. A ponderous four-volume manual of rules and regulations modeled on the FBI's has been introduced, and there is a surfeit of forms and paper work, creating an atmosphere of pettifoggery. "We even have Hoover's 'loyalty oath,' " complained one of the troopers, referring to the Elbert Hubbard poem extolling employee loyalty that adorns each bureau field office. Manifesting the FBI obsession with statistics, the troopers now have a citation quota system. "You have to be above the zone average or be hauled on the carpet," the troopers explained. "One trooper who was a bit low near the end of the month wrote up a dead traffic victim for five violations. Another managed to find five technical violations in one burned-out tail light."

Despite the intramural bickering, the police establishment presents a unified front in lobbying for more power and less outside control. Its principal objectives are to nullify Supreme Court decisions by legislation, legalize Big Brother devices in the interests of the "crime war," obtain more repressive laws, perpetuate the punitive theory over rehabilitation, and become a national-thought police system.

Such ambitions are subversive to a free society. The answer to the crime problem is not a vast police monolith but a war on the economic roots of crime and an enlightened penology. The answer to subversive thought is not police persecution but the championing of democratic ideals. It is not the police for whom the Communists have reserved their most vitriolic attacks, but the American liberals and non-Communist left, who compete for the minds of men.

In promoting a Big Blue Line as our bulwark against crime and Communism, the police lobby poses a viable threat to our democratic institutions.

16

Wanted: A New Breed

Not long ago a small city in New Jersey fired its police chief and his officers and placed newspaper advertisements seeking new police officers. The main requirement listed: that the candidate fit one of the city-owned uniforms. While extreme, the incident symbolizes what lies at the heart of the current police dilemma: the police ranks have been filled not by men recruited for their professional capabilities or potential but for their ability to fit into the old police mold. Only by a massive proselytization of an entirely new breed of police officer, and by a drastic restructuring of the system in which he will work, can American law enforcement solve the crisis now confronting it.

That crisis, as we have seen, is not predominantly one of violence in the streets, despite the self-serving cries of some police and politicians. The National Crime Commission has warned that "crime in the streets is an inaccurate label for the bulk of serious crimes in this country," and the rate of economic crimes is far outstripping the violent crime rate. Homicides have steadily declined since the bloody days of Prohibition, and homicide, felonious assault, robbery and rape combined are only 14 percent of the serious crime total, far too high in terms of human misery but a relatively small part of the crime picture.

There has been a metamorphosis in truly significant crime in the United States that the headline-grabbing criminality of stickup men, safecrackers, footpads and sex fiends has disguised. The silent rampage of organized crime—the syndicated rackets that thrive by means of slick, businesslike methods—has reached the point where the body politic is drained of an estimated $22 billion annually, yet law enforcement has been alternately unwilling and unable to cope with it. The same is true of "white-collar crime"—loan-sharking, embezzlement, business and consumer frauds, crooked pawnbroking, price-rigging, restraint of trade through duress or threats, blackmail and the like. This is the kind of crime that does not appear in statistics but rips at the moral fabric of society and gives a hollow ring to calls for law and order aimed only at the street level.

Even in its battle against conventional crime, the present police system has been found wanting. That only one out of four serious crimes is "cleared by arrest" is only half the story. In many cases, the suspect is known to the victim, so that the police task is for the most part one of gathering sufficient evidence to convict. In the forcible-rape category, for example, fewer than half the victims contend that their attacker was a total stranger. In "unknown subject" cases, which test the investigative prowess of the police, the clearance rate plummets to about one out of ten. A survey by the President's National Crime Commission revealed that the Los Angeles department, which has been widely acclaimed for its efficacy, cracked only 11 percent of its cases when it had to start from scratch in identifying the suspect.

Since most serious crime is committed by recidivists, even a modest increase in the crime-solution rate would appreciably reduce the number of crimes. When a professional burglar is apprehended, to give one example, a string of burglaries usually is cleared and more are prevented from happening. The "vast criminal army" that J. Edgar Hoover talks about actually is not so vast; a nucleus of professional criminals are committing crime after crime, and getting away with it far too long.

There is an urgent need for police improvement in crime prevention, and saturating the streets with more and more policemen is not the answer. As the President's Commission observed in its report, "One of the most puzzling aspects is that reported crime rates often seem to fluctuate with relatively little correlation with what the police do. For example, the ratios of police per thousand population in cities over 500,000 range from 1.2 to 5.4, but there is no discernible relationship between these ratios and reported incidence of crimes."

Crime prevention, then, is something quite different from deterrent muscle-flexing. Granted that much crime is incubated in the abject poverty of the slums, fostered by parental disregard, and lent impetus by the failure of our cities to provide constructive outlets for youthful energies, and thus is fundamentally a socioeconomic problem, the fact remains that the police have abdicated their responsibility toward wayward youth. Chief Parker's "We are not sociologists" remains the refrain, and a myopic one considering that more fifteen-year-olds are arrested today than any other age group, with sixteen-year-olds running a close second; and that a majority of persons arrested for both crimes against property and against the person are under twenty-one. The efforts of the police to establish rapport with the new generation have been largely token gestures. A wall of hostility divides the police from the less privileged youth, and it rises higher every time shortsighted police assume youthful delinquents to be incorrigible and treat them accordingly.

The police approach to community relations has likewise been unimaginative. Current community-relations programs, with the outstanding exception of that undertaken by San

Francisco's beleaguered Community Relations Unit, have most often developed into honeymoons with "respectable" groups already sympathetic to the police side rather than magnanimous attempts to communicate with the more hostile elements. This is not to say that the police should indulge wanton lawlessness, "mollycoddle" hardened criminals, or relinquish the authority that is rightfully theirs. It is to say, however, that they must abandon their hard line and get down to an earthy dialogue with the most troublesome elements.

That they were reluctant to do so was noted by the National Crime Commission. In a report dealing with the community relations problem, released on April 29, 1967, the commission virtually predicted the cataclysmic Detroit and Newark riots that were to occur in three months. The two cities were included in a dozen cities the commission singled out as potential danger spots because police relations with minority groups had sunk to explosively low levels. "Impatience, frustration and now violence are growing quickly in minority communities," the commission warned, "and these trends are likely to accelerate." The trouble stemmed in large measure from real and imagined grievances that led minorities to view the police as enemies and "as the protectors of white people, not as protectors of Negroes, as well." Unless the police confronted frankly and effectively the legitimate grievances of the minorities, trouble was in the offing.

The Newark tinderbox was touched off by alleged police brutality against a Negro cabdriver. A few days later Detroit was ignited by the arrests of 73 persons in a raid on a Negro after-hours club. The toll in Newark ran to more than 25 dead, 1,200 injured, 1,300 arrested, and more than $15,000,000 in property damage. Detroit was much worse: at least 38 deaths, 1,000 injured, 2,900 arrests, and more than $200,000,000 in property damage. What was perfectly obvious to all who would see was that the rioting was really a revolt and that the sops tossed the ghettos in recent years had merely ripened the conditions for revolution. But Mayor Hugh Addonizio of Newark had a typically official explanation. He described the riots as a "planned situation" fomented by criminal conspirators. Governor Richard J. Hughes agreed when Addonizio cited the statistic that 662 of the 1,381 Negroes arrested had "criminal records," but neither pointed out that many had never been convicted of the charges, nor did they take into consideration the dual standards of arrest that prevail in the ghetto.

The reaction of the police establishment of Detroit and Newark was largely to arm itself to the teeth. Police supply houses waxed fat with orders for such "humanitarian" equipment as grenade launchers, foam generators to make demonstrators slip and slide, leather sap gloves, blackjacks, Kelly come-alongs, shields, flat saps, brass knuckles, tear gas, gas masks, and armored riot vehicles that look like three-quarter-scale Sherman tanks. The garrison state came closer as New York police asked for 5,000 more men, and Chicago Mayor Daley, irate that two aldermen had been the victims of Negro robbery attempts, shouted at the City Council, "If it's necessary to put 5,000 more policemen on, I'll ask you for authority to put them on. We must put a halt to this violence" (ironically, Daley's call to arms came at the precise time that the Ku Klux Klan cell was discovered on the police department).

In Miami, Chief Walter Headley responded to a spate of holdups in what is termed the Central Negro District by "declaring war" on the Negro area. "Community relations and all that sort of thing has failed," he fumed, announcing that he would "use shotguns and dogs." Said the chief, "We don't mind being accused of police brutality. And in Washington, President Johnson added to police power by signing the controversial District of Columbia Bill which permits police to ignore the well-established Mallory Rule and grill suspects for as long as three hours before arraigning them. The President's Riot

Commission, set up to seek a reasonable solution to the problem, could only look on in dismay as the nation's police disdained diplomacy for raw power.

What should the new breed of police officer be like in order to challenge the crisis? Mayor Lindsay's New York Task Force roughly sketched him as a professional equipped to fight crime with courage and imagination, an individual who has earned the respect of all citizens by respecting and protecting all equally. The President's Commission, in its section on "Needed Qualities and the Selection Process," concludes that "the complexities inherent in the policing function dictate that officers possess a high degree of intelligence, education, tact, sound judgment, physical courage, emotional stability, impartiality, and honesty. . . . One incompetent officer can trigger a riot, permanently damage the reputation of a citizen, or alienate a community against a police department." At present, the commission admonished, "far too many of our officers who are charged with protecting life and property, and rationally enforcing our laws are not respected by their fellow officers and are incompetent, corrupt, or abusive."

This means that the threshold of acceptability into the police service will have to be greatly raised. As long ago as 1929, Berkeley Chief August Vollmer urged in "The Illinois Crime Survey":

> Higher standards . . . must be established. Whatever may be achieved in remedying police defects must be done through enlisting the services of intelligent men of excellent character, who are sufficiently educated to perform the duties of a policeman. . . . The police organization suffers in reputation and society pays the bill when policemen are dishonest, brutal, stupid, or physcially or tempermentally unsuited.

Unfortunately, police standards have little changed from Vollmer's day, and society continues to pay the bill.

The fact that the police have always placed a premium on

physical prowess over intellectual has not helped in dealing with the vagaries of human behavior. The present educational level of the police is deplorably low for a group that must constantly solve the human equation. A 1961 survey by the IACP of over 300 departments revealed that 24 percent had no minimum educational requirements and less than 1 percent had any college-level requisites. A 1964 IACP poll of 6,200 officers determined that only 30.3 percent had taken one or more college courses and only 7.3 percent held a college degree. In the New England states a majority of the officers were not even high-school graduates, and in the metropolitan Detroit area only one out of four had seen the inside of a college classroom.

Education is an indispensable prerequisite for the type of officer needed today. It tends to diminish authoritarianism, broaden the outlook, and instill self-discipline and reasoned thinking. To take advantage of the scientific aids now coming to the fore, the officer must additionally have a thorough grounding in the sciences.

Beyond education is that elusive factor called quality. The President's Commission has stressed that "the quality of police personnel at all levels of activity and authority is today's most important factor in effective law enforcement." What is quality in the law-enforcement officer? Answers the commission: an officer with determination and devotion "accompanied by breadth of outlook, social awareness, a high degree of education, good judgment and a willingness to take responsibility." The ideal police officer "should be a distinguished man."

At first glance it seems hopeless to seek 350,000 "distinguished men" to man the nation's police ramparts, and only by revising our concepts of the police system can the goal become realistic. In the first place, we do not need 350,000 policemen. As it is considerable police time is misspent. And the commission found that the quicker an officer arrived at the crime scene, the more likely the crime would be solved. Thus communications, planning, mobility and strategic deployment are more important than sheer manpower.

By insisting on quality men and training and equipping them properly, police officials can cut back on the ever-rising "authorized strengths" that are rarely met. But even with the fat trimmed off, most police executives are pessimistic that quotas can be filled with the higher standards. It is difficult enough under present standards, they argue, often poor-mouthing that today's young men are unwilling to accept the rigors of police work and are dissuaded by the general lack of respect for the police.

To a large degree, the police have not earned respect. One confirmation came in the form of a surprising report of research conducted by the University of Chicago's Opinion Research Center for the President's Commission. Questioning a cross-section sample of 10,000 citizens, the researchers found that only 49 percent of offenses recalled by the victims were reported to the police—and that 55 percent of those victims had not reported the offenses because they did not like or trust the police or believe in their effectiveness.

The argument that sufficient numbers of high-caliber men cannot be attracted to the "dirty work" of law enforcement went out the window more than forty years ago when an ambitious new director took over an FBI riddled with venality and inefficiency. Hoover radically streamlined the horse-and-buggy outfit by lopping off heads and setting unprecedented standards for recruitment. At the time, veteran policemen scoffed at the "college cops with a Boy Scout complex," but Hoover's pioneering proved that brains were superior to brawn in law enforcement and that well-educated, highly motivated men could be lured by the right inducements.

One inducement is decent pay. The median salary for metropolitan departments is now only $5,300 a year, hardly competitive with private industry. Even after long years of service, a policeman cannot expect to make much more than $8,000 a year, a marginal wage. Compared to the $16,500 a senior FBI agent can earn, the police scale is pitifully low, especially in view of the fact the police job is in many ways more demanding than the FBI agent's. As a patrol force, the police are confronted with instant decision-making, while the FBI ordinarily can afford to take its time. And the police face more physical hazards: thousands are injured in the line of duty each year, and in a recent five-year period 225 were murdered, as compared to only 19 FBI "martyrs" since 1924.

"This nation can't afford bargain-basement cops any more," declares former Sheriff Donald Clark of Portland, Oregon. In the first such action by a major police force, Clark in 1966 required that all applicants for the deputy position to hold at least a bachelor's degree. Concomitantly, he pushed to have the pay scale raised significantly from the present $6,996 a year maximum.

Former Detroit Police Commissioner George Edwards, now a federal judge, looks forward to the day when all police will possess a university degree and start at $10,000. Paradoxically, it is not the "Support Your Local Police" sloganeers who have been most vocal in advocating higher police salaries but civil rights leaders. "Pay a cop $10,000 to start," reasons Dick Gregory, "and then he'll have something to lose." In a *U.S. News & World Report* interview May 23, 1966, CORE national director Floyd B. McKissick said: "The quality of the policemen and the standards of police have got to be improved. I think there probably should be some national standards set in police qualifications and training. And there should be increased salaries for policemen, so police departments can attract better men—and men who are not bigoted and hold membership in the Ku Klux Klan or the John Birch Society."

More than money is needed to attract the "distinguished

men" described by the commission, however. The musty atmosphere of the police establishment—the anti-intellectualism, the boorish conservatism, the almost theological cant, the status quoism—will have to be thoroughly ventilated. "Police departments traditionally have resisted change and have been wary of the intellectual," the commission chided. "As long as this attitude prevails, the police will never successfully compete for the type of person they so desperately need."

Nor will ambitious, imaginative men put up with the present encrusted civil-service system, which dictates that the most competent younger man must wait out his time in deference to a mediocre individual with longer service. Since the police have always placed undue emphasis on seniority, waiting periods in most departments are especially long. Baltimore, for one, requires five years as a patrolman before sergeant eligibility, and another two years for the next higher grade. The British Home Office Committee on the Police Service concluded: "Seniority may be taken into account but should not govern promotion, and promotion by competitive examination would be quite unsuited to the police system because of the importance of initiative, tact, judgment and other personal qualifications which cannot be gauged by means of an examination paper."

Not only does the civil-service system retard enterprise and ambition, it serves to shield misfits, undesirables and incompetents. A former Los Angeles officer who regretfully turned in his badge for a less hidebound occupation, estimated that "in the detective bureau 20 percent of the men did 80 percent of the work." William A. Bradley, deputy superintendent of the Boston department, points out that civil service ties the hands of the administrator. "Once a man gets in there, it's almost impossible to get him out," he says. "And the system just doesn't provide enough incentives for the right kind of man."

One of the more recent proposals for providing incentive

is to divide the manifold police duties among three classes of police service. Advocated by the President's Commission, the proposal would delineate between community service officers, police officers, and police agents. The CSO would substitute for the beat patrolman, who has almost disappeared with the advent of motorization. Drawn from the neighborhood in which he would serve, the CSO would perform minor investigative duties and handle the numerous emergency tasks which presently consume so much police time. Educational requirements for the position would be minimal, and a minor police record reflecting mischievious rather than criminal conduct would not be disqualifying. The more promising CSOs could eventually work up to the next level: the police officer.

The PO would be mostly engaged in routine patrol, maintaining order at public gatherings, enforcing traffic codes and investigating crimes that are soluble by immediate follow-up investigation. Since the CSO will relieve him of many burdensome duties, he will be freer to concentrate on these functions and, presumably, be more effective. On occasion, he would be called upon to assist the police agent.

The PA would replace the current detective, but his responsibilities would be much broader. In addition to investigating major crimes, he would patrol high-crime areas, handle matters involving social unrest, and respond to delicate situations such as domestic disputes (one of the most common and touchy police problems) and juvenile "rumbles." And he could be summoned to the scene when a complex decision on arrest is to be made.

Obviously the police-agent position would require the highest order of judgment, intelligence, education, initiative and understanding of human behavior. Its holder would have to blend the skills of an investigator, diplomat and sociologist. This challenge, unfettered by miscellaneous and regulatory tasks, should attract many outstanding men to police service. But as the President's Commission cautions, "The police agent must be accorded the status and compensation of a skilled professional who requires a minimum of close supervision. A police agent should be permitted far greater latitude in his performance and should be judged by his ability to solve problems and to prevent as well as repress crime."

This is a bold and venturesome concept, and it has drawn the fire of many police executives. The main objection cited is that the three levels, with their gradients of status and pay, would stir jealousies and undermine morale. However, de facto levels of competency already exist; the patrol officer at the scene of a major crime, for example, must relinquish the investigation to the detective squad. As long as progression from one level to the next is based on demonstrated ability, the trilevel system should supply incentive and make for greater efficiency.

Elimination of hidebound civil-service rules would also help rejuvenate police administration. One of the most durable of police traditions is that leaders must "come up through the ranks." This nepotistic notion has survived largely through the myth that police work is so mysterious and complex that "outsiders" cannot possibly grasp it. The tradition has produced a poverty of leadership. A 1964 national survey by the IACP found that only 33.6 percent of police administrators had attended college at all, of which a meager 9.2 percent held one or more degrees. The paucity of education is part of a deeper deficiency, which was spelled out by the President's Commission: "Although a great majority of the chief administrators in our nation's police departments have achieved enviable records as outstanding police officers, only a few possess the ideal level of training and education in management and administration to administer a law enforcement agency."

The remedy is not to discourage promotion through the

ranks—for that would be inviting serious morale problems—but to open up line and staff commands to qualified outsiders, with merit being the sole determinant. This is termed lateral entry, and it already has been used at top levels that are unprotected by civil service. The appointment of O. W. Wilson, a university dean, to the command of the Chicago department was one example, and the naming of Ray Girardin, a crime reporter who had made an avocation of criminal rehabilitation and social psychology, as Detroit's commissioner was another. Lateral entry could immensely stimulate the police service, but safeguards would have to be installed to prevent the kind of transplanted nepotism that has afflicted the New York state police.

In its rather haphazard evolution, the police system has become a semimilitary bureaucracy. The organizational structure is patterned on military lines, the chain of command and sharp delineation of rank are military hallmarks, and the uniform and gun are military accouterments. Anyone who has witnessed the ceremonious muster of a police platoon, with the sergeant's bark of "Take your posts," realizes that in spirit as well as form the military theme is dominant.

The military atmosphere has had a detrimental effect on the police. The tight regimentation, which exceeds the need for reasonable order and discipline, stifles initiative and molds automatons. There is an accent on rote learning over individual judgment. There is far more emphasis on making arrests and following orders than on questioning traditional procedures or solving community problems. As the President's Commission expressed it, the atmosphere "is not an appealing environment for a person of professional stature."

Nor is it an environment likely to produce policemen capable of "instant judgment" and possessing the personal resources needed today. As long ago as 1934, a Harvard Law School survey of the Boston Police Department perceived that:

Too often the military aspect of organization pushes the essentially individual character of police work into the background. A policeman is regimented with his fellows. He is given a uniform, badge, and number; he is assigned to a squad and platoon; he carries a book of rules in his pocket and a schedule of duty calls in his mind. He is a cog in a machine. Everything seems to be numbered, labeled, covered by rules, and arranged far in advance. Yet, when he goes out on post he is alone and on his own responsibility.

In their closely regulated milieu, the police have developed a militarylike camaraderie and mystique that are morbidly preoccupied with victories won (the "big pinch") and dangers shared. A social gathering of The Finest is in many respects indistinguishable from a Rainbow Division reunion, except that the war is still going on. The talk inevitably moves to gunplay—and guns. The gun is the policeman's symbol of power and authority; it is the menacing bulge that sets him apart from ordinary mortals. The gun is also, in a sense, the policeman's equivalent of the child's security blanket. Former New York Commissioner Murphy, the evening he resigned from the force, was quoted by columnist Jimmy Breslin in the *Herald-Tribune* as remarking, "I'll keep this [the gun]. I'd feel undressed without the thing. When you get up in the morning, it's like putting on your tie." Chief Frank Rizzo of Philadelphia wears three guns, one on the hip, one in a shoulder holster, and one strapped to a leg.

The "pearl-handled revolver syndrome" and the strut and swagger that goes with it may be the policeman's compensation for his estrangement from society, but it also conditions a frame of mind that surely contributes to the incidence of homicides by police. One of the more interesting police statistics, should it ever be tabulated, would be the frequency of exhibitionism with guns in bars and at parties.

There is a certain adolescence to police exhibitionism, and

indeed the Philadelphia department, although it has not banned guns, has had the sirens removed from police cars. "They're adolescent enough without having sirens to blow," confided a deputy chief. In England, where the police have traditionally disdained carrying guns, the deliberate shooting of a police officer is a rare occurrence, and the police are more uniformly respected—by the citizenry and criminals alike.

One debilitating trait of the police bureaucracy is its habit of devouring its young. From the FBI down to the smaller departments, constructive criticism and dissent and the questioning of long-cherished assumptions simply are not tolerated. Many promising young men have enthusiastically enlisted in the police service; some conform, some quit, and a few, openly critical, are drummed out in a tattoo of pettifoggery.

In their *Introduction to Law Enforcement*, Germann, Gallati and Day score the process by which carefully screened recruits are "subjected to a 'brain washing' by poorly motivated senior officers that would do credit to the most expert and fanatical totalitarian." In a personal interview, Dr. Germann briefly described the process: "The new recruit is at first shocked by a system that indulges immoral and illegal habits by some officers. But he wants to get along in the system, so he tolerates them. In time he begins to accept them, and eventually he uses them himself. Ultimately, he may adopt them as his own—and his personality has changed for the worse." Obviously, this process is cyclical. The end product is a veteran officer who at one time or another will be responsible for breaking in other new recruits.

Thus the recruit, however decent his instincts, wishes above all to "get along," and in the end he is pressure-molded to the cynical image of the system. In large measure, this mutation accounts for the abundance of surly, truculent police officers who are unwilling to judge situations individually on their merits—and for much of the physical and verbal brutality that stigmatizes law enforcement. James W. Smith, a former California highway patrol officer who is now a police-community-relations consultant, recalls his own subconscious transformation. "I was assigned to the Watts area," he says, "and I found myself roughing up Negroes routinely in the back seat of the patrol car—not because I disliked Negroes, but because in the police group it was the thing to do."

Probably the crux of the police problem is that it is unreasonable to expect men who inhabit a totalitarian world of their own to police an outside world in a democratic fashion. The only solution is to rip the cocoon from the police system and expose it to the fresh air of informed public opinion. Several decades ago the eminent police consultant Bruce Smith thought he detected a tendency on the part of the police to break out of their cocoon. "There is ground for hope," he wrote in *Police Administration*, "in the fact that police of all ranks . . . are now more disposed to re-examine some of the basic assumptions concerning their exercise of authority. If this attitude of self-criticism continues, we may yet effect a close approach to a police regime that is vigorous without being oppressive, and scrupulous in its observance of civil liberties without losing its effectiveness in law enforcement."

The hope was premature. Progress in the police system has been mostly technological, not sociological, and the old attitudes are as entrenched as ever. "During the past 100 years the police have made great strides along the road toward professionalization," affirmed Douglas Gourley in 1953 in his *Public Relations and the Police*. But, added Gourley, a former captain in charge of the Los Angeles Police Training Division and now a professor of police science at Los Angeles State College, "the greatest advances have been those which deal with scientific techniques and equipment. The social problems in policing have not received their fair share of attention."

Recent federal measures aimed at improving law enforcement have concentrated on training, equipment and the scientific aids, skirting for the most part the issue of drastically restructuring and replenishing the system itself. In his statement urging passage of the Law Enforcement Assistance Act, President Johnson on March 8, 1965, talked in terms of building on the old foundation: "It means giving new priority to the methods and institutions of law enforcement—to our police, who are our front line, both offensive and defensive, in the fight against crime." In his State of the Union message the same year, he confined his advocacy of new anticrime programs to providing the police with training and equipment, crime laboratories, and police-academy-type centers. Although some of its proposals were far-reaching, the President's National Crime Commission bent to the will of the police bloc on its membership and the police lobby prompting in the wings, and did not recommend the sweeping changes needed.

The changes must be revolutionary: an opening up of the closed society; the recruitment of a visionary breed of policeman. It is the quality of the man behind the badge upon which the quality of our police system depends. There is no essential conflict between a social conscience and ability to enforce the law vigorously and wisely. The old mentality must be replaced by the new; the ranks must be filled with the kind of bright young attorneys, social scientists and similarly committed university graduates now flocking to such programs as Anti-Poverty and Vista and the various state programs. There is an untapped reservoir in the nation's schools of law, education, social sciences, physical sciences, and the like. Internship programs would bolster the regular forces. Civil rights cops like Michael Hannon of Los Angeles would have a respected place in the police system, rather than being the objects of contempt and scorn. Broad-minded men of the caliber of Lt. Dante Andreotti of San Francisco, whose bold and imaginative police-community relations unit is so unique as to be avant-garde, would sit in the chiefs' chairs.

In this modern police society, the William Parkers, Thomas Cahills, Michael Murphys and J. Edgar Hoovers will be portraits of the past in the police museum.

If these proposals seem preposterous, it is precisely this which indicates the vast changes that must come.